Christianity and Chinese Religions

Christianity and Chinese Religions

Hans Küng
Julia Ching

DOUBLEDAY
NEW YORK LONDON TORONTO SYDNEY AUCKLAND

PUBLISHED BY DOUBLEDAY
a division of Bantam Doubleday Dell Publishing Group, Inc.
666 Fifth Avenue, New York, New York 10103

DOUBLEDAY and the portrayal of an anchor with a dolphin
are trademarks of Doubleday, a division of Bantam Doubleday Dell
Publishing Group, Inc.

This book was originally published in German under the title *Christentum und
chinesische Religion* (© R. Piper GmbH & Co. KG; München, 1988)
The chapters by Hans Küng have been translated from the original German by
Dr. Peter Beyer.

Library of Congress Cataloging-in-Publication Data
Küng, Hans, 1928–
[Christentum und Chinesische Religion. English]
Christianity and Chinese religions / Hans Küng and
    Julia Ching.—1st ed.
    p. cm.
Translation of: Christentum und Chinesische Religion.
March, 1989—T.p. verso.
Bibliography: p.
Includes index.
1. Christianity and other religions—Chinese. 2. China—Religion.
I. Ching, Julia. II. Title.
BR128.C4C4813   1989   88-22114
261.2'951—dc19   CIP

ISBN 0-385-26022-9
Copyright © 1989 by Doubleday and Collins Publi
ALL RIGHTS RESERVED
PRINTED IN THE UNITED STATES OF AMERICA
MARCH 1989
FIRST EDITION

BG

Contents

Hans Küng:
China–A Third Religious River System

According to the calculations of the 1982 World Christian Encyclopedia, there are 1.4 billion nominal Christians in the world. By comparison, the Chinese alone number 1 billion. Does this fact alone not show what a challenge China presents for Christianity and that it is high time Western theology (which we should call "Western" and not just "theology") recognized this challenge?

For thousands of years, Europe and China have both thought of themselves as the center of the world. The small world around the Mediterranean proudly called itself *oikoumene,* the whole of the inhabited world. China saw itself as the "middle kingdom." For both, other regions and religions counted as mere peripheral zones. This was even easier for China, since the massive Himalayan barrier and the broad desert and vast steppes of the Central Asian plateau isolated it, allowing it to leave but a narrow passage for the entry of external cultural influences. Small wonder that Christianity and the Chinese religions were strangers until after the Jesuit mission of the sixteenth to seventeenth centuries, when they became more familiar with each other during the European Enlightenment.

When one compares Christianity with the religions of Indian origin, above all Hinduism and Buddhism, they all seem at least to share various words, usages, myths, and ideas of the Indo-European language group between the Ganges and the Mediterranean. But a comparison between Christianity and the Chinese religions, this third great world religious "river system" besides the Semitic-prophetic and the Indian-mystic? This is in fact my working hypothesis, one that will be confirmed again and again in the course of this book: within the single "religious history of humankind" (Wilfred Cantwell Smith, *Towards a World Theology* [Philadelphia, 1981]), the Chinese religions are not some kind of Far Eastern and exotic appendage of general religious history, to be treated as marginal or as an afterthought as the textbooks usually do. No, the Chinese religions must be taken seriously as a *third independent religious river system, equal in value to the others.* It is not without reason that it has gained world significance beyond its land of origin, in Japan and Korea, in Vietnam and Taiwan. But how is this to be understood, a third river system? As with the geological surface whose mountain ranges and river systems change completely over the millennia, so it is with the spiritual-religious landscape.

If we take as our vantage point the *origins* of human history—more precisely, the prehistoric, Stone Age beginnings of humanity with its primitive, preliterate religions—then at least four original, historical high religions can be seen to have developed subsequently. These arose in the context of the sedentary high cultures of the great fertile river valleys: along the Nile, in Mesopotamia, in the Indus Valley, and in the North Chinese lowlands of the Huang Ho, the Yellow River. The earliest *written* documents on religious institutions, ideas, and practices, dating from as far back as three thousand years before Christ, come from Mesopotamian Sumeria. The religions of the Mesopotamians, the Sumerians, the Babylonians, and the Assyrians, however, have disappeared like those of the ancient Egyptians and the much later Greeks and Romans.

Therefore, if instead of looking forward from the origins of human history, we look back from the *present*, then, taking into account various transitions and hybrid forms, we can distinguish three existing great religious river systems. What we are after is not a superficial and static "geography of religion" (for example, European-Indian-Chinese "worldview"), but rather a historically grounded and phenomenologically *dynamic typology of religion* that goes beyond specific countries and continents.

In the Near East, the *first great river system, of Semitic origin and prophetic character,* developed out of the primitive religion of nomadic tribes. Today, after much conflict and suffering, we have a renewed awareness of the internal coherence of this system as "the three Abrahamic religions." These, however, do not represent parallel developments but rather divergent ones. Their common distinguishing feature is a "piety of belief" (R. Otto). There is, first of all, Judaism as the religion of the Israelite patriarchs, the law, and the prophets. Out of it emerged Christianity, the religion characterized by faith in Jesus, the Christ or Messiah. Finally, there is Islam, the religion of the prophet Muhammad, whose holy book, the Qur'an, refers to the prophets of Israel, and to Jesus of Nazareth as a prophet.

To the east of these Semitic-prophetic religions, and clearly distinguishable from them, is the no less intricate *second great river system, of Indian origin and mystical character.* There, in reaction to the overdeveloped cultic religion of the late Vedic priesthood, that mystical and often ascetic religion came to be, centered on the experience that everything is one. An immediate experience of unity achieved through meditative practices, as well as a doctrine of unity first delineated in the Upanishads, formed the basis for the high religions of India that developed later. There was the reform movement of Mahāvīra, called Jina, the "victor," founder of Jainism. There was the reform movement of Gautama Buddha which spread all the way to China and Japan, albeit with several changes of paradigm. Finally, there are also the more recent Hindu religions, whether monotheistic or henotheistic.

What will become clear in this book is that a *third great river system* in the Far East is to be distinguished from both these. This one had its origin in *China.* The central figure here is neither the prophet nor the mystic, but rather the *sage:* this is a religion of wisdom.

Of course, Chinese culture and religion did not develop in complete isolation from all others, something that nationalist ideologues in China and, in a different version, Japan like to assert. The Chinese high culture of the Yellow River Basin did, after all, emerge relatively late, and it is by far the youngest of the early high cultures. Although Chinese sources are silent on the matter, ever since Wolfram Eberhard, some scholars have therefore assumed that decisive cultural developments after the Stone Age, such as bronze casting and even writing, were triggered by contact with the older Near Eastern cultural centers, notably Sumeria and Egypt. The domestication of horses and use of war chariots in China would also have been taken over from neighboring Indo-European peoples (cf. Herbert Franke and Rolf Trauzettel, *Das chinesische Kaiserreich* [Frankfurt, 1968], ch. 1). Such external cultural impulses were the more likely source of writing, bronze, domestication of horses, and chariots than their totally independent "new invention" in China as late as the second millennium before Christ. (To take but one of numerous indicators, the domestication of horses is today no longer attributed to one of the legendary Three Sovereigns or Five Emperors [culture-heroes], but rather only to the historical Shang dynasty.) Given that archaeology in China has barely begun to plow an infinitely vast and virgin field, a bit of light may gradually be shed on some of these questions; and new discoveries in Inner Mongolia should change our understanding of ancient China decisively.

Yet no matter which influences will eventually be demonstrated, what is important for us is that the early bronze objects, the writing, and also the religion showed *typically Chinese forms and motifs from the very beginning,* although ethnology and the study of religion have thus far had difficulty in specifying what "typically Chinese" is. In any case, in spite of similarities with, for instance, Indian developments, Chinese culture and religion are on close examination entirely different from what Europeans for the longest time have considered to be typically "oriental." The amazingly early beginnings of Chinese historiography soon gave way to complete monopolization by the court and by a state bureaucracy for historiography that led to an emphasis on tradition and stereotypical conformity. Even so, this in no way justifies the European view that became particularly widespread after Hegel, holding that we are faced with a static, "eternal China," almost without history.

To be sure, in the slowly flowing course of Chinese history, the Western observer will hardly be able to find the same kind of drastic discontinuities in architecture, sculpture, and painting, in dress and furniture as can be found in Western history. And yet, epochal upheavals are clearly evident, not least in the history of religion. One thing is of course undeniable: the *great value set on age and its wisdom* is a constant of Chinese history. This was reinforced by the absence of the Western dualism of state and church, nobility and clergy, a split which generated a great deal of conflict, to be sure, but which was also productive. In addition to this absence, China also lacked a developed theory of the state, the concept of the supremacy of law, and an independent judiciary.

Still, does such a historico-phenomenological characterization of Chinese religions as wisdom religions not encourage an oversimplified classification and schematization? Hardly, since we obviously have no intention of ignoring the way that religions have historically influenced each other and created hybrid forms. On the other hand, the fundamental differences must also be emphasized and their terminology clarified. For if we expand concepts such as prophet, mystic, and sage so that they lose all contours and even come to encompass their opposites, they become useless. (According to Aristotelian logic, the broadest concepts have the least content.) Let us demonstrate this with three particularly striking historical overlappings and mixtures.

1. Even among *Semitic* religions, there are of course *mystical tendencies.* It is possible that the mystical current of Greece and Asia Minor, which began its broad diffusion into Western piety through Plotinus' disciple, Dionysius the Areopagite (fifth or sixth century), had its source in India. Mysticism is grounded in the immediate and intuitive experience of unity. As such, while it is central for the Indian religions, for Judaism, Christianity, and Islam it remains an often suspect and even persecuted marginal phenomenon, notwithstanding Jewish Kabbalistic mysticism, the Christian mysticism of Germany, the Netherlands, and Spain, and Islamic Sufi mysticism. The great Israelite prophets always saw themselves as distinct from God. They were no more inward-looking mystics in search of cosmic union than was the Jesus of the synoptic Gospels (in spite of certain mystical traces in John's Gospel) or even the Prophet of the Qur'an.

2. Even among *Semitic* religions, there is a *wisdom literature,* as there was everywhere in the ancient Near East. And yet this also

remained a marginal phenomenon for Judaism, Christianity, and Islam. By contrast, the religious history of China is fundamentally and centrally characterized by wisdom literature.

3. Conversely, as we shall see, Chinese tradition also has something akin to *prophetic* or at least "enthusiastic" (originally shamanic) figures. The differences between the great prophets of Israel and the Chinese shamans are nevertheless as clear as those between Jesus of Nazareth and Confucius (K'ung Fu-tzu) or Lao-tzu. These latter became and remain the important sages of Confucianism and Taoism, two religions that, unlike Buddhism, are of Chinese origin.

The three great religious river systems not only have developed numerous tributaries over the millennia, but have also mingled anew with primitive popular piety and cults as well as flowing into one another. Some examples:

• Biblical-prophetic religion mixed with Hellenistic mystical elements and tendencies in Judaism, but especially in Alexandrian Christianity and then in Arab-Persian Sufism.

• Conversely, later on in India, the mystical religion of the Upanishads and the Vedanta amalgamated with the personally oriented Vishnu, Bhagavān, Krishna, and Rāma cults, all of which emphasized emotional commitment to the one God.

• And in China, not only did the two main wisdom religions of Confucianism and Taoism become intertwined, they also absorbed a large number of Mahayana Buddhist influences—not, however, without giving them a deep Chinese coloring.

It is nevertheless worth repeating that, in spite of all the admixtures, the fundamental differences remain! Moreover, the other types of religion should not be seen as mere precursors or deviations from one's own, something that especially Christian dogmatists have tended to do. Nor should one follow those historians and philosophers of religion who want to see mystical religion as the "authentic" religion from which prophetic religion then derives, or, conversely, who regard prophetic religion as superior to mystical religion. All the more should one guard against that tendency to which areas under Chinese influence are prone: amalgamating everything and then availing oneself of one or another religion as the need arises.

The dialogue represented by the lectures contained in this volume was held during the 1987 summer semester at the University of Tübingen. I hope that they will make clear that it is impossible to understand the Chinese people and, indeed, the entire vast Sinicized territory from Pyongyang to Taipei, from Turfan to Tokyo, without some knowledge of Chinese religion: above all Confucianism and Taoism, but also Buddhism and Chinese folk religion. This is admittedly a daunting undertaking and therefore it is of primary importance that we first gain some acquaintance with this continent so unfamiliar to us and with its religion. Providing this information and interpretation will above all be the task of the specialist, Professor Julia Ching of the University of Toronto, herself Chinese by birth and one of the internationally most established scholars of Chinese philosophy and religion.

Christianity and Chinese religion are to be *equal partners in dialogue, in terms of both value and status.* As in the "Paths to Dialogue with Islam (Josef van Ess), Hinduism (Heinrich von Stietencron), and Buddhism (Heinz Bechert)" that appeared under the main title of *Christianity and the World Religions* (Hans Küng et al.; Garden City, N.Y., 1986), the information about China will be juxtaposed with the *Christian response* of the theologian. Divergences and convergences will be examined, but such examination has to be limited to the most critical points. We cannot answer all the detailed questions or respond to all the counterarguments. What was dealt with in the above-mentioned work will not be repeated here: the whole question of mysticism, for instance, but above all Buddhism. Although the latter will be presented in its Chinese form here, I refer the reader to the aforementioned book for the *theological* treatment of this religion. Instead we will look into the possibility of a contextual, inculturated Christian theology in China. In contrast to the efforts at mutual understanding between Christianity and Buddhism, this possibility has hitherto received little discussion in the West. The aim of the responses will be to attempt something like a presentation of Christianity in the light of the Chinese religions: first the religion of ancient China, then Confucianism and Taoism. The different models for encounter between Christianity and Chinese religions will then be presented and discussed, all in the interests of cross-cultural and interreligious understanding.

The present aim is therefore not to deliver superficial and selective observations about the foreign religion, barely going beyond clichés. Rather, we are after serious *exchange of information, reciprocal challenge, and mutual transformation.* The end result will be to avoid all false exclusivities, rejecting uncritical syncretism and cheap harmonization in favor of gradual, *all-around critical elucidation, stimulation, interpenetration, and enrichment* of the various religious traditions. To be sure, such a process cannot be carried out by any religious or political authority, but must and will grow slowly "from below."

The signs of the times for a dialogue with China today are more propitious than before. Since the 1960s, there has been an unexpected revival of the scholarly study of Chinese religions in Europe, North America, Japan, and finally also in China. The dynamic role and function of Chinese religion in all periods and in all social strata of Chinese cultural life have been made clear in a very concrete fashion. At the same time, despite all the barriers that still exist, it cannot be denied that greater religious tolerance in China is currently leading to a revival of China's own hitherto suppressed religiosity. Not only are Confucians, Taoists, Buddhists, and Muslims increasingly beginning to profit from this atmosphere, but so are the Christian churches of China: three million Catholics (naturally, divided) and perhaps likewise three million Protestants (united by the regime). These churches are in the process of accepting the Communist Revolution as a historical fact, and of living their faith in a new way within a socialist Chinese society that is itself changing. Along the way, they are finding new, creative ways of inculturating their theology into Chinese life.

If there is indeed a renewal of the religiosity that was suppressed in the first phases of the Chinese Communist regime, then it would be particularly inappropriate on the part of the West to want to approach the Chinese phenomenon strictly from the scientific-technological or politico-economic point of view. In this case, economists, sociologists, development strategists, and above all, politicians must be encouraged to take China and its people seriously not only from an economic, technological, and political point of view, but also from the cultural (that is, from a philosophical, ethical, and religious) point of view. In China as elsewhere, economics and sociology without knowledge of philosophy and theology easily lead to that myopia characteristic of specialists. However, one who has seen more than a little philosophical and theological provincialism knows that naturally the same thing also applies in reverse! Happily, there are signs of change on both sides, and one purpose of this book is to expand the horizons of both sides.*

* Mention of prophetic and mystical religions in the Preface alludes to Friedrich Heiler's monumental work *Das Gebet* (Munich, 1921), translated into English as *Prayer* (London, 1932).

Note on Transliteration

The transliteration of Chinese names and terms is complicated by the fact that several systems are being used among scholars; which system is chosen depends on each scholar's special interests in the field of Chinese studies. The authors of this book decided to follow as a rule the modified Wade-Giles system of romanization, as is still done by specialists working on traditional Chinese culture in North America. But place names are usually rendered according to known, customary usage. There are, however, a few exceptions —for example, proper names of persons and places from contemporary mainland China—that are given according to the newer Pinyin system of romanization now in use there. In these cases, when deemed useful, the Wade-Giles forms are also given within parentheses.

Chronological Table

(Dates and entries before 840 B.C. are traditional)

LEGENDARY PERIOD

The Three Sovereigns
The Five Emperors   (Yellow Emperor, Yao, Shun, etc.)

ANCIENT CHINA

Early Royal Dynasties (3rd to 2nd millennium)

Hsia dynasty	Mythical founder: Yü, the Flood Controller
Shang dynasty (c. 1766–1122 B.C.)	Founder: King T'ang The religion of antiquity (oracle bones)
Chou dynasty (1122–249)	Rise of humanism Bronze inscriptions Spring/Autumn Period (722–481) Confucius (c. 552–479) Lao-tzu (?) Warring States Period (403–221) Mo-tzu (c. 468–376) Mencius (c. 371–289) Hsün-tzu (c. 298–238) Chuang-tzu (?) (Legalism, Yin-yang school, etc.)

IMPERIAL CHINA

Early Period (3rd cent. B.C.–5th cent. A.D.)

Ch'in dynasty (221–207 B.C.)	a united empire Burning of books (213 B.C.)
Han dynasty (206 B.C.–A.D. 220)	Confucianism as "state religion" (2nd cent. B.C.)

	Introduction of Buddhism (1st cent. A.D.?) Taoism as religion (Chang Tao-lin: 2nd cent. A.D.) The Three Kingdoms (A.D. 220–80)
The Six Dynasties (420–581)	China separated Kumārajīva in northern China (402–13) Spread of Buddhism and of Taoism

Middle Period (6th to 9th cent.)

Sui dynasty (581–617)	Buddhism as state religion in Japan (594)
T'ang dynasty (618–907)	Climax of Buddhism (7th–8th cent.) Nestorians in China (Hsüan-tsang, 596–664) (Hui-neng, 638–713) Persecution of Buddhism (845)

Later Period (10th to 20th cent.)

Five dynasties (907–960)	
Sung dynasty (960–1279)	(Jurchen rule in northern China, 1115–1234) (Jews in Kaifeng) Climax of Neo-Confucianism Chu Hsi (1130–1200)
Yüan dynasty (1260–1367)	Mongol rule Kublai Khan (r. 1260–94) Tantric Buddhism dominant (Franciscan missionaries in China) (Marco Polo in China)
Ming dynasty (1368-1644)	Wang Yang-ming (1472–1529) (Jesuit missionaries in China) (The Christian century in Japan)
Ch'ing dynasty (1644–1911)	Manchu rule Opium War (1839–42) (Return of Christian missionaries) T'ai-p'ing rebellion (1850–64) Boxer Rebellion (1900)

REPUBLICAN CHINA

Republic (1912–49)	May Fourth Movement (1919) Founding of Communist Party (1921) Sino-Japanese War (1937–45)
People's Republic (1949–)	(Expulsion of Christian missionaries) Cultural Revolution (1966–76) (Anti-Confucian campaign, 1973–74) Fall of the Gang of Four (1977) (A Policy of modernization and of religious tolerance)

I.
The Religion of Antiquity

1. *Julia Ching:* Chinese Perspectives

INTRODUCTION: ARE THE CHINESE RELIGIOUS?

Are the Chinese a religious people and is their civilization rooted
in religious beliefs? Had they gods, myths, and heroes as did other
peoples—Greeks, Hindus, and even Japanese? It may seem
strange to raise such questions, and yet these are questions which
have often been answered negatively by those scholars who spe-
cialize in one or another aspect of China's traditional and modern
culture. In the past, the image of China in Western scholarship was
that of a civilization that entered history full-grown, not having
passed through a childhood of dreams and heroic exploits but
rather appearing from the very beginning with a humanistic face
and rationalistic outlook, as reflected in its classical texts and the
persons to whom these were attributed: Confucius, Lao-tzu, and
others. But this was only so because the prehumanist stage was
largely overlooked.

I wish to emphasize that "Chinese religion" does not only refer
to the "great traditions" of Confucianism, Taoism, and Buddhism.
I wish to include a "great tradition" that was once alive, that has
been rediscovered through the writing it left behind: the religion
of antiquity, with its mythology, its divination and sacrifices, its
ecstatic or "shamanic" character. I believe that it is important to
know the past, not only for its own sake, but also in order to
appreciate the present better. I believe that Chinese civilization

in general, and Chinese religion in particular, are better under-stood when we see the *whole* picture, against four thousand years of historical background, including both the so-called "great tradi-tion" of the philosophers and the "little traditions" of the ordinary folk. Such a holistic panorama would permit us to understand better the ethical humanism that developed so early—by putting it in the right perspective.

I believe also that there is much that may be described as *ec-static* in the traditional religion of East Asia in general, and in ancient Chinese religion in particular. I use here the singular for "religion," which, in turn, has a plurality of forms and expressions. For "ecstatic religion," I shall borrow the description from I. M. Lewis *(Ecstatic Religion: An Anthropological Study of Spiritual Possession and Shamanism* 1971), who speaks of "the seizure of man by divinity" in ecstatic encounters. According to him, the Tungusic word *saman* means literally "one who is excited, moved, or raised," that is, a person of either sex who has mastered spirits and who can at will introduce them into his or her own body, or a person who permanently incarnates these spirits and can control their manifestations, entering into controlled states of trance in appropriate circumstances. He insists on the regular occurrence together of spirit possession and shamanism, particularly in the Arctic *locus classicus.*

In my opinion, ancient Chinese religion may be defined as *ec-static* religion, to the extent that it had an essentially shamanic character. And even following the emergence of ethical human-ism and the humanist repudiation of many of the myths and prac-tices of an earlier age, religious Taoism and certain forms of Bud-dhism, together with that product of their union which is called popular or folk religion, continued to manifest those features that can be identified as shamanic and also ecstatic. Let us, for a mo-ment, examine the evidence from today's folk religion.

THE ECSTATIC CHARACTER OF FOLK RELIGION

"He who shakes the Heavens comes from the west riding on a tiger and a dragon, bearing a holy seal. . . . Your voice like thun-der makes the *shen* (spirits) and devils tremble. . . . You can save a myriad of people. Now we invite you . . . to come before this altar. With your sword you can kill evil spirits. . . . Wake, wake, and save us." (See Alan J. A. Elliott, *Chinese Spirit-Medium Cults in Singapore* [London, 1955], p. 170.)

This is one of the invocations used to call for a spirit in a Chinese spirit-medium cult in Singapore. There, the male spirit-mediums are called *tang-ki* (or *dang-ki;* Hokkien dialect—literally, "divining youth"), not necessarily because they are young, but rather because they are not expected to live long. Such a person is subject to involuntary possession by one or more spirits, and serves as a medium for those who desire to seek out the will of the spirits as regards them. The trances vary with the importance of the occasion. The following is a description of what occurred in a spirit-medium temple: "First there is a gentle quivering of the limbs, which rapidly becomes stronger. Soon, the *dang-ki's* whole body sways and his head begins to swing round in circles. This may go on for two or more minutes, becoming faster and faster all the time. [His] hair, which is usually left very long, flies in all directions, and his neck appears to be at impossible angles. . . . As the drums rise to a crescendo, he staggers to his feet. . . . He slobbers at the mouth and rolls his head. . . . He prances around on his toes, staggering from side to side and muttering strange sounds. . . . It is now that he cuts his tongue with his sword, or . . . sticks spikes through his cheeks, hits himself with a prick-ball, or climbs a sword-ladder."*

After feats of self-mortification, the ceremony is concerned with personal consultations, involving the presentation by worshipers of charm papers and amulets, or the stamping of clothing and household ornaments with blood marks, or the interpretation of "speaking in tongues." Eventually, the *dang-ki* makes some final gesticulations, leaps into the air, and is caught in the arms of an assistant in an apparently unconscious state, from which he must be revived by having charm water splashed onto his face.

Besides such public ecstatic behavior, we know also of private or

* See Elliott, *Chinese Spirit-Medium Cults,* p. 63. The climbing of a sword-ladder is a widespread practice, also found in Japan, and may symbolize the shaman's "magical flight."

semipublic séances, which have more to do with communication with spirits of the deceased. In Singapore, such communication takes place through a female medium called by Elliott a "soul-raiser," and usually occurs in the privacy of the home. Ecstatic or trance behavior is involved also, as the medium prays to her god or spirit for assistance to seek out a specific soul. Here, it is interesting to observe that the souls raised are recently deceased kinsmen, rather than actual ancestors.

Spirit-mediumship as described above is expressive of what Elliott calls "shenism," that is, a belief in spirits, which is part and parcel of folk religion and cannot be assigned specifically to Taoism or Buddhism, even if the spirits involved might be Taoist or Buddhist. Spirit-mediums are not necessarily shamans, who demonstrate much more control over their own trances. Besides, what we may perceive in the reported ecstatic behavior is the interconnection between spirit-mediumship and divination, the latter being the purpose of the "act," as well as between spirit-mediumship and the cult of the dead—in this case, as noted above, not always the ancestors. This belief in spirits is also found in other East Asian societies, whether Korea or Japan or Vietnam. With the liberalizing religious policy in mainland China, more is coming to light there as well.

Our purpose here, however, is less to describe folk religion than to mention its existence before going back to the religion of antiquity, with its own practices of divination, ancestral veneration, and shamanism. I am not suggesting that any of the phenomena we witness in today's folk religion are lineally descended from those in ancient religion. But I wish to point out that various practices known in ancient religion still persist today, if in different manifestations.

HOW DEAD BONES TALK

If we go back four thousand years to the dawn of Chinese history, we find a society where ancestral religion, the belief in all kinds of spirits, and divination permeated daily life. Extant oracle-bone inscriptions, be these made on tortoise shells or the shoulder blades of cattle, continue to tell the tale of a literate civilization, that of the Shang dynasty (c. 1766–1122 B.C.). Its kings and nobles made important decisions only after having consulted the diviner-mediums, who, in turn, sought counsel from ancestral spirits, or from the supreme being, called Lord-on-high *(Ti,* or *Shang-ti),* from whom blessings and protection were expected. Such testimony to the religious character of early society is corroborated by that of the somewhat later ritual bronze inscriptions, which come from the early part of the Chou dynasty (c. 1122–256 B.C.), when the court diviners had diminished in influence but the ancestral religion, together with the belief in a supreme being called *T'ien* (Heaven), remained.

I propose to discuss certain topics regarding ancient Chinese civilization and religion, including mythology, divination, and sacrifice, paying particular attention to such specialist classes as diviners, prayer-men, and shamans, and to kings as religious as well as political leaders. My aim is to bring to light the essentially ecstatic or shamanic character of ancient Chinese religion. To do so, I wish first to go back to the beginning of Chinese culture and civilization, as these are known to us through the extant remains and records that have been unearthed.

The science of archaeology was introduced into China only in the early twentieth century. There it immediately made some important finds. The best known is that of the now missing Peking Man, *Sinanthropus pekinensis.* Its discovery is a story that illustrates the strange combination of mythical beliefs and scientific investigation, and in the case of the eventual loss of Peking Man, the loss too is a story that is once more shrouded in mystery.

The Chinese have always had a love-and-fear relationship with dragons, the mythical beasts with ancestral associations, believed to be life-giving and rain-giving, and at the same time fear-provoking because capable of bringing destruction. In chasing after the origins of the fossil fragments called "dragon bones" which were on sale in Peking shops, J. G. Andersson, the Swedish geologist and paleontologist, accidentally discovered in 1927 the site of the earliest human fossils in China, some thirty miles southwest of Peking, in Chou-k'ou-tien. From there, in December 1929, the head fossil was dug out, followed by other pieces that contributed to the assembling of the composite Peking Man of roughly five hundred thousand years ago. The opinion has since been voiced that the jawbones and teeth indicate genetic relations to the Mongolian peoples in general and the Chinese in particular.

The Peking Man specimen was lost during the Sino-Japanese War (1937–1945) in mysterious circumstances and has not yet resurfaced. But "dragon bones" apparently did not just come from human or mammal fossils. Even before the discovery of Peking Man, in 1898 (or 1899), Wang Yi-jung, then chancellor of the Imperial University in Manchu China, discovered that the surfaces of the "dragon bones" displayed engraved characters. He concluded that the hieroglyphic writings, which he did not understand, went back to a period more ancient than that of the bronze inscriptions with which he was familiar. After his death by suicide during the Boxer Rebellion of 1900, his friend, Liu Ô, a noted writer, inherited his findings and continued the task of searching and collecting, publishing in 1903 an assemblage of 1,058 pieces of "oracle shells" in a six-volume work. This led to the discovery in 1911 of the ruins of the ancient royal Shang capital at Anyang, making possible a scientific reconstruction of an ancient civilization that had a profoundly religious orientation.

Incidentally, "dragon bones" are still used as medicine in today's China, a continual reminder of the presence of the past in the postrevolutionary present. We suppose that they no longer include early fossils or oracular records, but the powder from bones continues to supply calcium and other substances that allegedly contribute to the healing of certain sicknesses.

Today, a revolution is still in the making, based on recent and ongoing archaeological discoveries that permit inferences of a very ancient history. The evidence may not yet be complete and is not sufficient to cover much of the distance of time between Peking Man and the Shang oracle bones, but it is impressive enough for scholars now to accept the Three Dynasties of traditional reckoning—not only the Shang and Chou, but also the Hsia (c. 2205–1766 B.C.), from which material remains, but no written records have surfaced, pushing the horizon of known Chinese history to four thousand or more years ago. Consequently, for our present purposes the term "ancient China" points to prehistoric China and includes the traditional Shang and Chou dynasties.

Archaeological discoveries have also thrown light on the religious character of prehistoric China, even the period before the Hsia. For the late fourth and early third millennia B.C., we have evidence of potters' marks resembling writing, of scapulimancy (etymologically, "shoulder-bone divination") using a variety of animal bones, and of clay phallus objects apparently involved in ancestral worship.

We may point besides to the evidence of mythology. Chinese myths of antiquity remain scattered and fragmentary, frequently interspersed in later texts which bear the mark of a de-mythologizer's editing. Just as archaeological discoveries have disclosed a past of war and violence, when warriors were buried with horses and chariots, so too the mythological records support an age of legendary gods and heroes, especially of those sage figures traditionally known as the Three Sovereigns *(San-huang)* and the Five Emperors *(Wu-ti)*.

WHO WERE THE SAGES?

The Chinese word *sheng* occurs frequently in the classical texts, where it refers to a wise and virtuous man, usually a ruler in remote antiquity. Etymologically, the oracle-bone graph for *sheng,* made up of a big ear and a small mouth, is closely associated with acute hearing, perhaps hearing the voice of the spirits, and perhaps also communicating something of what has been heard. The names of the so-called Three Sovereigns reveal their legendary character as well as their contributions to culture. They have sometimes been called the Supreme Sovereign *(T'ai-huang),* the Heavenly Sovereign *(T'ien-huang),* and the Earthly Sovereign *(Ti-huang).* They have also been identified with such figures as Fu-hsi (Animal Tamer), Sui-jen (Fire-maker) and Shen-nung (Divine Farmer), who bear names that bespeak their merits. As a group, these figures might represent the personifications of certain stages in the development of early culture, and are hailed as culture heroes in later texts.

About fifty years ago, Ku Chieh-kang, Yang Hsiang-k'uei, and others of the critical circle of Chinese historians proposed the theory that these legendary sages were god-figures. Their hypothesis was founded upon their critical examination of the fragmentary materials in the early texts, be these classics, history, or mythology. It associated the Three Sovereigns and the Five Emperors with the primeval Great One *(T'ai-i)*, which in turn represents the supreme being called God. According to them, the Three Sovereigns and the Five Emperors belong to the realm of mythology but became regarded as human beings during the later Chou period.

Were the ancient sages human or divine? The answer depends on whether we refer by the term "divine" to a supreme being, or to an ancestral spirit or deity of a tribal group. Scholars who consider the ancient sages as deity symbols do not always agree as to what it means to be a deity. Ku Chieh-kang and his circle think that the Three Sovereigns, and perhaps also the Five Emperors, all represented a supreme being, a personal God. But others prefer to regard the same sages as ancestral spirits, occupying a position lower than that of the supreme being. This is closer to a totemic theory, in which an animal or plant species is associated with a particular tribal group's identity. When the term "totemism" is applied to ancient China, it is thought that oracle and bronze inscriptions bearing a number of pictographs derived from animal symbols are to be associated with totemic clans. The sage Shun is associated with the phoenix and has been regarded as the ancestor of the Bird Tribe, while the Flood-controller Yü, allegedly identical with the mythical Kou-lung (Dragon), has been called the ancestor of the Reptile Tribe. But whether ancient China may be called a totemic society depends very much on how such symbols are interpreted.

The supernatural or perhaps totemic character of the primordial sages may not be directly relevant to a discussion of ecstasy in ancient Chinese religion. But it points to an age when communications between the human order and the divine were considered important, with the sages either representing the divine order or perhaps serving as mediators or ancestral spirits.

DIVINATION

Divining the future by the colorations, cracks, and other features of animal shoulder blades is a widespread and venerable custom. Speaking generally, in Europe, the Near East, and North Africa, the natural condition of the bone was read after the flesh had been scraped away ("apyroscapulimancy"), whereas in North and Central Asia as well as North America, the diviner created omen cracks by applying fire to the bone ("pyroscapulimancy").

Starting from the late fourth millennium B.C. the Neolithic inhabitants of northern China appear to have been the first people to use animal shoulder blades for divination, by heating them and interpreting the cracks which ensued. The practice reached its height by Shang times, with the widespread use of tortoise shells ("plastromancy") in addition to shoulder blades, the sophisticated preparation of the animal remains, chiseled to produce hollows and grooves to facilitate the application of fire and also structure the omen cracks, and the adding of inscriptions after the event, noting not only the occasion and result of the particular divinatory act, but also sometimes the coming to pass of the events, which proved the efficacy of the oracle. After the fall of the Shang, the Chou continued divination by shells and bones for a while before the practice died out.

From later ritual texts and historical records, such as the *Historical Annals* compiled during the Han dynasty (about first century B.C.), we know something about how the shells and bones were prepared for divinatory uses, probably after the animal victims themselves had been offered in sacrificial ritual. The assumption was that the dead animals would have special power in contacting others in the spiritual world, especially ancestor figures. We also know something about how the ritual itself took place (usually under the direct supervision of the king and at his court, perhaps in the ancestral temple), how the questions were asked (usually of the ancestral spirits), how the fire was applied, and how the cracks appeared. And we know as well that the persons who engraved the records on the shells and bones were not the same persons as those who probed or interpreted. But we do not know how the prognostication was made, on what basis the simple yes or no reply (from the ancestors) was chosen. So far, the notations of replies left behind in the inscriptions do not offer enough correlation with the shapes and angles of cracks. There is also evidence that divination manuals were followed, which are no longer extant. But did these also explain the logic of prognostication, or was that perhaps left to a higher form of reasoning?

In the oracle records, a word is often placed between the name of the ancestor and the word for "king," a word which means "guest" *(pin)* in modern Chinese. There is speculation that it refers to the king "receiving as guest" a specific ancestor or God himself, or at least to a kind of possibly ecstatic séance in which the two met. How it happened remains unclear. But apparently, music and dancing were part of the divination ritual, during which alcohol, served from bronze vessels, was possibly consumed in some quantity—and these could all have contributed to a ritual trance. It has been suggested that the "guest" might have been the prototype for the later (but ancient) institution of the spirit's impersonator *(shih),* into whom the spirit allegedly descended and to whom ritual offerings were made. But then, another question remains: did spirit-possession take place only during the sacrificial ritual, or did it also take place during the divination ritual, which was frequently a preamble to an important sacrifice? As available records do not enlighten us on these points, it may be useful to find out more about the religious specialists such as the diviners and the prayer-men.

Who were the diviners of ancient China? Were they mere ritual specialists, or were there also among them men alleged to have superior powers and given to trancelike sessions, whom we call shamans? The task of clearly identifying the diviners by functions remains difficult but has been rendered easier by those names which are engraved on the shells and bones, and by the ritual texts of later ages, the *Institutes of Chou (Chou-li)* and especially the *Ceremonials (I-li).* Where the performance of the divination ritual is concerned, functions were divided between the person(s) who posed the question *(chen-jen),* the person(s) in charge of the specific ritual itself, including the burning, and the person(s) who interpreted the results. Most probably also present were a master of ceremonies and various assistants. And besides, in the case of royal divination, there were the official recorders or archivists. Since royal divination revolved around decisions concerning state matters or the ruler's private life, the assumption was to involve the supernatural order in the human and natural order, to receive blessings from above, and to avoid punishments and calamities. In this sense, divination in ancient China (and in modern times as well) differed little from divination elsewhere, such as in ancient Sumero-Babylonian religion.

Shang divination involved mainly the use of shells and bones, and occasionally yarrow stalks. With the fall of Shang, the tortoises gradually fell into disuse, while the stalks were increasingly used in the Chou and later times, especially in association with the *Book of Changes*. But yarrow plants are perishable materials and have not survived in the company of oracle bones. Our knowledge about them comes from the texts, and from surviving contemporary usage. The diviner appeared to have the dual responsibility of performing the ritual and of interpreting its outcome with the help of one of the three divination manuals. These have as their kernel the sixty-four hexagrams *(kua)*, which, in turn, are derived from the eight trigrams, composed of broken or unbroken lines. In divining with the help of the *Book of Changes*, today's diviners still have recourse to yarrow stalks, playing with these as with a deck of cards. Since it is a time-consuming process, it is being replaced in many parts of Taiwan and Southeast Asia by the use of coins, placed in turtlelike containers. As far as we know, such divination is performed rather mechanically, without any ecstatic behavior.

Also concerning divination in antiquity, there was a kind of official, *chan-jen,* in charge of dream interpretation; these officials apparently performed their duties with the help of their knowledge of stars. And then there was another class of astrologers with the duty of interpreting celestial phenomena, including the eclipses of the sun and the moon. Here too, we have no direct evidence of any ecstatic character of divination.

The fall of the Shang dynasty appears to have mitigated the enthusiasm for court divination, even if the practice itself remained important and became widespread among the common people. However, we hear voices of doubt from the third century

B.C. regarding the power of divination. These offer significant clues of the growing dissatisfaction with the dependence on the supernatural, and the advent of a radically different age, the age of humanism. According to the story in *Ch'u-tz'u* (*Songs of the South*), the exiled minister Ch'ü Yüan called upon the great diviner Chan Yin to settle the turmoil in his mind. His questions were so phrased as to allow for simple affirmative and negative answers:

> Is it better to be painstakingly honest, simple-
>   hearted and loyal,
> Or to keep out of trouble by welcoming each change
>   as it comes?
>
>   .   .   .
>
> Is it better to risk one's life by speaking
>   truthfully and without concealment,
> Or to save one's skin by following the whims of
>   the wealthy and high-placed?
>
>   .   .   .
>
> Is it better to be honest and incorruptible and to
>   keep oneself pure,
> Or to be accommodating and slippery, to be
>   compliant as lard or leather?

It is said that the great diviner threw aside the divining stalks, excused himself, and said:

> There are cases in which the instruments [of
>   divination] are of no avail,
> and knowledge can give no enlightenment.
> There are things to which my calculations cannot
>   attain,
> over which the divinity has no power.
> My lord, for one with your mind and with
>   resolution such as yours,
> The tortoise and the divining stalks are unable to
>   help.*

* See David Hawkes, trans., *Ch'u Tz'u: The Songs of the South* (Oxford, 1959), p. 89, 90.

If the answers Ch'ü Yüan sought seemed simple enough, the questions he asked were obviously not such that the tortoise and the stalks could answer. He was ruminating over ethical decisions, and these were not meant for oracles. But the diviner's admission of impotence was itself of significance, indicating the limits of divination as well as the rise of a new age, when human beings were to rely more upon themselves, their own moral intuitions, rather than upon the instruments of divination.

SACRIFICE

Divination always points to something else; it may be a helpful device, but it is not a substitute for more important rituals. It presupposes a belief in spirits and in their power to protect the living. Besides, as the abundant oracle records have shown, divination in antiquity was associated with sacrifice and frequently served as a preparation for sacrifice.

Like the ancient Hebrews, the ancient Chinese had a three-tiered worldview—of heaven above, the abode of the dead below, and earth, the abode of the living, in between. They believed that at death, the upper soul *(hun)* rises up to heaven while the lower soul *(p'o)* descends into the earth. While this belief was formulated only in Chou times, it was already implicit in the religious beliefs of Shang times, and in Shang practices of divination and sacrifice. But the dead were not, so to speak, "imprisoned" down under. The royal ancestors, perhaps considered the most powerful among the dead on account of a special relationship with the gods, were represented as somewhere "on high," in the presence of God, and continued to have power over the living, whether to protect and bless them or to punish and curse them. Although departed, they continued to expect, for their nurture and enjoyment, sacrificial "blood" offerings.

The Chinese word *chi* (sacrifice) is said to derive from a graph representing the offering of meat, and possibly also wine, to some spirit. Originally, the practice began as a simple act of providing food for the dead. But later ritual texts describe an elaborate system of state sacrifices, each with its own name, offered to heavenly and earthly deities as well as to ancestral spirits.

What kind of offerings were made in ritual sacrifices, and how were such rituals carried out? There is ample evidence for responding to these questions, from both the oracle and bronze inscriptions as well as from later classical texts. The usual victims were cattle, goats, and pigs, with young bulls being preferred for the most important sacrifices. Other objects, such as jade and silk, were also offered. In the case of animal victims, the selected animal had to be the best available, perfect in itself. This was led to the site, and then killed, and opened up by the chief priest celebrating the event, with some assistance from the other participants. The fat was burnt to make smoke inviting the spirits to descend, and the internal organs were prepared and cooked. In all cases, special halls and yards in the royal ancestral temples were available for various kinds of sacrificial rituals, and bronze vessels of different sizes and shapes were at hand to hold the raw and cooked offerings.

OF GODS AND SPIRITS

Generally, we know of four classes of gods and spiritual beings. The supreme being was God, called Lord *(Ti)* or Lord-on-high *(Shang-ti)*, who reigned over a host of nature deities just as the king below ruled over his court. The exact etymological meaning of the term *Ti* is not clear, and various explanations have been offered. He is usually considered the supreme deity and is frequently referred to in Western literature as God. In divination, questions regarding eclipses of the sun and the moon were especially posed to him, such natural events being then regarded as manifestations of heavenly displeasure with earthly conduct.

In Shang times, the supreme God *(Ti)* was represented as a being remote and impersonal, perhaps a creator God. In Chou times the preferred term for God was *T'ien* (Heaven), originally probably a human with a big head, a word often found on bronze inscriptions to designate a personal God who was interested in human affairs, and possibly the supreme ancestor figure worshiped by the Chou royal family. The conquest of Shang by Chou probably led to the confusion and combination of two originally distinct cults, and to the subsequent usage of both *Ti* and *T'ien* to designate the supreme being, regarded as a personal God.

The second class of gods were the nature deities. These include such heavenly deities as sun, moon, wind, clouds, rain, and snow, and such earthly deities as the earth *(she)* itself and its product, grain *(chi),* rivers and mountains, and what have been called the eastern and western mother goddesses—perhaps identified with the sun and moon, perhaps also the spouses of the Lord. They were all under the direct control of Ti. The cult that they received in antiquity, and the veneration they continued to receive in later ages, albeit in different forms, witness to the mixed character of Chinese religion throughout the ages: never exclusively an ancestral religion, but rather a combination of the cult of ancestors with that of other spirits.

Then there are the high ancestors, frequently semidivine figures to whom the royal lineage was traced, and to whom the later ancestral spirits, both male and female, as well as the spirits of deceased ministers, looked up. The Three Dynasties were each allegedly founded by members of a different clan—people who traced their descent from the same mythological ancestor. The Hsia dynasty goes back to the sage-hero Yü, allegedly born out of a rock. The Shang dynasty had for its principal high ancestor a mythical hero whose mother became pregnant after devouring a dark bird's egg. The Chou dynasty goes back to Chi, meaning "Lord Millet," whose mother had allegedly trodden on Ti's divine footprint.

The fourth class of spiritual beings are the other ancestral spirits, on a level lower than that of the high ancestors. These are the ancestral spirits of the governed, rather than those of the kings and the aristocrats. The worship of such certainly less pretentious spirits was little known until a much later age. Perhaps one might associate with these departed spirits the so-called ghost *(kuei),* the graph for which shows a human being wearing a huge mask, possibly to signify a feeling of strangeness.

HUMAN SACRIFICE

Was human sacrifice practiced in early antiquity? Today's scholars answer in the affirmative, seeing it as a universal religious phenomenon. In the case of China, we find mention in the *Histori-cal Annals* of the Ch'in capture of Duke Hui of Chin, who was nearly offered in a sacrifice to the Lord-on-high but was saved after the intervention of the Chou king as well as that of the Ch'in duchess, his own sister (645 B.C.).

Human victims were not always offered on altars of sacrifice. There were those also who accompanied their lords and ladies to the other world in the burial chambers of ancient Egypt as well as China. The *Book of Songs* preserves the record of the sorrow of these men before the event:

> "Kio," sings the oriole
> As it lights on the thorn-bush.
> Who went with Duke Mu to the grave?
> Yen-hsi of the clan Tzu-chu.
> Now this Yen-hsi
> Was the pick of all our men.
> But as he drew near the tomb-hole
> His limbs shook with dread.
> That blue one, Heaven,
> Takes all our good men.
> Could we but ransom him
> There are a hundred would give their lives!

The first Ch'in emperor and dynastic founder took with him all those who constructed his underground mausoleum, as well as all the childless ladies of his harem. (And we have today the impres-sive life-size terra-cotta army of men and horses, recovered from their burial place by archaeologists. These had served as secondary burial companions to the dead emperor.) The classical texts con-firm the practice of human sacrifice in antiquity, but without giv-ing it approbation. The *Book of Rites* gives the story of a disciple of Confucius telling his brother's widow that such behavior was con-trary to the rites and should not be followed.

* Arthur Waley, trans., *The Book of Songs,* (London, 2nd ed., 1954), p. 311. Duke Mu of Ch'in died in 621 B.C.

WHO WERE THE PRIESTS *(Chu)?*

In Western languages, the word "priest" denotes a religious specialist with a special ability to communicate with the divine, devoted especially to cultic worship, and belonging to both a profession and a class. As such, the priest may occasionally appropriate the function of other specialists, whether medicine men, diviners, or magicians, but functions usually as someone with specialist knowledge of the deity and expert skills permitting the performance of cultic duties. The priest's mediating powers depend upon his ability to influence the supernatural powers of the deity, whereas the magician's powers to manipulate nature rest upon *techniques* properly applied, such as spells and incantations.

Our question here is: What about the religious specialists of ancient China? Were they priests, magicians, or both? Was there an equivalent to the priestly class as this was found in other ancient societies, especially in the Near East? Who were the people called *chu* dedicated to the cult? The problem here is that whereas we find a differentiation of sacrifices depending on the persons— gods, spirits, or ancestors—to whom they were offered, we do not have a term which is exactly parallel to the English word "priest." Scholars tend to characterize ancient Chinese religion generally as a religion of the shamans, known as *wu,* or *wu-chu.* But who were these persons? Is it possible to make a meaningful differentiation between the religious specialists of ancient China, between diviners, priests, and shamans?

According to the Han dynasty lexicon, the *Shuo-wen chieh-tzu,* the *wu* is a person who serves the invisible spirits and can call these down by dances. The word also refers both to a person who is skilled in dancing and to someone holding in two hands the instruments of magic or divination. The *wu* refers to a person who apparently reaches a state of trance through ritual dance and is able afterward to transmit the wishes of the spirits to human beings. In Chinese, *wu* is often used in association with the other word, *chu,* which signifies communication through the mouth with the divine. Indeed, the oracle-bone script for *chu* offers the picture of a human being kneeling in front of an altar. But the Han lexicon calls *chu* a female *wu.* The term *wu-chu* can refer to the same individual; it can also refer to two persons, or two kinds of persons, with distinct functions—especially in antiquity. When it is used particularly to refer to the *wu* or shaman, his or her special skills include praying in rain dances and communicating with the spirit world—perhaps also predicting good or evil fortune, healing sicknesses, and interpreting dreams. One explanation is that the word *wu* refers to a mediator between the human world and the divine, while the word *chu* refers to the mouthpiece of God who transmits his messages to human beings, that is, an expert in ritual incantations.

The *chu* appear to have been members of the official clergy, to whom was entrusted especially the worship of ancestors in antiquity, and they may be described as the priests and deacons of the state cult, with special responsibility for sacrifices. Their status appears to have risen, at the expense of the *wu,* especially in the Warring States time. Their duties included praying for blessings from on high, especially for a good harvest. To the extent that their incantations were considered effective in themselves, these persons may be also called magicians. However, they did not have the gift of ecstasy, as had the *wu.*

"SHAMANISM"

We have so far discussed diviners and prayer-men, or priests. What about the shamans themselves? Is there a clear distinction among the three classes of religious specialists in ancient China, and if not, may we speak of a shamanic character of all the religious specialists?

The word "shaman" comes from a North Asian, specifically Siberian context (Tungusic *saman)* and denotes a person, male or female, who has a special ability of communing with the gods, or with one of the gods, through knowledge and mastery of a "technique of ecstasy." Shamans are by definition ecstatics. They are said to become shamans through initiatory ecstatic experiences such as pathological sicknesses, dreams, and trances, followed by theoretical and practical instruction at the hands of the old masters. But it is always an ecstatic type of experience, including what resembles a mystical marriage with a god, that determines his or her "vocation." Allegedly, they possess the ability to have visions, to *see* the spirits, whether of deceased humans or of animals, and to be able to communicate with these in a secret language (resembling animal language), such as during a séance. They are also described as being able to levitate, to make magical flights into the sky and magical descents into the underworld (presumably in a trance state), to have mastery over fire, and to cure sicknesses. And, especially in China, they are alleged to have power over rain.

Arthur Waley has described the *wu* of ancient China as intermediaries in spirit-cults, experts in exorcism, prophecy, fortune-telling, rainmaking, and the interpretation of dreams, as well as magic healers. "Indeed the functions of Chinese *wu* were so like those of Siberian and Tunguz shamans that it is convenient . . . to use shaman as a translation of *wu.*" *(The Nine Songs* [London, 1955], introduction, p. 9.)

In contrast to the *chu*, who were priests and prayer-men in the employ of the state cult, the *wu* were rather individuals chosen from out of all the social classes by their own gods, and they sometimes served only these gods. Some of them belonged to a particular god, but most of them were able to enter into relations with several gods, or especially with the spirits of the deceased. To classify the *wu* by their functions, we may speak of the simple spirit-mediums, the healers, the exorcists, the interpreters of dreams, the rainmakers, and others.

The following passage from the *Dialogue Between the States (Kuo-yu)* may be helpful: "Anciently, men and spirits did not mix. But certain persons were so perspicacious, single-minded, reverential and correct that their intelligence could understand what lies above and below, their wisdom *(sheng)* could illumine what is distant and profound, their vision was bright and clear and their hearing was penetrating. Therefore the spirits would descend upon them. The possessors of such powers were, if men, called *hsi,* and if women, *wu.* They supervised the positions of the spirits at the ceremonies, took care of sacrificial victims and vessels as well as of seasonal robes." *(Dialogue Between the States, Dialogue of Ch'u,* pt. 2.)

And so the *wu* and the *hsi* of ancient China were mediators between the divine and the human. By Shang times, the female shamans had been reduced to being specialists in rain dances, while the male shamans were growing in importance. But unlike their Siberian counterparts, both played a minor priestly role in sacrificial rituals. Like the *chu*, who were official prayer-men, they too uttered prayers and incantations. Besides that, however, the *wu* had special gifts: that of calling upon the gods to descend, to look with favor upon the prayers of men, and also of summoning back the soul of a sick or deceased person.

The *wu*'s special gifts are especially described in the collection of poems called *The Nine Songs*, derived from the *Songs of the South*, that issued from the mid-fourth-century-B.C. kingdom comprising parts of today's provinces of Hunan, Hupei, Anhwei, Honan, and Szechuan, which together included about a third of the then known China. There, the relationship between the shaman and the deity is described as a fleeting love affair, either that between a female deity and a male shaman, or between a male deity and a female shaman, and the mood is often wistful:

> I have washed in brew of orchid, bathed in sweet
> scents,
> Many-colored are my garments; I am like a
> flower. . . .
> The Spirit in great majesty came down;
> Now he soars up swiftly amid the clouds. . . .
> Longing for that Lord I heave a deep sigh;
> My heart is greatly troubled; I am very sad.*

Another important function the shamans performed was that of summoning back the soul of a sick or deceased person. At one time, the soul was summoned wherever death had occurred, when a relative would climb on to the roof holding the deceased's garments and crying out for the person to return. (See the *Book of Rites*, chapter on the evolution of rites.)

In a poem entitled "Summoning the Soul," we have the follow-

---

* See Waley, *The Nine Songs*, p. 27.

ing dramatic plea on the part of the shaman, arguing the inhospitality of the other regions as reasons for returning:

> O soul, come back! In the east you cannot abide.
> There are giants there a thousand fathoms tall,
> who seek only for souls to catch,
> And ten suns that come out together,
> melting metal, dissolving stone. . . .
> O soul, come back! In the south you cannot stay.
> There the people have tattooed faces and blackened
>   teeth;
> They sacrifice flesh of men,
> and pound their bones to paste. . . .
> O soul, come back! For the west holds many
>   perils:
> The Moving Sands stretch on for a hundred
>   leagues . . . ,
> And you will drift there for ever,
> with nowhere to go in that vastness. . . .
> O soul, come back! In the north you may not stay.
> There the layered ice rises high,
> and the snowflakes fly
> for a hundred leagues and more. . . .
> O soul, come back! Climb not to the heaven above.
> For tigers and leopards guard the gates . . .
> O soul, come back! Go not down to the Land of
>   Darkness,
> Where the Earth-God lies, nine-coiled,
> with dreadful horns. . . .
> O soul, come back! Return to your old abode.*

The distinction between shamans and prayer-men existed, but it was not a clear one. And all distinctions blur when we speak of the ancient institution of kingship, with its religious as well as political character.

---

* Hawkes, *Songs of the South,* pp. 104–7.

THE KING AS CHIEF DIVINER, CHIEF PRIEST,
AND CHIEF SHAMAN

If the king was ultimately in charge of divination and diviners, he was similarly, in his capacity as chief priest, in charge of sacrifice and the priesthood, and he has also been described as the chief of shamans, in charge of the *wu* in his kingdom. Accepting that the king was a religious as well as a political leader, should we also consider his office to be not only a charismatic one, with reference to his purported claims of divine or semidivine ancestry, but also a *shamanic* one? Was the first king of each dynasty, so to speak, a powerful shaman in his own right? And were his descendants considered as having inherited his shamanic powers as well? Here we are led to probe into an examination of kingship in itself.

The Chinese word *wang* (king) is found frequently on oracle bones. The graph is sometimes supposed to represent a fire in the earth, other times an axe, but in any case designates without doubt the political ruler and his royal ancestors. The French scholar Léon Vandermeersch sees a relation between this word and another term, originally denoting "male," and explains it as the "virile king," father of the ethnic group, heir of the founder-ancestor's power. Thus he places kingship in a familial and patriarchal context. (See *Wangdao ou la voie royale* [Paris, 1980], vol. 2, pp. 13–18.) As already explained, the ancient kings also claimed some kind of divine descent, whether we are to understand it totemically or otherwise. Divine descent symbolizes without doubt a direct access to the supernatural, and the kings of antiquity were already called *T'ien-tzu* (literally, "the sons of Heaven"), even if the kings and other rulers of historical China, unlike the emperors of Japan, never claimed for themselves any personal divinity. This is like the contrast between Mesopotamian and Egyptian concepts of kingship. Whereas in Egypt the king was a god descended among men, the Babylonian king was not a god but a human being charged with maintaining harmonious relations between society and the supernatural powers.

Were the ancient kings also shamans *(wu)*? One way of answering this question is to look at the stories concerning the early dynastic founders. The mythical Yü, the Flood-controller, of the Hsia dynasty has been characterized as walking in a particular gait, described as the shaman's dance step. The information about King T'ang, the founder of the Shang dynasty, that we find in classical texts is much more rational. According to several accounts, T'ang's conquest of Hsia was followed by many years of drought, during which he was told by the diviners that Heaven could be placated only by a human sacrifice. Thereupon he purified himself, placed himself on the firewood, and prepared to offer himself to the Lord-on-high. But no sooner was the fire lit than rain came and quenched it.

T'ang's prayer is cited in the terse language of the *Analects* (20:1): "I, the child Li, presume . . . to announce to thee, O most great and sovereign God. . . . If in my person, I committed offenses, they are not to be attributed to . . . the people of the myriad regions. If [the people] in the myriad regions commit offenses, these offenses must rest on me alone, the one man. . . ."

T'ang's gesture of self-sacrifice is a supreme example of a king's acting as both priest *(chu)* and victim while serving a shamanic *(wu)* role for the sake of getting rain. And he did so after divination, as would have been expected. The sense of expiation for sins committed either by himself or by the people should also be noted.

A phrase frequently found in the *Book of History* introducing royal pronouncements is *Wang jo yüe.* The difficult term is *jo.* Some philologists have explained it as "The King, *seized by the spirit (jo),* said." In this light, the kings appear to have made many speeches in a trance state, communicating what they had heard from the divine, or at least they were *perceived* as having done so. The loss of the etymological meaning of the word *jo* has caused Chinese exegetes and Western translators to understand it to mean "The King said *to the following effect."* In ancient China, the king was the One Man of the classical texts, the ultimate mediator between the divine and the human. At all times, he was the paradigmatic priest and shaman as well as the political ruler and military leader. And, as in the case of T'ang, he was responsible for all that happened in nature and society. True, the feudal lords officiated at many rituals, each in his own realm, and the patresfamilias officiated at family rituals, each in his own household. But all did so to the extent that they exercised, in their own domains, those powers of mediation that the king exercised for all under heaven.

Many Western scholars (and many mainland Chinese), following the leadership of Karl Marx, Max Weber, or Karl Wittfogel, have looked to universal economic laws—such as "the Asiatic mode of production," the regulation of river and canal construction, or the creation of a bureaucracy for the mobilization of hydraulic power —in explaining the rise of ancient China as a political society under an all-powerful ruler. K. C. Chang, archaeologist and historian of ancient China, has offered an alternative explanation: that political power was accumulated by those individuals and families who claimed a better access to the gods, through divination, shamanism, and a newly invented system of writing (See K. C. Chang, *Art, Myth, and Ritual* [Cambridge, Mass., 1983], ch. 7). I should like to take a middle position, accepting the essential role of socioeconomic factors in the development of all political societies, while agreeing that religious beliefs dominated the social and political destiny of ancient China, of its people as well as of its kings and rulers.

The ancient kings of Shang and of early Chou, together with some of their wise ministers, were regarded as sages *(sheng)* in the company of the paradigmatic Three Sovereigns and Five Emperors, including the mythical Yellow Emperor, Yao, and Shun. They were actually shamanic rulers, even if the shamanic character belonged more to the institution of kingship itself, on account of the royal ancestors who apparently had certain charismatic powers, than to every individual royal successor. Let us also remember here that the ancient graph for "sage" or *sheng* is constituted by a big ear and a small mouth. Could not the greatness of the historic sage kings and ministers of the Shang and Chou dynasties be attributed to their powers, real or alleged, of hearing the voices of the Lord-on-high and of the ancestral spirits, and of being able to speak for them, as their mouthpiece?

SHAMANIC KINGSHIP IN ANCIENT JAPAN

Among China's neighbors, we find the same kind of sacred kingship and early shaman-rulers. The "divine" character of the Japanese emperor already reveals something of its shamanic origin. Actually, many of the early rulers were women, that is, shamanesses. The best-known example is the charismatic Queen Himiko of the Yamato state, who reigned during the late second and early third centuries, A.D. Her story is described in the Chinese chronicle *Wei-chi:* "[The people of Wo] made a young girl their queen with the name Himiko [literally, "child of the sun"]. She served the ghosts or spirits [literally, "the way of the ghosts"] and had a special power that bewitched the people. She was already grown up but never married, and her brother helped her to govern the kingdom. After she became queen, only a few persons were able to see her. She was waited upon by a thousand maids. But only one man always attended her, served her meals, transmitted her words, and had access to her living quarters. . . ." (See "Biography of the Japanese," in *Chronicle of Wei,* a part of *Chronicle of the Three Kingdoms,* ch. 30. *Wo* was the Chinese name for the Japanese.)

This charismatic queen appears to have been enthroned when she was only fourteen or fifteen, and her reign continued for sixty-eight years. Her personality and character appear typical of a shamanic queen. Some historians have even identified her with Amaterasu Ōmikami, that is, the Great Sun Goddess and the mythical ancestress of the imperial family. (Consult Ichiro Hori's chapter on Japanese shamanism, in *Folk Religion in Japan: Continuity and Change,* ed. Joseph M. Kitagawa and Alan L. Miller [Chicago, 1968], p. 188.)

THE ECSTATIC CHARACTER OF ANCIENT RELIGION

To hear the voice of the gods and to act as their mouthpiece: was this not basically the function of the *wu-chu,* the shamans and priests of antiquity? Perhaps not all the historic kings in China and Japan had the special gift of communicating with the divine, but they appeared to have descended from ancestors with such shamanic and ecstatic powers. It was a case of the institutionalization of shamanic (and ecstatic) charisma. In this charismatic role, the king served as the chief diviner, the chief priest, and the chief shaman—at least in name. If certain later kings lost their powers, they continued to make use of those religious professionals who did possess and exercise the gift of ecstasy, of calling down the deity at will. All of religion in ancient China, whether divination, sacrifice, rain dance, or so-called magical healing, was predicated upon this special relationship between certain gifted persons and the deities. All of ritual pointed symbolically, and sometimes also actually, to a primeval union between the human being and the gods, a union that was shamanic and ecstatic.

We have made frequent mention of ancestors and ancestral spirits, whether in relation to divination, sacrifice, or kingship. In a society and culture dominated by the belief in ancestral spirits, the bond between the human and the divine was especially assured by communication between the ancestral spirits and their living descendants. The heart of all rituals was that by which such communication was maintained. The formal celebration of the ritual reveals its ecstatically shamanic character. We possess no literary description of an ecstatic experience as such, but we find reference to the performance of rituals in which the son had to serve as the family priest, while a grandson or nephew was usually appointed, after divination, to serve as *shih* (literally, "corpse") or ancestral impersonator, a living reminder of the ancestor to whom sacrifice was being offered. But he was much more than a dramatic impersonator. He was regarded as the carrier of the ancestor's soul, the *shen-pao,* "possessed by the soul of the ancestor," just as shamans were called *ling-pao,* "persons possessed by spirits." It was believed that the ancestor spirit received in this person the offerings made to him, and also spoke in person through this mouthpiece, expressing gratitude for the offerings and promising protection and happiness to the family. The following gives a vivid description of a royal ritual offered to ancestors, at which more than one impersonator was present:

With correct and reverent deportment
And oxen and sheep all pure,
We proceed to winter and autumn sacrifices.
Some flay and others boil [the flesh]
Some arrange [the meat] and others adjust [the
    pieces]
The priest sacrifices inside the temple gate. . . .
Grandly come our ancestors;
Their spirits *(shen-pao)* enjoy the offerings. . . .
And respond with great blessings. . . .
The great impersonator arises
Bells and drums send him off. . . .
May your sons and grandsons
never fail to perpetuate these services!*

Was the above a mere description of a ritual performance, a reenactment of a primordial séance, or should we believe that, in a mood of intoxication, ancestral spirits appeared, at least sometimes, to descend into their impersonators and commune ecstatically with their descendants?

Spirit-medium and Shaman: A Brief Conclusion

Is there a clear difference between a shaman and a spirit-medium? The question is relevant, since we have begun the presentation with a description of spirit-medium practices in today's Singapore, and we are now concluding the presentation by repeating the suggestion of ecstatic behavior and possible shamanic influences in ancient Chinese religion. Here, let me recall that Arthur Waley has made a distinction between a shaman dancing and a medium in motionless trance. I agree that such a distinction can be made, that is, between the charismatic shaman and the impersonator *(shih)* serving as medium who was not always a professional. I also perceive a possible distinction in behavior, such as between a

* Consult James Legge, *The Chinese Classics* (Oxford, 1861–72), vol. 4, pp. 369–73. Explicit mention is made of drinks, and of the role of women in assisting and serving.

private individual absorbed in meditation, reaching perhaps a transformed state of consciousness, rendering him or her somewhat "motionless," which I shall consider as a kind of "personal religion," and the professional shaman or spirit-medium engaged in a public or semi-public performance including so-called magical feats, which is what I understand by "shamanic religion." Perhaps this distinction is discerned better today than in antiquity, and is in part derived from the difference between the semiamateur medium, unable to control the trance state completely, and the professional shaman who does so at will. Besides, today's accounts of the trance behavior of spirit-mediums in public include a whole spectrum of ecstatic behavior, ranging from motionless passivity to violent acts of self-injury and what may appear much more "shamanic" in Waley's terms.

In *The Catalpa Bow* (London, 1975), Carmen Blacker suggests a parallel distinction in the case of Japanese folk religion. While she calls both kinds shamans, she distinguishes between the medium *(miko),* someone who enters into communication with the spirits and is used by them as a "transmitter," and the "ascetic" of *Shugendō,* primarily a healer who banishes malevolent spirits responsible for sickness and madness. The "ascetic" usually has acquired these powers after a severe regimen of ascetic practice, including fasting, standing under a waterfall, and a symbolic or "magical" journey to another world. As Carmen Blacker and others attest, the founders—and even more, foundresses—of many of the New Religions in Japan were persons with shamanic power. Examples are the nineteenth-century Nakayama Miki, foundress of Tenrikyō; Deguchi Nao, foundress of Omoto; and the twentieth-century Kitamura Sayo, foundress of Tenshō Kōtai Jingukyō, more popularly known as the Dancing Religion.

And so, what can we say about the continuation of archaic religiosity in today's folk religion among the Chinese as well as in all East Asia? Divination is still practiced; shamanism is always important, although the understanding of priesthood has changed very much with the historical development of Confucianism, Taoism, and Buddhism. What was practiced at the royal court and by the nobles four thousand years ago is still found today—in different forms, of course, and as peripheral rather than central concerns.

The state religion of divination, shamanism, and sacrifice is no longer, having fallen long ago with the Shang house. But the *practices* of divination, of having trances, and of making sacrificial offerings, especially *cooked* offerings to the ancestors, persisted through many centuries. And the ecstatic union between human beings and the gods or spirits, so much a part of ancient religion, would contribute to the philosophical ideal of harmony between the human and the divine (or the "natural") that became part and parcel of Confucian and Taoist humanism.

What can be said about the relevance of these practices today, to the China and East Asia of today. What similarities and differences are there between East and West? And what can be said from a theological perspective about these phenomena? We await now Professor Küng's response.

2. *Hans Küng:* A Christian Response

No religion is only a doctrine of God, a theory about God, thinking about God; no religion is only a philosophy. Like the prophetic religions of Judaism, Christianity, and Islam, Chinese religions did not simply arise from intellectual reflection, especially not from an effort at strictly rational proof of another, higher reality. Conversely, it is also true that religions did not arise, as earlier scholars of the history of religions suggested in an oversimplified manner, from the purely irrational and nonintellectual levels of the human psyche. No, today's specialists would to a large extent agree that religions are grounded in an experiential unity of knowing, willing, and feeling. Neither in the prophetic nor in the Chinese religions is this unity simply understood as one's own achievement. What I say is also supported by looking at the ancient sages of early Chinese religion, to which the classics refer. There as well, religion is originally a response: a response, no matter how determined, to an encounter with or experience of the holy, Heaven, the divine, God, or whatever one calls it.

The picture of China that Julia Ching has drawn from its origins is quite different from that which we Europeans know from the Enlightenment. This is not an exclusively rationalistic and humanistic picture such as the classical texts and persons, above all K'ung Fu-tzu, allegedly give. This is rather a *total* picture of China in historical depth and with social differentiation:

• which includes not just Chinese humanism, but also those ancient strands of the tradition from the prehumanistic phase that are still present today;

• which does not present (as was normal throughout the centuries in China) the historiography of the dominant as the dominant historiography;

• in which not only men but also women (as shamanesses, priestesses, diviners) play a significant role;

• which not only brings the "great tradition" of the philosophers and scholars into play, but also the "little tradition" of the people.

But, to take up Julia Ching's question, how is a Christian theologian to respond to all this?

THE PERSISTENCE OF ARCHAIC RELIGION IN TODAY'S FOLK RELIGION

Phenomena that are four thousand years old were presented here purely from the viewpoint of the academic study of religion. What does a Christian theologian have to say to this as a theologian, given that he cannot proceed in the same phenomenological and descriptive way? It is more his task to present the spiritual challenge of all these phenomena for Christianity and for religions today. The position of many apologists who say, "In our religion everything is completely different," would be too simple and would justifiably provoke the response from comparative religionists that "with you, it is always the same!" Sober historical observation will differentiate: similar phenomena can be arranged and interpreted in nevertheless different overall contexts. Therefore, I want to begin my response on the level of historical comparison, and then proceed to contemporary religious phenomena.

Let us, for example, compare the function of *kingship*. Neither the Chinese emperor, the "son of Heaven," nor the king of Israel, sometimes called the son of God, was divine. Yet, in ancient China there was no separation of kingship and priesthood; the king functioned simultaneously as the high priest, the chief diviner, and the head shaman. He therefore possessed all-embracing power. There was thus no difference between state and "church." While, in the

Europe of the thirteenth century, the pope and emperor still fought over power, in China the absolutization of the emperor's power was already essentially complete. Indeed, in Japan the emperor was already deified from early on.

In ancient Israel, however, the king was and remained an entirely human being and never became a god-king, despite the title of son of God. Although common in the rest of the ancient Near East, the deification of the king and the assertion of his power over the forces of nature was thus excluded in advance. "According to the Jewish conception, the king was neither Son of God by nature nor did he automatically enter into the sphere of the divine through his accession to the throne. Rather, he was recognized as son through a declaration of the will of Yahweh, and in this way acquired a share of Yahweh's right to rule, possession, and legacy" (Georg Fohrer, *Geschichte der israelitischen Religion* [Berlin, 1969], p. 140). The power of the Israelite king was thus limited in advance through Yahweh's superior authority and his clear commandments ("Thou shalt," "Thou shalt not"). It was further limited through the priesthood and a certain right of codetermination on the part of the people at his installation. Here we already have the basis of certain later developments, such as the distinction between church and state in the West, and the lack of such a distinction in China (including the frankly cultic veneration of Mao).

Kingship may appear foreign to us; the sociocultural and religious-historical context may seem distant. Yet much that we have heard about ancient Chinese religion does not just belong to a distant past. It survives close to us and in the present, especially in the bizarre world of *folk religion.* And folk religion represents an interreligious phenomenon that therefore also involves Christianity. For there are undeniable structural similarities between archaic religions of the past and folk religions of today—in all parts of the world.

As scholars of religion, we should therefore affirm the following:

First: *early Chinese society* was a deeply religious one. It was characterized by shamanism with its ecstatic elements and sacrificial cults that assumed a special relationship of human beings to the divine. The ritual enactments of this ancient religion referred symbolically to an original unity between the people and their gods. But this means that, seen globally, China is not the entirely incomparable and (ir-)religious foreign element that some philosophers of the European Enlightenment assumed it to be. Rather, with all the similarities and differences one might observe, China is part and parcel of the single "religious history of humankind" (Wilfred Cantwell Smith). Next to the other two still-existing great religious river systems of Semitic-prophetic and Indian-mystic origin, China has shown itself ever more clearly (the significance of "sage" = *sheng* [holy] is striking) to be a third completely independent system. To be sure, it is composed of different religious tributaries, but there are nevertheless many points of contact as well as parallels with the other river systems.

Second: with all the differences regarding kingship, and naturally priesthood and shamanism as well, it cannot be denied that religious phenomena, belief practices, and ritual performances similar to those in China were also found in India, in Mesopotamia, in Greece and Rome, and even in Christianity. And in all the great religions—not in their pure teachings but definitely in their concrete lives—it is obvious that *certain elements of archaic religiosity have persisted until today.* To put it concretely, the veneration of ancestors, sacrifice, divination, and faith healing are found not only in China, but also in Christianity, particularly in that form, configuration, or stratum of Christianity which today is called folk or popular religion. As a theologian, I want to discuss problems such as the ancestor cult, sacrificial practices, and divination in a differentiated and comparative manner.

VENERATION OF ANCESTORS—BUT HOW?

It is well known that ancestor cults in the most diverse forms are not uniquely a Chinese phenomenon. In the late nineteenth century, when it was still thought possible to establish the original religion of humankind historically, many scholars agreed with the English philosopher Herbert Spencer *(Principles of Sociology* [London, 1876–96])) that the ancestor cult could be considered the root of every religion; their position led to an emphasis on the conservative side of religion (authority of the elders, social control, traditional attitude).

From as early as the *Paleolithic and Neolithic periods,* the ancestor cult was undoubtedly also widespread among Indo-European peoples (whether out of fear or piety vis-à-vis the dead). The background for this was a particular worldview and a belief in survival after death in whatever form. Prehistoric research has shown that, even in the time of Peking Man and Neanderthal Man, "belief in a survival after death seems to be demonstrated, from the earliest times, by the use of red ocher as a ritual substitute for blood, hence as a symbol of life. The custom of dusting corpses with ocher is universally disseminated in both time and space, from Choukoutien on the western shores of Europe, in Africa as far as the Cape of Good Hope, in Australia, in Tasmania, in America as far as Tierra del Fuego" (Mircea Eliade, *A History of Religious Ideas* [Chicago, 1978], vol. 1, p. 9).

Since the cult of the ancestors *(manes,* hence "manism") was strongly rooted in particular among the Greeks and Romans (striking parallels to China!), *Christianity* was, already in its early history, forced to come up with its own answer. The obligation of filial piety toward father and mother was deeply rooted in the patriarchal religions of not only China, but also Israel. Combined especially with the Christian belief in resurrection, it was a promising foundation for a properly Christian cult of the dead which, of course, found its place more in community and church than in family and clan.

Christianity was a *religion of the Fathers,* but unlike the ancient Chinese religion, it was never strictly speaking an *ancestral religion.* Israel believed in the God of the Fathers, but not in deified Fathers in the sense that, for instance, the God of the Shang dynasty was apparently originally an ancestral spirit. This Judeo-Christian (and subsequently Islamic as well) belief in the one transcendent God had consequences particularly for the cult of the dead. Christian Church Fathers pointed out early on that prayers and sacrifices to the dead were opposed to the first commandment. The true God did not permit beside him any quasi-gods to whom prayer was due. But there was never any precept against *praying for* the dead. Only *praying to* the dead was considered theologically impermissible—initially, at any rate. A Christian re-interpretation of the *sacrificial offerings* already being carried out by the people was likewise unavoidable in this connection. The church only tolerated them if they were understood as food offerings for the dead, but not as sacrificial offerings made to the dead. The Christian theological distinction said yes to the veneration of the ancestors, but no to the ancestor cult (manism).

Yet this is of course theory. In *practice,* this distinction is not so easy to maintain and enforce. In the Middle Ages, the Cluniac Reform sought to respond to certain folk needs, yet the ancestral cult took on exorbitant proportions with the conceptions of purgatory and of indulgences. And in the light of the radical critiques by the Reformers, the Council of Trent felt itself forced into issuing a specific decree on purgatory (1563) that insisted on an end to such superstitious and profit-seeking practices. The medieval conception of indulgences was of course not fundamentally criticized. Prayers and the liturgy for the dead were justifiably defended by the council (cf. Denzinger, *Enchiridon Symbolorum,* Freiburg in B., 1960, p. 983).

In China, however, there was an epochal, even if completely superfluous, *rites controversy* precisely on account of the veneration of the ancestors (more on this in Response IV). A half century after Trent, Matteo Ricci and with him the Jesuit missionaries allowed their Chinese converts to venerate their ancestors and Confucius, practices that were central for the Chinese. When they were later denounced precisely for this by rival orders, it proved futile for Emperor K'ang-hsi to issue an official affirmation that K'ung Fu-tzu was only venerated as a teacher and not as a god, and that the veneration of ancestors was a memorial and not a divine service. Finally, in 1704, the Roman Congregation for the Doctrine of the Faith (at that time, the Holy Office of the Inquisition) decided "definitively":

• that the ancient Chinese were idolators and the more recent ones atheists;

• that Confucius himself was a public idolator and a private atheist; and

• that the Chinese rites were therefore forbidden to Christians.

All in all, after the case of Luther and the case of Galileo, this was perhaps the weightiest of the numerous fallible papal decisions in matters of faith and morals! It was only 350 years after Ricci's death that it was corrected by Pius XII in 1939, at the beginning of the Second World War—of course, as always with Rome, without admission of guilt and once again too late.

Today churches in China, above all the Protestant congregationalist ones, are trying to find a path to genuine *inculturation,* between liturgical purism on the one hand and carefree syncretism on the other. Here the question may be asked: in a time of the deliberate suppression of death and the "death of man" in Western industrial societies, might not perhaps a veneration of the dead as has been preserved in China right through its democratic and Communist revolutions offer a new challenge for modern society and for Christianity? In a society that has successfully suppressed history, suffering, and death—where everything functions in a technically perfect manner right up to the day of death and burial —the "memory of the dead" takes on the character of incisive social criticism. Indeed, it has a humanizing function and a group-cohesive effect: solidarity with the victims of history, as the Catholic theologian Johannes-Baptist Metz has justifiably emphasized again and again. For Christianity in China particularly, such veneration means giving its own *rites de passage* new meaning in dialogue with Chinese piety. It means discussing anew such crucial experiences as birth and death, suffering and guilt, profound individual and social conflicts, but now in the Chinese context. All this is a challenge to Marxist as well as Western technological society (cf. Uwe Gerber, "Kontextuelles Christentum im neuen China," *EZW-Texte,* Information No. 94 [Stuttgart, 1985], pp. 21f.).

Sacrificial Practices: Processes of Interiorization and Spiritualization

Sacrifices are often designated as sacred action par excellence, in which the human person gains the clearest realization of his or her religion. In this or that form, they are a part of most religions. Concretely, however, human history is witness to an enormous *diversity of sacrificial practices* according to who sacrifices and what is sacrificed, where, when, and how, why and for whom the sacrifice occurs. Morphologies and typologies of sacrificial performances have been worked out. Yet, thus far, no unanimous theory has emerged regarding the origin of sacrifice—whether as attempted bribe or homage, as expression of fear or gratitude, as magic, as reenactment of a primordial event, or from the notion of a scapegoat.

We presume that, through a complex process of development— at least since Neolithic if not perhaps since Paleolithic times— different forms of sacrifice emerged simultaneously. And what had already formed in archaic cultures developed in early high cultures into often very complicated rituals. It is especially in China and Israel that we can observe how offerings (often firstfruits), mostly fruits or animals, were brought to God, sanctified, sometimes even destroyed, in order to make contact with an invisible power and thereby avert evil or invite beneficial influence. The idea of "do ut des" (tit for tat) often played a role. An *animal,* earlier (everywhere, not just in China and Japan) even a *human being,* could be the part that represented the whole ("scapegoat"), taking upon itself the sins of the community and the individual, thus destroying or expelling them. In the exposition, we heard about *King T'ang,* who offered himself as a sacrifice. One can draw an analogy between this event and the offering by Abraham of his son (likewise prevented at the last moment from above!), a last trace of human sacrifice that earlier was undoubtedly also common in the Palestinian region. On the other hand, for ancient Chinese religion the practice of sacrifice for expiation indicates that the concept of sin as an insult to the highest being was not at all unknown.

In time, of course, a more *ethical and spiritualized understanding* of sacrifice emerged in some religions. For these, the attitude of the one making the sacrifice took on more and more significance. It was understood that a sinful person cannot bring God an adequate sacrifice. Already for the Israelite prophets critical of the cult and in the Psalms, the most pleasing sacrifice was the unconditional surrender of the heart to God. And then, with the destruction of the second temple in A.D. 70, the entire Jewish sacrificial cult disappeared. It had become to a great extent a mere exercise in obedience and evidently nonessential for the continued religious existence of the Jewish people. To be sure, there are still Orthodox Jews today who, true to the letter of the Hebrew Bible, earnestly demand the rebuilding of the temple and the restoration of the sacrificial cult.

Although in the context of Jewish sacrificial practice, the Jew *Jesus of Nazareth* stood entirely in the tradition of prophetic critique of sacrifice and cult: "So if you are offering your gift at the altar, and there remember that your brother has something against you, leave your gift there before the altar and go; first be reconciled to your brother, and then come and offer your gift" (Mt. 5:23–24).

Against such a background and in the light of the execution of Jesus demanded on account of the law, it was quite understandable that the New Testament writings interpreted Jesus' *offering of his life* on the cross, together with his statements at the Last Supper as a living sacrifice for sinners and for sin. In this context, the New Testament stresses that this unique sacrifice of atonement must under no circumstances be understood in the Jewish or pagan sense. No, Jesus did not offer external gifts; he offered himself. Also, according to the New Testament, this sacrifice was not meant as a conciliatory appeasement of a wrathful God. It is after all not God, but man that must be reconciled, specifically through a reconciliation utterly and entirely initiated by God.

It was the Epistle to the Hebrews that elucidated this realization which permeates the entire New Testament: the sacrifice of Jesus served as the perfect self-sacrifice once and for all. Unlike the sacrifices of the Old Testament, it therefore rendered further expiatory sacrifices superfluous. And even if the primitive church already considered the Lord's Supper a way of participating in the unique sacrifice on the cross, this was nevertheless not looked upon as a repetition or completion, let alone a surpassing, of that expiatory sacrifice. To be sure, the event does summon the community and the individual to "sacrifice." But what is expected is not external offerings (as is falsely insinuated in the Roman Catho-

lic Offertory), but rather the sacrifice or offering of the human
being himself or herself. Not material offerings—bread and wine,
fruits or animals—are therefore demanded, but spiritual offerings
of praise to God, thanksgiving, faith, obedience to God's will, and
active love in daily life.

Such *radicalization of the understanding of sacrifice* in the New
Testament also includes a revolutionary critique of the Israelite
(and pagan) *priesthoods*. It is now impossible to see New Testament duties and offices—as occurred in an early process of sacral-
ization—as a continuation of the "Old Testament" cultic priesthood. In the entire New Testament, the word "priest" (Greek
hiereos, Latin *sacerdos,* cultic priest) is used only for Israelite-
Jewish or pagan officials, but never for officeholders in the church.
No, the one entirely nonsacral, unique, final, unrepeatable, and
therefore definitive sacrifice of the one everlasting, eternal High
Priest, Christ, fulfills, elevates, and abolishes the work of all human
priesthoods. To the *one* High Priesthood and Mediatorship of
Christ now corresponds the (spiritually understood) priesthood of
all believers. The heads of the communities should, however, following the example of Jesus, be the *servants* of all.

The foundations for the medieval understanding of the *Eucharist,* that memorial and thanksgiving celebration of *all* believers,
were already laid in the primitive church. It was seen as a specific
sacrificial act of the bishops and priests *for* the believers. In opposition to it, the Reformation justifiably brought the original Biblical
perspectives to bear again. Biblically, the unique sacrifice on the
cross justifies only an offering of praise and thanksgiving to God
and otherwise an offering of love for the neighbor. In contrast to
Trent, the Second Vatican Council emphasized both theoretically
and practically the Eucharist's character as a memorial banquet,
without of course wishing to exclude a certain sacrificial character
completely. The most recent documents of ecumenical consensus
have brought about a decided convergence of the Christian confessions on this question.

In *global* perspective, the historical convergence seems to me
to be important. Not only did all blood sacrifices cease in *Judaism*
with the destruction of the second temple; not only did *Christianity* internalize and spiritualize sacrifice after the death of Jesus;

but *Islam,* the third of the great prophetic religions, also demanded the surrender of the heart in place of blood sacrifices (sura 22, 37f.). The three Abrahamic religions therefore show significant consensus on this point. This consensus corresponds to developments in *China,* where, after the downfall of the last Chinese emperor, the sacrifices in the Temple of Heaven in Peking ceased. No, today no one should want to restore material sacrifices, whether plants, animals, or even human beings.

DIVINATION AND THE OTHER DIMENSION OF LIFE

What is divination? Divination is that "ability," based on extrasensory perception, to make pronouncements about the hidden future or events and relations of the present using different means (on which, by contrast, the pure "seer" is not dependent). This is a *universal phenomenon* that already existed among primitive peoples! It was most highly developed in the archaic high cultures, and certainly not only in the Chinese. Even today, we seem to find a primal human desire to know about the meaning of all of personal life, about the insecure future, about certain obscure life circumstances; to find unknown causes of illness, or to uncover the untraceable guilty party. Whether as conscious divination (partaking of the knowledge of the "gods"), or as "mania" (of those "raving" in ecstasy); be that done on the basis of personal charisma or institutional position; from shoulder blades, tortoise shells, yarrow sticks, or coins as in China, or from the flight of birds and the entrails of sacrificial animals as in Rome; or, as everywhere today, simply from reading palms or viewing the constellations of cards and stars. All this has little to do with the usual logic of science, but a lot to do with the prescientific "logic" of the "believer" who consciously simply accepts the possibility of such extrasensory knowledge of the future and hidden connections, along with quite specific rules of the game.

Now, to the extent that diviners, who combine visionary talent with methods, are authenticated through the conceptions and forms of a particular *religion,* their authority is hard to contest. For, the more divination is woven into the structures of a concrete, living religion, the more it is supported by the belief in the trust-

worthiness of that religion. Even the empirical experience of
failed prophecy is hardly of any consequence here. Conversely,
the more divination in the course of modern development is "pro-
faned" to become a professional and gainful "art," the more the
diviner becomes dependent on the people, his "clientele."

Until now, however, *hardly any empirical research* has been
done to test the factual reliability of divination. This is especially
regrettable in light of the fact that many people "faithfully" concentrate entirely on the successes of such predictions (for instance,
horoscopes) while ignoring the failures. No investigation has been
done regarding the extent to which the individual diviners themselves believe in the efficacy of their methods, and the extent to
which they are aware of the circumstantial character of these
methods. It would also be difficult to assess the extent to which the
predictive power of, for instance, the *Book of Changes* can be
explained with reference to meaningful coincidence (Carl Jung's
"synchronicity") and intuitive sensitivity. This is what C. G. Jung
claims in his well-known introduction to Richard Wilhelm's 1949
translation of the *I-ching.* This must remain an open question here
along with others, such as certain questions regarding shamanism
and parapsychological, transpersonal, and shamanic potentialities
(cf. Holger Kalweit, *Urheiler, Medizinleute und Schamanen:
Lehren aus der archäischen Lebenstherapie* [Munich, 1987]).
What makes things tend to occur at the same time? Using unscien-
tific divination methods that are qualitatively and synchronisti-
cally oriented rather than quantitatively and causally oriented,
Jungian depth psychologists are trying to defend divination methods as a legitimate way of researching the unconscious (cf. Marie-
Louise von Franz, *Wissen aus der Tiefe: Über Orakel und Syn-
chronizität* [Munich, 1987]).

And what about the *Bible?* It is ambivalent on this matter. Israelite law forbids sorcery, divination, the interpretation of signs,
and necromancy (Dt. 18:10f.; Lev. 19:26); but it permits the oracle,
the interrogation of God's will through a priest (Dt. 33:8), prophets
(Dt. 18:15; cf. 1 Sam. 28:6), and seers (1 Sam. 9:9). Dreams also
count as such a "source" (cf. Num. 12:6; 1 Sam. 28:6). Saul, the first
king of Israel, (according to 1 Sam. 28) expels all spirit-mediums
and diviners from his realm around 1000 B.C. Yet, in dire straits

(having been disobedient, he received no answer from God either through dreams, through the sacred lottery, or through the prophets), he himself consults the spirit-medium of Endor.

There is, of course, a fundamental difference: the role of ethics, of the moral law. In the Hebrew Bible, neither the priest (who had entirely different tasks to perform than did a diviner) nor especially the prophet is indifferent vis-à-vis questions of moral principles like the diviner, who, after all, simply answers questions put to him by individuals or groups. Accordingly, the diviner also cannot develop the same social criticism as, for instance, the prophet, who defines himself on the basis of an individually experienced calling instead of through an often highly complicated normative discipline (cf. Joachim Wach, *Sociology of Religion* [Chicago, 1944], pp. 356f.).

And the *New Testament?* We all know of the star that led the wise men to Bethlehem and of how Joseph was instructed in dreams. . . . Nevertheless, in the New Testament, the diviner plays a role neither in the presbyterial system of Jerusalem nor in the charismatic Pauline communities. Sorcery is explicitly condemned in the Acts of the Apostles. And yet, divination is in no way thereby eliminated. Indeed, in spite of all the condemnations by church authorities, in spite of all the criticism from theologians, in spite of all the enlightenment and then all the scientifico-technical rationality (or perhaps just for this reason), this phenomenon in all its shades and variations has been amazingly persistent. This is true not only for the Middle Ages, in which astrology, for instance, was an established science. It is also true for modern society, and here not only among the lower classes, but also in the upper social strata—the Soviet Union and the People's Republic of China included.

This phenomenon calls for a nuanced judgment. The irrational, pseudoscientific, psychological, and commercial aspects, it seems to me, must be criticized. By contrast, the "existential source" of the yearning for divination is to be taken seriously. The traditional religions in particular are not to be spared criticism in this matter. Could they adequately diminish the amount of "anxiety" that is concealed behind the need for divination? Certainly no dogmatic belief (in no matter how many truths of faith) can succeed against superstition in times of anxiety and affliction. But this may just be possible for a Biblical faith, one that puts unconditional, unshakable (and in no way irrational) trust in God, particularly when faced with anxiety and affliction.

One has to consider seriously whether it is not precisely the rationalistic one-sidedness of the scientific attitude and worldview and the spiritual vacuum of our time which today again make room for divination, just as in times past the attraction was for oracular, mantic, shamanic, sibylline, and magic powers. This would be indicative of religio-spiritual alienation in our society! No, in a postmodern view of things, the "particle of truth" in such practices would have to be integrated into a holistic understanding of the human person. In any case, it is no wonder that Europe and North America are witnessing such a boom in the religious and pseudoreligious literature market for books about shamanism and astrology. Is this the expression of a backward-oriented nostalgia? Not necessarily. It could be a postmodern longing for a new, recognizable continuity between humanity and nature, outer life and inner strength, rationality and spirituality, science and mystery, cosmic consciousness and authentic life.

WHAT LIES BEHIND FOLK RELIGION?

It has become clear that, while Chinese folk piety is in some respects more sober than that of other religions (for example, those in India), there is no lack of analogies with Christianity, so long as the sobering reality of the other religions is not measured against the lofty ideals of one's own: this would be applying a double standard. It would be like saying, "What they do is superstition; with us it is profoundly religious symbolism. . . ."

After the end of the eighteenth and beginning of the nineteenth centuries, it was *no longer* possible to understand religion *only from above*, only from the point of view of the educated, dominant, mostly clerico-elite upper strata. (Ancient Chinese religion was also an aristocratic religion; its priests stood in the service of the king!) Under the influence of Giovanni Battista Vico's and Johann Gottfried Herder's discovery of the "folk" and the *"Volkgeist,"* religion now had to be understood *also from below,* from the perspective of the less educated lower strata. "Folk religion" refers to all those forms of religious expression—those practices, styles, and attitudes—that cultural anthropology, the history of religions, and the sociology of knowledge have been investigating for a long time already; and to which Christian theology, especially Latin American liberation theology, is now finally paying some attention. Such folk religion often manages without its own sacred scriptures, historical records, and systematic organization. Originally it was rooted mostly among the rural peasantry, in a milieu tied to the natural rhythm of the seasons, with the accent on New Year and harvest, birth and death. It was oriented primarily toward earthly, material needs, toward economic, physical, and psychological requirements. And yet, such folk religion has evidently even managed to survive in the large urban agglomerations of modern industrial society, albeit in a greatly transformed form with even greater emphasis on the individual and the family. This has been the case especially when it has been supported by new means of communication.

Such folk religion is thus of archaic origin, as widely distributed as it is persistent, and even to some extent resistant to the modern Enlightenment. Its existence *undermines the sharp distinction between magic and religion* so widely held earlier. To be sure, it is possible to make a conceptual distinction between the two basic attitudes of a coercive magic and a supplicatory religion; but a doctrinaire evolutionary scheme is impossible today. Contemporary empirical field research (Bronislaw Malinowski and A. R. Radcliffe-Brown) has demonstrated the untenability of interpretations such as those put forward by the cultural anthropologist E. B. Tylor, the ethnologist and scholar of religion James G. Frazer (development from magic to religion and finally to science); and which even Sigmund Freud still presupposed in his critique of religion. No, magic and religion cannot be distinguished concretely as two successive stages. The magical survives in the religious, and the religious can become magical again: a prayer can become a magic formula, a religious symbol can become a fetish, an offering can become a magic ritual. Magic and religion to this day exist simultaneously alongside and within each other, just as religion for its part has in no way been superseded by science.

However this may be, what is hiding behind this folk religion that will apparently not die? As has been indicated, what is evidently behind these ancient and yet still contemporary religious phenomena are *basic human needs:* the need for protection and help, for consolation and encouragement, for an explanation and interpretation of human existence and this world. Religion as *remedy for the people!* These religious phenomena are grounded in an existential depth such as is seldom achieved by the legal, political, and even aesthetic realms, insofar as these are actually "secular" and separated from the religious at all. It is no wonder then that people will defend themselves with hands and feet, with their mind, their hearts, and their feeling, if they are attacked at this profound religious level and threatened with the loss of what is most sacred to them. The thesis that predicts the disappearance of religion and increasingly secularized, "progressive" societies must accordingly be critically reexamined—even for Western countries.

Moreover—and this is why we speak of the holy here—all these religious practices, all the rites and symbols, teachings and myths, are in some form grounded in the transcendent. They are supplied with *supernatural, heavenly, divine authority* and secured with temporal, even otherworldly and eternal sanctions. In human consciousness, therefore, even that which has become historical can easily acquire a divine and unchanging character. It is no wonder then that this kind of religiosity has proven itself to be extremely resistant and is now also venturing to reemerge, often unbroken and unchanged, into the light of day in China, now that the antireligiousness of the Communist Party is beginning to give way to a limited tolerance.

This is becoming especially apparent in *Taiwan.* In spite of an enormous injection of personnel, money, and time, in spite of forty years of unhindered missionary work, Christianity is stagnating there. Only 3 1/2 percent of the nineteen million Taiwanese could be won over to Christianity; and a large proportion of these are from the non-Chinese aboriginal population. And yet, Chinese folk religion is experiencing an unparalleled revival after extended political and cultural suppression under the Japanese colonizers (1895–1945). This flowering of a Chinese folk piety mixed with Buddhist, Taoist, and Confucian elements can be seen above all in the restoration and new construction of numerous temples. In Taiwan there are apparently around twelve thousand altogether. How is this development to be explained? It is more than a matter of economic prosperity; it also has to do with the search for spiritual sources in the traditions of one's own people and with the yearning for religious security in the cycle of the seasons, with all the feasts and pilgrimages that the new media of communication encourage.

But traveling today from Taiwan to the *Chinese mainland,* one immediately notices that the beginnings of a similar trend can be observed wherever a temple has been restored to religious (and not just museum) use. Even on ordinary weekdays, one can find thousands of joyful people, old and young, visiting these temples. And much as plain folklore and increasing tourism may also be involved (as in Christianity), all these various practices with incense sticks and divination lots, these prostrations before a god, before the Taoist Three Pure Ones, or before the deified Buddhas are certainly not *just* folklore! Thus for instance, the "All Souls' Day" (to use a Christian expression) that is celebrated in all Sinicized countries and now again on the Chinese mainland is supposed to free all the wandering souls from their suffering. (At least in Taiwan, even something like the consecration of altars to Chiang Kai-shek and Sun Yat-sen can be observed—of course not by a pope, but rather by the pious popular will or the state.)

It need not be denied that such folk religion can be an *opium of the people* instead of a remedy for them. Mao Tse-tung and the Chinese Communists undoubtedly had good reason for their rejection of religion. In *Tibet,* even today the folk and religion are one as perhaps nowhere else. If one compares the temples there, abounding in gold and treasures, with the bitter poverty of the people, then, even after (in spite of all strategic interests) the completely irresponsible Chinese aggression and occupation of Tibet (1951) and the flight of the Dalai Lama (1959), one may still ask whether here (as, for instance, in Christian Latin America) religion has not been used to keep the lower classes in dependency and passivity, superstition and fatalism. A limited modernization such as the Chinese are now attempting could therefore have other than negative consequences—and need not stand in the way of the desirable return of the Dalai Lama as the spiritual head of the Tibetan people.

Nevertheless, even in Tibet (as in Latin America, South Africa, Korea, or the Philippines), one can see that religion is not only the "expression of real distress" of the people, but also, at the same time—again quoting Karl Marx—"the *protest* against real distress." In any case, the Communist Party, whether in the Soviet Union, in the People's Republic of China, or particularly in Tibet, has not been able to do away with religion. The lesson could have been drawn from the history of religion: although great religions are subject to epochal changes of paradigm, they are nevertheless as tough as anything. The survival of religion in the entire Sinicized world through the millennia until today is a fact: not only in the fast-growing countries of South Korea and Taiwan, but also more subtly in highly industrialized Japan, ever more clearly after the Cultural Revolution in the People's Republic of China itself, and, since 1980, strikingly in the underdeveloped "autonomous region" of Tibet.

The folk religion under discussion here, drawing as it does upon archaic sources, has acquired a very special power of perseverance because it has from ancient times (and surely not just in Tibet) been the *expression of the cultural identity of the people.* Culture and religion are often almost identical, so that even urbanization, although it may threaten it, can hardly suppress this religion completely. The result is the transformation of the religion. Of course, this persistent folk religion puts Christianity before a grave dilemma.

THE DILEMMA OF CHRISTIANITY IN THE FACE OF FOLK RELIGION

The decisive question is, how can an originally foreign religion such as Christianity ever put down roots among a people if it itself wants nothing to do with the religion of this people, especially with the folk religion and the folk culture? *Either* Christianity is critical of the folk religion and therefore remains foreign to the people, *or* it accommodates itself and therefore is threatened with the loss of its identity. This dilemma arose when early Christianity was faced with Hellenistic and Roman culture, and when medieval Christianity was faced with Germanic and Slavic culture. Now, at the latest since the onset of modernity, it also presents itself in the face of Indian and Chinese-Japanese high culture. This is a dilemma that, today as well, is answered in different ways by different churches and often even within the same church. The discussions especially in Japan, Korea, and Taiwan are evidence of this. But how is one to handle this dilemma?

Much exemplary work—done in Japan, for example, by Jan Swyngedouw, in Taiwan by Yves-Émil Raguin or by the Presbyterian Tung Fang-yen—has shown that folk religion can in no way be simply dismissed as idolatry, human projection, or superstition. Rather, it must be appreciated with all its spiritual and cultural richness. What is often declared to be *belief* and what *superstition;* what is said to be religiously correct, legitimate, and orthodox and what is considered illegitimate or heretical; indeed, what is called true and what false religion—these are questions of definition that are answered in quite different ways in different epochs and contexts. They depend, on the one hand, on the reigning orthodoxy of the majority and, on the other hand, on the better judgment of the time. This can be seen not least in the Latin root of superstition, *superstitio,* a word that had a negative and pejorative (instead of descriptive and analytic) connotation from early on *(superstitio;* from *superstes,* surviving, witnessing; see Mary R. O'Neill, "Superstition," in *The Encyclopedia of Religion,* ed. Mircea Eliade [New York, 1987], vol. 14, pp. 163–66).

Certainly Christianity, at least in its first thousand years, demonstrated that it was not less capable than other religions of creatively integrating earlier religious attitudes, convictions, and practices. It not only transformed pagan shrines, sanctuaries, and festivals, but also took over the entire Latin calendar vocabulary with its references to the old gods (Mars, Jupiter, Venus). In the sixth century, Gregory the Great recommended to the Christian missionaries in England that they proceed gradually, something for which John Paul II in the twentieth century (as in the case of the African churches and their problems with polygamy and degrees of marriage) again has no understanding.

Of course, even discerning Christian interpreters of Chinese folk religion are not of the opinion that all forms of religious expression are to be accepted uncritically just because they manifestly belong to a religion or a people. The Church Fathers spoke out *against* an undifferentiated *syncretistic amalgamation.* The humanists (Erasmus of Rotterdam) and the Reformers (Luther, Zwingli, Calvin) quite rightly directed their vehement protests against the late medieval externalization, materialization, and commercialization of religion (in connection with saints, prayers, masses, pilgrimages, shrines, bones, relics, candles)—not to mention the later radical critique of popular superstition by the Enlightenment, the natural sciences, and medicine.

Replacing the word "superstition" with the term "folk belief," as ethnologists suggest, is therefore problematic. Belief itself is after all also folk belief. Yet belief and superstition cannot simply be put on the same level with the help of the term "folk belief." A separation of the "spirits" is unavoidable. The folk belief in witchcraft that was still prevalent among the Reformation churches will serve as sufficient illustration. The Enlightenment was correct in insisting on the philosophical and theological unavoidability of criteria for distinguishing between responsible belief in God and irresponsible belief in witches in popular piety.

Indeed, all too often Chinese folk religion, like the Christian one, has been a purely *utilitarian piety.* People pray to those gods or saints from whom they expect the greatest understanding and eventually also the greatest advantage for themselves. In Taiwan, one can choose from more than 240 deities, while Christians have no fewer saints and helpers at their disposal. This is religion as wish fulfillment. The danger is obvious: an overemphasis on the popular threatens to stifle everything ethical. The result is that, sooner or later, the critical thinkers and above all the intellectuals will leave. The disdain for and eventual persecution of religion under Lenin and Stalin (a former Orthodox seminarian) as well as under Mao and the Cultural Revolution presupposed that the *moral claims* of religion had long since lost *credibility.*

My plea is as follows: Christian faith will have to guard against an overemphasis on folk religiosity without thereby allowing an excessive rationalism to take over, something that would result in the extinction of religion among the masses. A *rational critique* of folk religion is possible *without* succumbing to an *arid rationalism,* be it a modern Protestant or a Neo-Confucian variety. No human being lives by concepts and ideas alone; images and symbols are indispensable. Religion operates not only through pious speeches and sermons, but often even more through actions, gestures, and productions. It acts not only through intellectual achievements, but also through bodily expression, through art, music, and dance.

In short, respect for folk religion does not mean that popular beliefs and practices, no matter how archaic and folklike they may be, cannot be subjected to cautiously enlightening criticism, to a process of self-enlightenment and self-purification. As we heard, this sort of process began in China early on, so that belief and superstition, religion and magic could eventually be distinguished there. I have given the examples of ancestral cult, sacrificial practices, and divination. Nevertheless, it cannot be overlooked that, in contrast to Chinese religion, Christianity—along with Judaism and Islam—stands in the great tradition of decidedly prophetic religions. And the *prophet,* at least the great individual prophets, are in the final analysis entirely different from the ecstatic *shaman,* with his paranormal powers, his quest for visions and knowledge, his healing journeys through time and space, and his search for special ways of power. Here, and here in particular, lies the central difference between Christianity and Chinese folk religion to the extent that it is characterized by shamanism.

THE DIFFERENCE BETWEEN SHAMAN AND PROPHET

To be sure, *prophecy,* in the wider sense of professional cult or court prophets who serve at a sacred shrine or royal court, is not a peculiarly Israelite institution. It can be found in many religions, including in China (cf. H. H. Rowley, *Prophecy and Religion in Ancient China and Israel* [London, 1956]). In the ancient Near East, *early forms* of prophets were the *seer* (probably nomadic and brought to Palestine by the Patriarchs) and the ecstatic *nabi* (found in the lands of Palestinian culture and fertility cults). In the case of ancient Israel, especially Elijah and Elisha are known as early representatives of prophethood. According to popular traditions and legends, their prophecy was still associated with magic (mantic practices, miracle tales, and magical words of Yahweh) and with ecstasy. So too, King Saul heard the seer Samuel's prediction that he would meet a "band of prophets . . . with harp, tambourine, flute, and lyre before them, prophesying. Then the spirit of the Lord will come mightily upon you, and you shall prophesy with them and be turned into another man" (1 Sam. 10:5f.).

Yet in *classical prophecy, magic is overcome.* The prophetic speech and action of the great individual prophets did not work mechanically but was rather founded entirely on the will and power of Yahweh. Experience with spirits became secondary to the word of Yahweh; the ecstatic had, if any, only peripheral significance. The great prophets were indeed taken over by God, but, entirely unlike the shamans, they were not experts in ecstasy who could put themselves in a trance state with ingenious techniques using drums or bells, dance or narcotics. None of the prophets would, so to speak, deliberately leave his body in order to undertake lengthy spiritual journeys up to heaven or down to hell, there to solicit the help of good spirits and drive out the evil.

No, unlike the shaman, *the prophet was no medicine man* who practiced the art of healing; and also *no companion of the dead* who led the souls of the deceased to the other world; and especially *no priest* in charge of public sacrifice. The true prophet stood in tension, indeed usually in opposition, to the king as political and military leader, and particularly to the priest, to the holder of a sacred office and the guardian of the tradition. He also distanced himself from the professional prophetic guild of the court and temple which included the "false prophets." He needed no complicated initiation and no authoritative ordination.

What was decisive for the prophet was and remains the passively received divine *call*, the detailed and particular *mission.* His goal was not the shamanic manipulation of the invisible and the unavailable (that is, magic). He wanted to serve the Invisible and Unavailable One (that is, religion). He was to be the messenger of God, entirely directed to *"pro-phetizing,"* by which is meant a *pro*-clamation and sometimes also a *pre*-diction. This then was the task to which the prophet devoted himself with all his passion, with unyielding determination, with words of power, and also with symbolic actions. This was the *proclamation of the word and will of God for the present and the future,* for the people and the individual. Unlike the shaman or the priest, the prophet did not act in the service of the religio-political establishment. His action had a *critical function.* It was often quite vehemently critical of the cult, the regime, and even of society as a whole.

Unlike the shaman or even the priest, a prophet could therefore never represent a utilitarian religion. A prophet was thoroughly ethically oriented and always represented a moral, indeed a liberating religion. Herewith we are faced with the question of how to evaluate the elements of the archaically grounded folk religion.

BELIEF OR SUPERSTITION?

We have heard that, unlike the old folk religions, many of the more recent folk religions manage to get along without their own sacred writings. We must therefore reconsider the question of criteriology that is addressed mainly in connection with the high religions. To the extent that a folk religion makes no appeal to normative texts, traditions, or configurations, it cannot, unlike any high religion, be judged by comparing it to its origins or canon (Bible, Qur'an, Gita, or Christ, the Enlightened One, the Prophet). To that extent, the *general religious criterion of the authentic or canonical* cannot be applied here (on the problem of criteria, see Hans Küng, *Theologie im Aufbruch: Eine ökumenische Grundlegung* [Munich, 1987], ch. C 2. English translation: *Theology for the Third Millennium* [New York, Doubleday, 1988]).

And what about the *specifically Christian criterion?* Does a religion let anything of the spirit of Jesus Christ come out in theory and in practice? Certainly this criterion can at least be applied to those folk religions that claim to be *genuinely Christian.* This claim is made by certain Afro-Brazilian cults as well as by the Unification Church of the Korean Reverend Sun Myung Moon. This specific Christian criterion is also appropriate if a cult claims at least to be *Christian as well.* An example would be the I-kuan-tao in Taiwan, which may be translated as "five religions in one." This religion claims to be Taoism, Buddhism, Confucianism, Islam, *and* Christianity at the same time. The critical question of whether the spirit of Jesus lives here or there can and should be

addressed to such Christian or "also-Christian" religions so that
one can distinguish the Christian from the non-Christian. But
what about the *non-Christian* folk religions? Unquestionably, the
specifically Christian criterion can only be applied from the outside here, and this is of help neither for the religion concerned nor
for dialogue. What should be done, then?

Is it perhaps, as some people think, only a question of *that* one
believes, not *what* one believes? We only have to look at the just
recently reissued, ten-volume work *Handwörterbuch des deut-
schen Aberglaubens* (A Manual of German Superstitions; ed. Hans
Bächtold-Stäubli [Berlin, 1927–42]) in order to see how many irrational, contradictory, indeed absurd elements (from aphrodisiacs
to number mysticism) religion would have to integrate if it wanted
to integrate *everything*. No, basically Thomas Aquinas distinguished superstition and true religion correctly: "Superstition is
the vice which is opposed to religion through excess, because it
offers divine veneration to him to whom it is not due or in a
manner in which it is not due" *(Summa Theologiae* II–II, 92, 1). Yet
his subsequent long discussion about the different forms of superstition (divination in particular) shows that, concretely, the boundaries are difficult to draw—and that deviance from orthodoxy does
not require the immediate resort either to the Inquisition, as in
the Middle Ages, or to the lawmakers and the police, as today.

The Chinese have in general been of the opinion that *all* religions are *good* for people, for all religions teach people to do good.
As we know, the Marxist critique of religion countered this notion
with the accusation that religions as a whole are superstition that
corrupts people. In 1979 (three years after Mao's death and two
years after the excommunication of the Gang of Four), I was the
first theologian to have the great opportunity to visit China officially and to speak positively on the belief in God at the Chinese
Social Science Academy in Peking. I asserted as the first of nine
differentiating theses, that "we have to *distinguish between religion and superstition.*" And the explanation:

• *Religion* does not recognize anything as absolute authority that
is relative, conditioned, or human, but only the absolute itself,
which in our tradition we have called God since time immemorial.

By the Absolute I mean that hidden first and last reality that not only Jews and Christians but also Muslims worship—and that Hindus seek in Brahman, Buddhists in the Absolute, and of course traditional Chinese in Heaven or the Tao. Religion is certainly one of the most important factors in the history of this great country. It is and remains a social and political factor not only in Tibet, but elsewhere as well.

• *Superstition,* however, recognizes as absolute authority and demands blind obedience to something that is relative and not absolute. Superstition deifies either material things, a human person, or a human organization. In this respect, any personality cult, for example, reveals itself to be a kind of superstition!

• *Consequences:* However, not all superstition is religion; there are other, very modern forms of superstition. Not all religion is superstition; there are true religions. Yet any religion can become superstition wherever it transforms the nonessential into the essential, something relative into something absolute (cf. *Die Zeit,* October 19, 1979).

Here "superstition" is not used in the restricted sense of magic, but in the broad sense of pseudoreligion or surrogate religion. Yet even the appeal to the one God can in no sense suffice as an adequate criterion for daily religious practice and especially for folk religion. Indeed, what horrors and absurdities have been justified with an appeal to God's authority!

THE QUESTION OF THE *HUMANUM*

The *theological* criterion for distinguishing religion and pseudoreligion needs to be concretized through the anthropological and *ethical* criterion for distinguishing true and false religion. This general ethical criterion can certainly be applied to folk religion. It is not by chance that religious people in China also ask, Do religions really always teach the good? Have they always done so during their long histories?

Yes, religions should help human beings do the good so that they may be *truly human.* This *general ethical criterion* can in fact be applied to folk religions:

• To the extent that folk religious teachings or practices protect, sanctify, and fulfill human existence, life, integrity, freedom, justice, and peace, we are dealing with true and good religion, and not superstition.

• To the extent that folk religious teachings or practices oppress, injure, and destroy physical or mental human existence in the individual or social dimension, we are dealing with superstition, with false and bad religion.

The problem, of course, is that this general ethical criterion can certainly be applied both to the relatively limited cult of Kuan Kong, the god of the Taiwanese trader, and to that great and ancient folk religion—Shinto—that became the Japanese state and emperor cult. In our century, however, it was state Shinto in particular that lent ideological justification to Japanese militarism and its aggression in China and Southeast Asia. The millions of dead that, in spite of Hiroshima, should not be forgotten hardly allow us to talk in this case of a true and good religion. The same holds for that "Christianity" that sought to justify the persecution of the Jews, the butchery of thousands of Latin American Indians, the burning of witches and heretics, as well as the Opium War in China and so much else. The question of the *humanum* in religion requires our further attention (cf. Küng, *Theologie im Aufbruch*, ch. C 2).

Therefore, let me make one last observation by way of transition. With the *humanum*, I have brought not just, for instance, a Greco-Christian category into play, but also an authentically Chinese one. We shall see that *jen*, translated as goodness, benevolence, and humanity, is the central teaching of Confucius. And in this sense, Confucianism is a *humanistic* and *moral* religion in contrast to utilitarian folk religion. Indeed, with its accent on human relationships, Confucianism often counts as the moral religion par excellence, definitely capable of being put on a level with the ethos of Christianity. Nevertheless, even a moral religion can seek to dominate, can become oppressive—or it can liberate. This will occupy our attention in the next section, where we compare Confucius with Jesus of Nazareth.

II.
Confucianism: Ethical Humanism as Religion?

1. *Julia Ching:* Chinese Perspectives

INTRODUCTION

Anyone visiting Peking today will wish to see, not just the imperial palace, but also the Temple of Heaven, situated in a wide park outside the former Forbidden City. There are several old structures there, including the well-known, circular prayer hall for good harvests, with its blue tiles (blue being the color of Heaven). What is, however, even more impressive are the three circular open-air marble terraces, under the sky itself. Here is the altar for the cult of Heaven. The middle of the topmost terrace is the place where the emperor used to make sacrifices to the Lord-on-high at the time of the winter solstice.

Visitors to the Temple of Heaven often ask, to what religion does it belong? The correct answer is, to Chinese religion. But exactly what is Chinese religion? Tradition has transmitted a plurality of traditions including Confucianism and Taoism. One would have to say more specifically that Chinese religion includes a dimension of nature worship which was transformed by Confucianism and Taoism and incorporated into each system in a different way. And, to the extent that the cult of Heaven has been approved by the Confucian tradition, one might even designate the Temple of Heaven a *Confucian* temple. The *Book of Rites,* a Confucian text, contains precise instructions for the performance of this cult to Heaven. But then, what is Confucianism? This is the question we are treating here.

Before we answer the question in some detail, let us point out that Confucianism appears to be attracting increasing attention in the world today, and its "work ethic" is being given credit for the rapid economic development of the Pacific Rim. In August 1987, an international scholarly conference on Confucius and Confucianism was held in Qufu, Shantung, the birthplace of Confucius. It was jointly organized by the Confucius Foundation of China and the Institute for East Asian Philosophies in Singapore. In November 1987, another international scholarly conference on Confucius and Confucianism took place in Taipei, Taiwan, under the auspices of the Confucius and Mencius Society and the Society for Chinese Philosophy. The Chinese Department of the University of Hong Kong celebrated an anniversary with a conference on Confucianism and culture in December 1987; another conference, on Confucianism and Christianity, is to take place at the Chinese University of Hong Kong in June 1988. Besides, the Adenauer Foundation in West Germany is also supporting a conference on Confucianism in the fall of 1988. Is Confucianism also experiencing a revival in China today? Has it a future tomorrow? Are its values useful also for the world outside China?

To answer these questions thoughtfully and systematically, we should first look into the origins of the school of Confucius, which is called Confucianism. And, in a book such as this one, we should also discuss the question of whether Confucianism is a religion, and even whether it has a religious dimension. This is a question that has been discussed recently, and is still being discussed today, in the People's Republic of China. There, however, such words as "philosophy" and "religion" still tend to be value-laden; to call a tradition a religion is therefore to put it in a place that is lower than that of philosophy, but higher than that of "superstition."

To begin with, there has been little dispute about Confucianism's being called an ethical humanism. Indeed, the concern for humanity and human nature is usually considered to be its strength. We shall therefore start by considering the rise of Confucianism in ancient China as an ethically humane philosophy, in our discussion of whether it has as well a religious dimension. But we shall not limit ourselves to antiquity or the historical past. We shall also consider the strengths and weaknesses of Confucianism in the recent past—and even today, as it faces the future.

THE RISE OF ETHICAL HUMANISM

The word "religion" *(tsung-chiao)* did not exist in the Chinese vocabulary until the late nineteenth century, when it entered through Japanese translations of European works and terminology. This was also true for the word "philosophy" *(che-hsüeh)*. Before that, the custom was to represent "doctrines" *(chiao)* of various spiritual and intellectual lineages, which functioned very much like philosophical and religious teachings.

What of the argument that the long absence of the word "religion" in traditional Chinese language signifies the absence of religion itself historically, or of any understanding of the phenomenon as it has been known in the West? Such a position of linguistic determinism would imply that the Chinese also never developed any humanism, since the term *jen-wen chu-i* or *jen-tao chu-yi* is also a modern coinage. And yet, those who object to describing the Chinese as religious and otherworldly usually represent them as humanistic and this-worldly.

At the dawn of Chinese history four thousand years ago, we find a society where ancestral religion, sacrifice, and divination permeated daily life. Later, the Chou people transformed the Shang religion which they inherited by appealing, in the last analysis, to the supreme Heaven, a personal deity who cared for people on earth and rewarded and punished them not capriciously but according to the rational morality of their behavior. Thus, the will of God became comprehensible, unmysterious, and the final guarantee of human rational behavior. And, through this transformed religious belief, human history itself became rational and comprehensible. The human being became increasingly conscious of his own ability to determine his own destiny as well as that of history.

Whereas the Shang kings led the people in the service of "ghosts and spirits," the Chou rulers made use of ritual and music to *educate* the people. We are now at the dawn of a new era, that of Chinese humanism. The early Chou kings appear to have been wise rulers, even inspired leaders, conscientious in their performance of duties toward Heaven, the ancestors, and the people. But the later successors to the Chou mandate lacked their ancestors' political wisdom. The royal domain was shaken by barbarian intrusions, while feudal lords grew impatient with the decline of central authority and began competing for hegemony among themselves.

The following poems, coming from the period following the eighth century B.C., express a sense of questioning of religion and God, in a time of disorder and uncertainty:

> You parents who gave me birth!
> Was it to make me suffer this pain?
>
> .   .   .
>
> Those innocent among the people
> Will be reduced to servitude with me.
> Alas for us!
> From whence will help come?
>
> .   .   .
>
> There is the great God:
> Does he hate anyone?*

We hear here echoes of Job complaining about God's silence during his own sufferings. The Book of Job concludes with Job's renewed faith and the return of God's blessings. In the Chinese case, the questioning of religious belief was also reflected in the philosophical thinking of the times. The emergence of Chinese humanism took place during those centuries of unrest. A series of great minds of the sixth century B.C. and afterward, making up the Golden Age of Chinese philosophy, further contributed to the rationalist atmosphere of philosophical reflection; they focused upon the place of the human in the universe, and the need of finding social order and harmony. While these thinkers had different ideas on many points regarding religion and morality, their common impact was to strengthen the sense of human autonomy and rationality, associating human destiny, fortunes and misfortunes with the activities of human beings themselves rather than

* Consult Legge, *The Chinese Classics*, vol. 4, pp. 315–16.

with the authority of the ghosts and spirits. Consequently, the system of religious orthodoxy, in belief as well as in ritual order, would not be discarded, although its importance was relativized.

Humanism characterizes the mature Chinese civilization, with its interest in philosophy, history, and literature. But if we are only to examine Chinese humanism in its mature phase, after the rise of the Han dynasty (206 B.C.–A.D. 220), we may be surprised at the dissimilarity between pre-Han and post-Han civilizations. Divination, sacrifice, and shamanic séances still took place after the Han, but their roles had grown marginal.

Like ancient Greek humanism, which also emerged at a time of intense questioning of religious beliefs, producing Socrates, Plato, and Aristotle, Chinese humanism had many voices, belonging to outstanding individuals. But tradition speaks more of their schools of thought than of the individuals as such. We hear, for example, of Confucianism, Taoism, and Legalism, what Arthur Waley calls *The Three Ways of Thought in Ancient China* (London, 1939).*

A certain question may be asked: did humanism become a closed system, a purely *secular* Weltanschauung, or was it also open to the transcendent, even to the divine? Before answering this question, we should first define the term Confucianism.

What do I mean by Confucianism? A Western designation of a Chinese tradition, the term itself is ambiguous, representing an ideology developed by a man of the name Confucius (552?–479 B.C.). It is actually a misnomer; the Chinese themselves have usually preferred *Ju-chia* or *Ju-chiao,* the school or teachings of the scholars. Etymologically, it has been claimed that the word *ju* is related to the word for "weaklings" or "cowards," and referred originally to those dispossessed aristocrats of antiquity who were no longer warriors but lived off their knowledge of rituals, history, music, numbers, or archery. Eventually, *Ju,* as the name of a school or thought, came to refer to the ethical wisdom of the past that Confucius transmitted to later ages, as well as the entire development of the tradition after his time.

Confucius and the school named after him offered a moral or ethical answer to the question regarding life's meaning and order

* Hans Küng will make further mention of Legalism in his response.

in society, an answer that would dominate Chinese philosophical thinking for about two millennia. But how did this answer arise in the classical period? Obviously, it was not produced in a vacuum. And yet, the search for its genesis in the society of its times is beset with problems. Many of the sources for the period in which Confucius and his followers lived are colored by Confucian ideas and either come from a later age or were edited at a later period. But then, must we accept Confucius as a kind of Melchizedek figure, emerging in time, without immediate intellectual predecessors, a lone voice that eventually won a hearing for two thousand or more years? And then, what can we say about his life, given the paucity of solid historical evidence, and the abundance of legendary materials?

WHO WAS CONFUCIUS?

In recent history, the *questioning* into Chinese tradition as such and Confucianism in particular involved also a *quest*—that for the historical Confucius, as distinct from the Confucius image of popular veneration. The development in the 1920s and 1930s of a more scientifically critical historical method facilitated this task to a certain extent. It might be studied in terms parallel to the quest for the historical Jesus.

First of all, it should be mentioned that "Confucius" is the Latin rendering of K'ung Fu-tzu, or Master K'ung; the sage's full name was K'ung Ch'iu, also styled K'ung Chung-ni. He was a native of the small state of Lu, and his birthplace is near modern Ch'ü-fu (Shantung). Little can be established about his life, forebears, and family, although legends (including very early ones) are abundant. He is sometimes said to have been a direct descendant of the Shang royal house whose grandparents came from the state of Sung, although he described his own circumstances as humble. The highest public office he occupied was at age fifty, as a kind of police commissioner in his home state for about a year. In over ten years of travel, K'ung visited many other feudal states of his time, seeking, but never finding, a ruler who would use his advice. In his old age, he devoted more time to teaching disciples, while also occupying himself with music and poetry, and with occasional conversations with rulers or ministers.

And how did Confucius perceive himself, his own accomplishments? The following passage gives us insight into his own self-consciousness, his sense of mission. It also discloses Confucius' high regard for rituals, and for the virtue of propriety which flows from them, and it should help us appreciate the fundamentally religious character of his personality, with its profound sense of reverence for the will of Heaven.

> At fifteen I set my heart on learning [to be a
>   sage].
> At thirty I became firm.
> At forty I had no more doubts.
> At fifty I understood Heaven's Will.
> At sixty my ears were attuned [to this Will].
> At seventy I could follow my heart's desires,
>   without overstepping the line.*

From his own account of spiritual evolution, it might also be inferred that Confucius was a religious man, a believer in Heaven as personal God, a man who sought to understand and follow Heaven's will. But he lived in an age of turmoil, during which the ancient religious beliefs were questioned, and he contributed to the rationalist atmosphere of philosophical reflection. And our knowledge of ancient religion, with its emphasis on divination and sacrifice, helps us to understand the reaction of the humanist philosophers, who distanced themselves from such and heralded in a new age of ethical wisdom.

While Confucius' teachings are best found in the *Analects*—the record of his conversations with his disciples—Confucianism regards as its special texts the Five Classics. These are books of widely divergent genres, including, as already mentioned, the *Book of Changes* or *I-ching*, the *Book of History* or *Shu-ching*, the *Book of Poetry* or *Shih-ching*, as well as the *Classic of Rites (Li-*

* *Analects* 2:4.

*ching)** and the *Spring and Autumn Annals* or *Ch'un-ch'iu.* (A sixth classic, the *Book of Music,* is no longer extant.)

In the past, the Five Classics had been attributed to Confucius; he was thought to be either their editor or, especially in the case of the *Spring and Autumn Annals,* a direct author. Contemporary scholarship no longer takes this seriously. The core of many of these classical texts goes back to Confucius, and even to the time preceding him, which shows the ancient lineage of the school of Ju. Each of them underwent a long period of evolution, receiving accretions postdating Confucius. The situation was complicated by the fact of the burning of books by the Ch'in emperor (213 B.C.), and the later restoration of the texts with the help of scholarly memory. During the Han dynasty (125 B.C.), these Classics were made the basis of the state examinations, obliging all aspiring scholar-officials to master their contents, and thus establishing the supremacy of the Confucian school. Its classical texts were inscribed in stone, and they collected eventually a corpus of commentaries and subcommentaries that established various traditions of textual exegesis.

WHAT IS THE VIRTUE OF HUMANITY *(JEN)*?

It has sometimes been said that the great merit of Confucianism is its discovery of the ultimate in the relative—in the moral character of human relationships. Confucius himself taught a doctrine of reciprocity and neighborliness: "To regard every one as a very important guest, to manage the people as one would assist at a sacrifice, *not to do to others what you would not have them do to you." (Analects* 15:23.) The last part of this quotation offers what has come to be called the *negative* Golden Rule.

Within Confucianism, the well-known Five Relationships include the ruler-minister, father-son, husband-wife, elder and younger brother, and friend and friend. Three of these are family relationships, while the other two are usually conceived in terms of the family models. For example, the ruler-minister relationship

* This ritual corpus includes the *Ceremonials (I-li),* the *Book of Rites (Li-chi),* and the *Institutes of Chou (Chou-li).*

resembles the father-son, while friendship resembles brotherliness. For this reason, the Confucian society regards itself as a large family: "Within the four seas all men are brothers" *(Analects* 12:5).

The responsibilities ensuing from these relationships are mutual and reciprocal. A minister owes loyalty to his ruler, and a child filial respect to the parent. But the ruler must also care for his subjects, and the parent for the child. All the same, the Five Relationships emphasize the vertical sense of hierarchy. Even within the horizontal relationship between friends, seniority of age demands a certain respect; and if the conjugal relationship bears more natural resemblance to that between older and younger brothers, it is more usually compared to the ruler-minister relationship. And the duty of filial piety—the need of procuring progeny for the sake of assuring the continuance of the ancestral cult—has been for centuries the ethical justification for polygamy.

Confucius' central doctrine is that of the virtue of *jen.* In etymology as well as in interpretation, *jen* is always concerned with human relationships. It is associated with loyalty *(chung)*—loyalty to one's own heart and conscience—and reciprocity *(shu)*—respect of and consideration for others *(Analects* 4:15). *Jen* is also related to *li* (propriety or ritual). But the latter refers more to social behavior, and the former to the inner orientation of the person. *Jen* is translated variously as goodness, benevolence, humanity, and human-heartedness. It was formerly a particular virtue, the kindness which distinguished the gentleman in his behavior toward his inferiors. He transformed it into a universal virtue, that which makes the perfect human being, the sage.

Jen is rooted in human sentiment as well as in a fundamental orientation of life. *Jen* means affection and love. "The man of *jen* loves others." This is the interpretation of a great Confucian thinker, Mencius (321–289?) *(Mencius* 4B:28). Indeed, he loves *all* and *everyone* (7A:46). In somewhat contradictory language, Mencius states that such a man "extends his love from those he loves to those he does not love" (7B:1). Hsün-tzu (c. 298–238), another Confucian thinker, concurs with this definition of *jen* as love. So does the *Book of Rites.* But the Confucian interpretation of *jen* as universal love differs from that of Mo-tzu (fifth century B.C.), who advocates a love of all without distinction. The followers of Confucius emphasize the need for discernment, even for distinction. They reserve for parents and kin a special love *(Doctrine of the Mean,* ch. 20), since the roots of *jen* are filial piety and brotherly respect *(Analects* 1:20).

If the natural feelings underlying kinship call for special consideration, the natural feelings aroused by the neighbor's—*any* neighbor's—need for help are also recognized. This is especially underlined by Mencius, who gives the example of a man witnessing a child falling into a well *(Mencius* 2A:6). The natural first impulse is to rescue the child, and this comes before any desire for praise or fear of blame. The following of this impulse is an act of commiseration, or love of neighbor. This example serves as a kind of Confucian parable of the Good Samaritan, illustrating the meaning of universal love.

For the follower of Confucius, parental love for children can be extended to cover other people's children, just as filial respect for the aged can be extended to cover other people's parents and elders; thus the natural order serves as a starting point and an experiential guide in achieving universal love.

Familial relations provide a model for social behavior. Respect your own elders, as well as others' elders; be kind to your own children and juniors, as well as those of others. These are the instructions of Mencius *(Mencius* 1A:7), and they have provided inspiration for generations of Confucians. They have been the reason for the strong sense of solidarity not only in the Chinese family, but also in Confucian social organizations, even among overseas Chinese communities today.

But Confucianism regards not just social behavior. It gives a definite importance to rituals, including religious rituals. Indeed, it has sometimes been called a "ritual religion" *(li-chiao).* The Chinese word for "ritual" *(li)* is related etymologically to the words "worship" and "sacrificial vessel" with a definite religious overtone. The ancestral cult was surrounded with ritual; so was the worship offered to Heaven as supreme Lord. But the term came to include all social, habitual practices; it partook even of the nature of law as a means of training in virtue and of avoiding evil. And it refers also to propriety, that is, proper behavior. Propriety carries a risk of mere exterior conformity to social custom, just as a ritual might be performed only perfunctorily, without an inner attitude of reverence. Confucius emphasized the need of having the right inner dispositions, without which propriety becomes hypocrisy *(Analects* 15:17). He insisted that sacrifice is to be performed with the consciousness of the presence of the spirits (3:12). And he emphasized that the importance of the rites does not rest in the external observance, such as in the offering of gifts and the accompaniment by musical performances: "What can rites do for a person lacking in the virtue of humanity *(jen)?* What can music do for a person lacking in humanity?" (3:3.)

Speaking of sacrificial rites, we should give attention to Confucius' announced distaste for an item of ritual usage: the human effigies or wooden burial figures *(yung)*. These were made with moving limbs, to better represent human beings capable of serving their lords and ladies in the world of the dead. Confucius is reported to have said that those who made such figures did not deserve to have posterity *(Mencius* 1A:4). It was an unequivocal condemnation of human sacrifice, even when performed symbolically.

CONFUCIANISM AFTER CONFUCIUS: MENCIUS AND HSÜN-TZU

Confucianism was further developed by Confucius' followers, including Mencius and Hsün-tzu. These differed not merely with Confucius himself on certain issues, but even more between themselves. Yet they shared enough to contribute together to the building up of the Confucian tradition. On the other hand, Mo-tzu was once a follower of the Confucian school but moved away from it to begin a distinctive "Mohist" school of thought. In one way, he was much more an upholder of the ancient religion from which Confucius had begun to distance himself. He asserts that ghosts and spirits exist, that they take cognizance of human affairs, and that they have the power to reward or punish any individual for his good or evil deeds. But, in reaffirming the ancient belief in God—the Lord-on-high, or Heaven, the source of all life—he insists on God's universal love for all beings. But he also discloses a rationalist's disapproval of funerary rituals, and he ridicules the Confucians for lavishing attention on them.

When we come to the *Book of Mencius,* we find a clear evolution in the meaning of the term Heaven. Whereas Confucius only makes infrequent mention of the personal deity, Mencius speaks much more of Heaven—but not always as personal deity. According to Mencius, Heaven is present within man's heart, so that he who knows his own heart and nature knows Heaven *(Mencius* 7A:1). Heaven represents, therefore, a greater immanence. It also refers more and more to the source and principle of ethical laws and values.

Nevertheless, Mencius continues to hold in esteem the practice of offering sacrifices to the Lord-on-high and to ancestors. "Though a man may be wicked, if he adjusts his thoughts, fasts and bathes, he may sacrifice to the Lord-on-high" *(Mencius* 4B:25).

Hsün-tzu sees a difference between a "gentleman" of education, who uses his rationality, and the common people, who believe in fortune and misfortune. Whereas we earlier found divination in the royal ancestral temples of the Shang dynasty, and rain dances sponsored by the state, we find in *Hsün-tzu* the beginning of the movement away from such religious practices on the part of the higher classes, and the identification of such practices with the "superstitious" commoners. It is the beginning of the separation between Confucianism as an elite tradition and so-called popular religion at a grass-roots level. "You pray for rain and it rains. Why? For no particular reason, I say. It is just as though you had not prayed for rain and it rained anyway. . . . You consult the arts of divination before making a decision on some important matter. But it is not as though you could hope to accomplish anything by such ceremonies. They are done merely for ornament. Hence the gentleman regards them as ornaments, but the common people regard them as supernatural." *(Hsün-tzu,* ch. 11.)

The Chinese word for human nature is *hsing,* a compound including the term for mind or heart, and life or offspring. Philological scholarship demonstrates the association between etymology and early religious worship. The human being is he or she who has received from Heaven the gift of life and all the innate endowments of human nature, especially the faculty of moral discernment. Mencius says that the sense of right and wrong is common to all *(Mencius* 2A:6) and is that which distinguishes the human from the beast. From this flows another belief, that of the natural equality of all, which exists in spite of social hierarchy, or any distinction between the "civilized" and the "barbarian."

The Confucian tradition has sometimes been criticized for its inability to explain the place of evil in human existence. Traditional thought affirms the presence of evil, explaining it either as the product of contact between an originally good human nature and its wicked environment, as Mencius tends to say, or as inherent in human nature itself, which is the position of Hsün-tzu. Interestingly, while the two thinkers differ regarding the original goodness or wickedness of human nature, they concur in assenting to human perfectibility. Mencius declares that all have the potential of becoming sages. Hsün-tzu explains that the evil in human nature desires its opposite, and that education can train nature to seek goodness.

At the time that Christian missionaries entered China, they found Confucian scholars usually upholding the basic goodness of human nature, explaining evil as a deflection from the good, a perversion of the natural. Besides, the Chinese language lacked a clear equivalent for "sin"—the term *tsui* has a double significance: of crime as well as of sin. The resultant ambiguity has led some people to the incorrect assertion that the Chinese (and the Japanese) had no guilt-oriented morality, with its internalization of the consciousness of moral evil, but only a shame-oriented one, which is external and superficial, being based on mere human respect. Certainly, Confucian education sought to instill a strong sense of moral responsibility, inseparable from guilt consciousness. In our own days, mainland Marxist scholars have tended to emphasize, with Hsün-tzu, the original wickedness of human nature, apparently in order to justify political and social control. But even this is beginning to change.

Of course, a sense of shame remains strong, especially in Japan. Some years ago, a Japanese soldier who survived after the war in the Philippines by hiding in a cave returned to Japan, and surprised his welcomers with the words "I am so ashamed! I am so ashamed!" He meant that he was ashamed to be alive, since he ought to have died for his emperor. (In the case of Japan, Shinto naturalism, even more than Taoist naturalism, precludes any theory of moral weakness.)

"CIVIL RELIGION" AND THE ANCESTOR CULT

Much more than Christianity, Confucian teachings are oriented to improving the political order, as a means of achieving universal love. The teaching of *jen* is extended to the political order, where it is defined as benevolent government, a government of moral persuasion, in which the leader gives the example of personal integrity and selfless devotion to the people. Confucian teaching prompted generations of scholars to strive for participation in government. For the human is never regarded as dualistic, as matter and mind, body and soul. It is always accepted as *one*, as existing in society, as striving as well for physical well-being, for social harmony, and for moral and spiritual perfection. The Confucian sage has been described as possessing the qualities of "sageliness within and kingliness without." In other words, he should have the heart of the sage, and the wisdom of the king.

And what happens should the ruler be less than sagely, as most rulers turned out to be? Mencius teaches that political power is legitimated by a mandate bestowed by the supreme Lord, Heaven. In this context, we owe to Mencius the formulation of the doctrine of rebellion or revolution known popularly as the "removal of the mandate" *(ko-ming)*. It was Mencius who said that killing a tyrant was not regicide, since the tyrant no longer deserved to rule *(Mencius* 1B:8); it was Mencius who declared, "The people come first; the altars of the earth and grain come afterwards; the ruler comes last" (7B:14).

The Confucian emphasis on political responsibility has had positive as well as negative effects. On the one hand, such an emphasis has kept the tradition active and relevant. On the other hand, it has also permitted the tradition to become manipulated by the political establishment. The Confucian tradition was, however, broad enough to include political conservatives as well as moderate and radical reformers; there always were men who remained independent of the state, while seeking to change or transform it.

To mention scholars and activists in China alone, we can think of the eleventh century's Ssu-ma Kuang as well as Wang An-shih, the seventeenth century's Tunglin scholars as well as Huang Tsung-hsi, and the twentieth century's K'ang Yu-wei and Liang Ch'i-ch'ao.

Confucian emphasis on political and social responsibility explains why during much of history Confucianism served the function of a "civil religion" (to use the language of the American scholar Robert Bellah). From the time of the Han dynasty on, an elaborate state cult was evolved which has been, rightly or wrongly, attributed to Confucian teachings, which include expressions of very ancient beliefs in a supreme deity, in the natural powers as deity symbols, and in the intercessory powers of deceased worthies or heroes. There were the great rituals performed by the emperor himself—for the worship of Heaven and of earth, and of his imperial ancestors; there were also intermediate rituals, for the worship of the sun and the moon and numerous spirits of earth and sky; and there were the lesser sacrifices to minor gods, including those of mountains, lakes, and rivers as well as those well-known historical figures—in particular, wise and incorrupt magistrates—honored as "city gods." Besides, surrounded by his disciples, and also by later worthies, Confucius himself became the center of a cult which included the others. While not deified, he received official sacrifices as the teacher par excellence and was especially venerated by the scholarly class. The Confucian emphasis on rituals assured a continuity with the past and offered also a ritual as well as moral education for the would-be gentleman.

The ritual surrounding the cult of Heaven developed very early, existing already at the time of Confucius, and remained in many respects the main feature of Chinese religion until the twentieth century. The Temple of Heaven, built during the Ming dynasty (1368–1661), still stands in an outer quarter of today's Peking. It witnessed the practice of this cult and remains a monument to more than six hundred years of recent history.

With the establishment of a republic in China (1912) the cult of Heaven came to an end. But its memory remains as witness to a theistic belief present at the heart of traditional Chinese religion and persisting throughout the ages, in spite of the changes in the philosophical interpretation of this belief. (There was as well a cult to earth, and even cults addressed to the sun and the moon—all of which offer evidence of the assimilation of nature worship into the "civil religion").

Much better known than the cult of Heaven, the cult of ancestors goes back to the dawn of Chinese history, although originally it was the exclusive privilege of the nobility. It became associated with the state orthodoxy while remaining very much a family practice—an expression of a community of both the living and the beloved deceased. While the ancestral cult may be regarded as a religion in itself, its persistence has also been considered another indication of the religious character of Confucianism. Even today, in many Chinese houses in Hong Kong, Taiwan, and Southeast Asia—as well as in Korea and Japan—the ancestral shrine is maintained. Here, a number of tablets are kept, each traditionally representing a dead ancestor or—as in today's society, sometimes together with photographs—a deceased member of the family. The tablets are customarily made of wood, and sometimes of paper. In front of these tablets are placed incense and offerings.

We have earlier spoken about the Chinese attitude toward life after death. The Confucian belief was that the human being is compounded of two souls: an upper, or intellectual soul, called the *hun,* which becomes the spirit *(shen)* and ascends to the world above, and a lower, or animal soul, called the *p'o,* which becomes the ghost *(kuei)* and descends with the body into the grave. These ideas were also accepted by the Taoist religion, which greatly elaborated them.

The ancestral cult was a memorial service, held in earlier times at ancestral temples, and after that at gravesides or at home. Wine and food libations were usually offered, with silent prostrations in front of the tablets. The ancestors were alleged to have tasted the food before the whole family partook of the meal. Conversion to Christianity frequently represented a rupture with this tradition, since the converts were either forbidden, or no longer expected, to continue the cult.

The proper observance of rituals is meaningful when accompanied by certain interior dispositions. Otherwise, it tends to formalism and even hypocrisy—and these are problems which have plagued Confucian society through the ages, just as they have plagued the Christian religion. Besides, as does any official ortho-doxy, Confucianism abhorred dissent, thus stifling creativity and spontaneity. It took the combined popularity of Taoism and Bud-dhism to arouse a movement of return to the roots of Confucian inspiration, a movement which has sometimes been called Neo-Confucianism.

NEO-CONFUCIANISM AS "SCHOLASTIC PHILOSOPHY"

The historical process by which Confucianism became institu-tionalized first happened around the first century B.C., when it became a "state religion." Much later (from the tenth century A.D. on), some independent thinkers sought to go beyond ideology to recover the lost truth, until, in its turn, the new synthesis they created became established as state doctrine. I refer here to Neo-Confucianism.

As a term, Neo-Confucianism is also a Western coinage. The usual Chinese usage is to refer to the later development of Con-fucianism as the "Metaphysical Thought" *(Li-hsüeh*— literally, "the learning of principle"). This was a *new* expression of Con-fucian thought, based on a smaller corpus of classical texts reinter-preted in response to Buddhist challenges. In this respect, the Neo-Confucian movement parallels scholastic philosophy in the West, which sought to reinterpret Christian teachings with the assistance of Greek philosophical concepts.

Neo-Confucian thinkers concentrated their attention on the Four Books: The *Analects* of Confucius, which contains the con-versations between him and his disciples; the *Book of Mencius,* also a collection of conversations; as well as the *Great Learning* and the *Doctrine of the Mean,* two short treatises derived from the *Book of Rites,* the former making moral and spiritual cultivation the beginning of good rulership, and the latter concentrating on the inner life of psychic equilibrium and harmony. Thus the move-ment oriented itself increasingly to metaphysical and spiritual questions, and even assimilated much from Buddhist and Taoist philosophies in its own discussions about the world and human psychology. The result was a new Weltanschauung, oriented to the quest for self-transcendence in the achievement of sagehood. This took place especially during the Sung and Ming dynasties.

An interesting phenomenon accompanying the development of this new Confucianism was the emphasis on oral transmission. Whereas before, scholars had spent their time annotating the classics or writing their own treatises, based always on appeal to the authority of the classics, another genre came into vogue during the Sung dynasty, as students of famous philosophers noted down for publication the conversations they had with their masters. These recorded conversations *(yü-lu)* expressed the attitude of the men who considered themselves to be primarily teachers communicating to their disciples the ineffable teaching of the ancient sages, which could be easily distorted when given too ornate a form.

But recorded conversations were not the only publications of the Neo-Confucian thinkers. Of these thinkers, Chu Hsi (1130–1200) was probably the greatest mind, and the most prolific author. Though he was not accepted as an orthodox thinker during his own life, his commentaries (on the Four Books) were eventually integrated into the curriculum of the civil service examinations (1313), making his philosophy the new state orthodoxy for six centuries to come.

THE PHILOSOPHY OF CHU HSI

Chu Hsi's philosophy is all the more representative of the Chinese humanist tradition, as it is a conscious synthesis of previous philosophies, comprising as it does the naturalist legacy of the Taoists and Buddhists, and the psychist and culturalist legacy of the Confucians themselves, modified also by an undercurrent of Buddhist influences. His theory of human nature draws from both sides. For Chu Hsi, as for the mainstream of Chinese philosophy, the human being and the cosmos are each paradigms, one of the other, so that evil loses its significance in the affirmation of human perfectibility, as expressed through the doctrine of sagehood.

A terse expression of the world regarded as an ontological paradigm is given in Chu Hsi's philosophy of the Great Ultimate *(T'ai-chi)*. This Great Ultimate is a symbolic expression of cosmology which emphasizes the interrelatedness of the world and man in macrocosm-microcosm terms; it also hides within itself a secret Taoist formula for alchemy and yoga; and it points possibly to early Chinese beliefs in a supreme deity under symbols of astral bodies.

Chu Hsi interprets the *T'ai-chi* with the help of the concept of *li*, those "principles" which constitute all things. *Li* may be defined as forms or essences, as organizing and normative principles, belonging to the realm "above shapes." It is prior—although not in a temporal sense—to its coordinate, *ch'i*, translated sometimes as "ether," or "matter-energy," which belongs to the realm "within shapes." All things are constituted of both *li* and *ch'i*, which are somewhat comparable to the Aristotelian form and matter, with the difference that *li* is passive and *ch'i* is dynamic.

The Great Ultimate is the most perfect *li*, a kind of primal archetype. It is also the *totality* of all the principles *(li)* of the myriad things, as brought together into a single whole. It serves in Chinese philosophy the function of the Form of the Good in Platonism, and that of God in Aristotelianism.

The history of Chinese philosophy after Chu Hsi may be described as a debate between those who, like him, wish to give more importance to *li*, and others who wish to give more emphasis to *ch'i*. The protagonists of *li* tended to presuppose a pre-established pattern of harmony in the universe and in human nature, to be recaptured and maintained by a proper balance of reason and the emotions. The protagonists of *ch'i*, on the other hand, were inclined to minimize the opposition between reason and the emotions. In other words, the tendency was toward either idealism, as in the first case, or materialism, as in the second. It is interesting to note that Chinese Marxist scholars have consistently sought to discover in *ch'i* a materialist ancestry for Chinese Marxism.

In the metaphysics of Chu Hsi, the human being represents the summit of the universe, participating in the excellence of the Great Ultimate and possessing the nature which has come to him or her through the interaction of *yin* and *yang* and the Five Agents metal, wood, water, fire, earth. Human nature is originally good, or "sincere" *(ch'eng)*. Whence, then, comes evil, that ugly fact of human life and experience?

The explanation is that *li*, though wholly good in itself, loses its perfection when actualized through *ch'i*, owing to the limitations imposed by the latter. This is true of physical things as well as of human nature, owing to impediments to the "manifestation" of *li*. Physical endowments vary: there are differences of "translucency" or "opacity" in *ch'i*. Persons who receive the *ch'i* in its purity and transparency are endowed with a natural ease for sageness; those who receive it in its impurity and coarseness will experience a stronger attraction for evil.

And how, specifically, is the task of self-cultivation to be carried out? Chu Hsi proposes the double effort of maintaining an attitude of reverence *(ching)* toward one's own inner nature and its capacity for goodness, and "the investigation of knowledge and the extension of things." In other words, he envisages a certain moral and spiritual attentiveness over oneself which is accompanied and strengthened by the development of knowledge, both about oneself and about the world.

We reach here a most controversial aspect of Chu's teachings, disputed especially by his contemporary and rival thinker, Lu Chiu-yüan (1139–93), as well as by Lu's spiritual heir of three centuries later, Wang Yang-ming (1472–1529). They point out a serious problem in such a doctrine of cultivation which makes of intellectual pursuit the cornerstone of moral striving: that it necessarily makes intellectuals of sages. This implies the inaccessibility of sagehood to all those who are deprived of the possibilities of intellectual development. Lu and Wang prefer to emphasize the potential for greatness in each and every human being, and "the power of the human mind and heart to choose good" *(liang-chih)* and to perfect itself by the practice of virtues; they see intellectual pursuit as a useful but not necessary component of cultivation. They prefer the dynamism of moral action, as the expression of the whole personality, oriented to the highest good.

Interestingly, Chu Hsi gives some importance to the practice of meditation, or "quiet-sitting." What is implied here is a *cyclical* movement: the return to one's original nature, the recapture of the springs of one's being, and the enabling of this state of original equilibrium of nature and the emotions to permeate one's daily living. Such a form of meditation differs from the scripture reading which precedes much of Christian meditation, and the tradition of point-by-point reflection on the Gospel episodes. It differs also from the Buddhist tradition of meditation by visualization—in which the person imagines the presence of Buddhas or bodhisatt-vas—but comes closer to the Ch'an (Zen) ideal of emptying the mind or heart of its concepts and feelings. Unlike Buddhist medi-tation, however, Confucian meditation has as its goal less the at-tainment of mystical experience (which is not excluded), and more the enhancement of one's moral nature. Here we are speaking of *spirituality* as well as moral doctrine. And it is especially as a spirituality—both the school of Chu Hsi and the school of Wang Yang-ming—that Neo-Confucianism has deepened the religious character of the Confucian tradition.

Neo-Confucianism was the official philosophy for China during the last thousand years that preceded the establishment of a re-public; the textual commentaries written or compiled by its repre-sentatives were, all that time, the basis of the civil service examina-tion system. The Jesuit missionaries, including especially Matteo Ricci, tended to prefer classical Confucianism to the later develop-ment. They thought that the earlier philosophy lacked a belief in the deity, and that this "vacant place" could be taken over by the Christian God. They also opposed the metaphysical dimensions of Neo-Confucian philosophy, which bore a pantheistic imprint of Buddhist influence. More recently however, leading Chinese scholars of the twentieth century have complained of this mission-ary attitude as one that overlooked the rich spiritual dimension of the Neo-Confucian tradition. And indeed, it is existentially impos-sible to separate Neo-Confucianism from the Confucian tradition.

However, we should remember that Confucianism is not just part of the Chinese heritage; it is also a Korean heritage and a Japanese heritage, and it continues to exercise its moral influence in the East Asian cultural circle outside of China.

CONFUCIANISM IN KOREA AND JAPAN

Of the two countries, Confucian influence appears stronger and more visible in Korea than in Japan. Historically, Confucianism in Korea, like its counterpart in China, has been associated with education, and with a civil service examination. Once introduced, the philosophy of Chu Hsi became supreme in Yi dynasty Korea, producing such Korean thinkers of the Songni hak (Learning of Human Nature and Principle) as Yi T'oegye (1501–70) and Yi Yulgok (1536–84), whose discussions centered on the relationship between human nature and the emotions. Confucian influence is especially discerned in the Korean emphasis on filial piety, shown also in ritual mourning for the dead—a reason why Koreans had traditionally preferred to wear white (the color of mourning in East Asia), since they were always mourning for some member of the large, extended family.

Confucian thought and culture spread from China usually through Korea to Japan, and retains its importance today as a diffused moral philosophy. Unlike Korea, Japan never adopted a civil service examination, although Confucianism has been traditionally associated with the task of education. The Tokugawa period (1600–1868) especially encouraged the development of Confucianism and Neo-Confucianism at the expense of Buddhism and Christianity. As people, however, whereas the Chinese and the Koreans were scholar-officials, the Japanese Confucians were scholar-samurais, fighting men who always wore swords and lived in readiness for an honorable death, according to the code of ethics called the Bushidō (Way of Warriors). This shows a principal difference between Confucianism in Japan and the same tradition in China and Korea. Of the five relationships, the Chinese have emphasized the parent-child relationship, thereby celebrating filial piety, where the Japanese samurai have focused more on the ruler-minister relationship, with the commitment of absolute loyalty from generation to generation. In this light, we can better understand the Japanese "emperor cult," and its tendency to divinize the emperor—a cult which was never found in China.

CONFUCIANISM AND MODERNIZATION

In reassessing the relevance of Confucianism, one must not overlook certain obvious problems. In the Confucian social order, human relationships tended to become hierarchically fixed and rigid—with the superior partners, the fathers, husbands, rulers, exercising more right and privilege, and the inferior partners performing more duty and submission. Historically speaking, this was the combined product of Confucian philosophy and the combined influence of the Legalist theory of power and *Yin-yang* philosophy with its arbitrary correlation of cosmic forces and human relationships.

In the past, the strength of Confucianism lay in its being a school of moderation between certain extremes—retreat from society as advocated by Taoists and Buddhists, and complete immersion in the social and political order according to the followers of the philosopher Mo-tzu or those promoters of power politics called the Legalists. But moderation also facilitated compromise—especially when state intervention brought in state orthodoxy, causing the classical texts to be studied and memorized by those more eager to climb the bureaucratic ladder than to become sages. What importance, however, has Confucianism today, long after the triumph of the Communist Revolution?

In the late nineteenth century, when China was shaken politically and psychologically by Western intrusion, Chinese intellectuals began a soul-searching questioning of the country's cultural heritage, particularly Confucianism. It was regarded as a weight and a burden—intellectual shackles on the mind, preventing the country from modernization. Its strongest critic was probably the writer Lu Hsün, whose short stories attacked the "cannibalistic" ritual religion which stifled human freedom and individual initiative in the name of passive, conformist virtues. These critiques satirized the dehumanizing elements in a fossilized tradition that was until then inextricably bound up with the sociopolitical establishment. They were also expressive of the newly awakened nationalism, desirous of asserting independence against the onslaught of the Western powers and Japan. It was in the midst of these antitraditionalist, anti-Confucian voices of the May Fourth Movement (1919) that the Chinese Communist Party was born (1921). What began as a search for intellectual freedom entailed as well a repudiation of the monopoly of tradition, especially of the Confucian social structure. With the Communist takeover of the mainland (1949), vigorous discussions and debates took place over the merits and demerits of the Confucian tradition.

The Marxist critiques of the 1950s followed in direct line the arguments voiced during and after the May Fourth Movement. During the Cultural Revolution (1966–76), however, the anti-Confucius movement entered a new phase, with diatribes (1973–74) linking the fallen defense chief Lin Piao with Confucius. It was the most vehement attack ever mounted, and it has since been officially denounced as part of a political conspiracy aimed at the now deceased premier Chou En-lai. Curiously, Chinese Marxist scholars have tended to portray Confucianism in *religious* terms—in order to discredit it. And arguments as to whether Confucianism is a philosophy or a religion are usually posited upon the superiority of philosophy over religion. Since 1984, however, the People's Republic has celebrated the official birthday of Confucius (September 28), thereby joining Taiwan and South Korea in honoring the sage.

Let us also look at the rest of East Asia—at South Korea, Japan, Taiwan, Hong Kong, and Singapore, which all belong to the same traditional cultural circle with China as its center. They offer a different model of understanding, since they have sought to confront the problems of modernity without formally repudiating the traditions of the past.

Till rather recently, modernization in East Asia has been attributed to Western influences. Then the last decades witnessed not only the coming of age of modern Japan as an economic giant, but also the rapid growth of the Pacific Rim countries. These countries and regions have never formally repudiated their cultural heritage. In Japan, the economy is capitalist and the government is a liberal democracy. There, traditional symbols (including the emperor system and religious beliefs associated with Buddhism and folk religion), as well as an ancestral cult and Confucian ethical values (especially the "work ethic"), continue to dominate the life of the people, including that of many of their intellectual leaders. For some time already, Japanese scholars have argued about the causal phenomena leading to the modernization of their country. Although the stimulus from the West has been essential, their argument has favored a modernization process that has not been merely that of "Westernization." Increasingly, this "traditionalist" interpretation focuses upon an examination of the forces already present in Tokugawa Japan which prepared the country for an acceptance of Western science and technology. Among these forces, the most prominent is Confucian (and Neo-Confucian) rationalism, that dominant school of thought in the cultural circle which includes China and Korea as well. It is a well-known fact that the earliest Japanese "modernizers" were usually from the samurai class, who had a Confucian classical and literary education, could afford Western scientific and technological training, and were motivated by a desire to "enrich the country and strengthen the armed forces," a slogan directly attributable to the utilitarian branch of Confucianism. Such a desire fostered nationalism, and in its Japanese manifestation, nationalism *was* the moving force behind the country's phenomenal economic success. The same slogan and this same desire inspired the Chinese and Koreans as well—whether Marxist or anti-Marxist—in their modernizing endeavors.

If nationalism promotes a work ethic in East Asia, family solidarity does the same among those North Americans of Chinese, Japanese, or Vietnamese origins, who are known to excel in work and in study. This is also being increasingly recognized in Western society itself. Besides, Western business circles are becoming increasingly aware of the need to better understand the Confucian ethos behind trade and industry in East Asia. This points to the importance of finding the traditional in the modern, of a process of cultural and possibly religious integration which has been going on in contemporary East Asia. It is a process with important implications for Christianity, as a new generation of Asian Christians, whether Korean or Chinese, assert themselves as Christians of Confucian background and values.

The recent decision in Singapore to incorporate Confucianism into the school curricula (1984), and the proposal by the former prime minister Yasuhiro Nakasone of Japan to do the same in his country, witness to the desire to strengthen Confucian values. This is not to say that a Confucian background or education is expected to accelerate modernization, but rather that it is being seen as a corrective to some of the by-products of modernization, such as extreme individualism or moral permissiveness, and that it is perceived as capable of contributing to a greater sense of cultural cohesiveness and Asian identity, and as an antidote to the continual spread of Marxism.

CONFUCIANISM AND FREEDOM

Confucianism is the common intellectual heritage of East Asia and even mainland China is demonstrating a greater willingness to acknowledge the need of "critically inheriting" the values most associated with Confucian family and social morality. In a modernizing world, Confucianism represents an "inner-worldly asceticism" (to use Max Weber's terminology) in the name of a secular goal. Indeed, whereas Confucianism serves as a stabilizing force, nationalism has acted as a catalyst for innovation and even revolution. Nationalism is innately selfish, a kind of collective egoism, whereas Confucianism makes important universal assertions about the moral and social orders. But the two are not mutually exclusive. The two need each other and have helped each other. For many intellectuals of the 1920s in East Asia, nationalism *was* religion. It alone gave meaning to life in society. And it made possible in China the political triumph of Marxism, in the name of national survival and modern transformation. For many people today, nationalism is still the most powerful force for social transformation, albeit a morally ambiguous force. It motivates the peoples of the developing world to attempt to "catch up" with the developed and highly technological societies of the West and Japan, in order not only to enjoy better economic well-being, but also to earn a greater sense of dignity and self-respect.

Confucianism represents a cultural universalism based on the harmony of the natural and social orders, respect for the past, and the sanctity of family life. Marxism, on the other hand, argues for the triumph of human effort over the natural universe, and the sanctity of labor. Unlike Marxism, Confucianism acknowledges the moral autonomy of the individual conscience, even if traditional Confucian society—like contemporary Marxist society—tends to subject the individual to the collective. Confucianism and Marxism proclaim the brotherhood of the human race even if both are being used to promote the special interests of nationalism. In mainland China, where Marxism formally defines the program for action but has not succeeded in developing its own revolutionary ethic, Confucianism maintains a certain amount of diffused influence.

However, Confucianism also could become an end in itself, as an ideology which enslaves minds rather than the truth which sets them free. In the past, Confucianism was manipulated and misused by Japanese militarists to motivate and justify their invasion of China and their efforts to establish an East Asian "co-prosperity sphere." In our own days, Confucianism has been used by regimes in the Asia-Pacific area to uphold an authoritarian "patriarchy." For this reason, the idea of introducing Confucianism into the school curricula was met with some consternation in certain quarters in both Singapore and Japan, among Christians (and not just for fear of competition) as well as among Japan's socialists. They fear the use of Confucianism by the government for imposing passive virtues of submission and for promoting conservative politics.

Confucianism can remain genuine and viable only as one value system among others, in a society where freedom and responsibility are esteemed. In this sense, the tradition-bound Confucian society of the nineteenth and early twentieth centuries was actually in need of liberation—from the bondage of vested interests which drew their authority from its name. In this sense as well, the Confucianism which continues to tolerate semidictatorial systems is still in need of such liberation. Once free, Confucianism as a universal value will then become true to itself as a rational *calling* —in a special way, as the calling of the intellectuals (Chinese *ju*). But the scholar or intellectual must strive as well to acquire *jen*, the virtue which makes a person a perfect human being, relating in responsibility toward and harmony with other human beings.

This is perhaps a partial answer to the questions regarding the relevance of traditional religions in East Asia. Traditional religions will remain relevant if they are ready to respond to new needs and new problems, which include the need of self-transformation as well as that of responding to human freedom and equality. And, to the extent that they are already doing so, they will also play an essential part in the making of a future China and a future East Asia.

We have come to the crux of the problem of modernization: that of education for freedom, for initiative and responsibility. Under authoritarian governments, education depends solely on political power for its support and even survival. In the case of China, the Marxist advent to power put an end, at least during a period of many years, to rational discussions concerning alternative social systems and forms of government, until the recent liberalization that revealed the disenchantment of the country's intellectual elite, whose usefulness is being rediscovered. In South Korea, growing literacy and higher education have created a demand for greater freedom and political participation, a demand made especially by the intellectuals—university teachers and students. They are actually acting in accordance with a great tradition, that of the *reformist* Confucian scholar-intellectual, whose first loyalty was always to a conception of a superior order—that of his conscience —and whose education was especially oriented to social and political responsibility. Here we may applaud the recent (1986) decision by Taiwan to permit the growth of a nongoverning "opposition" party.

Education may not bring political power, but education should always seek to actualize the best of our human qualities. And modernization will mean little unless it can enable more people in the East and West to actualize and develop the best of themselves. They may then be able to treasure their particular national identities while also transcending them—to remain loyal to their own cultural heritages while also inheriting the common, *human* heritage. They may then live according to the Confucian calling by being among "the first to take on the worries of the world, and the last to enjoy its pleasures." (These words come from the eleventh-century Chinese scholar-official Fan Chung-yen.)

True, in China much more than in Japan, the *calling* of the intellectual is discussed and perceived, among other reasons because of the distinctiveness of an educated class in a country where education has not yet become a universal privilege. This calling is directed especially to political responsibility, to changing and transforming society. But it is not limited to such. It is also a calling to the discovery of moral values and inner worth, and to the achievement of spiritual greatness.

CONCLUSION

Is Confucianism a philosophy or a religion? In this chapter and in this book, my definition of religion includes a consciousness of a dimension of transcendence that I perceive as having been present in Confucianism from the very beginning, even though this has not always referred to a belief in a personal deity. I recognize also the tendency in the tradition to identify the transcendent with what is immanent, to acknowledge the presence of the way of Heaven in the way of man, to an extent that the issues have become often ambiguous. But the very insistence upon the priority of the way of Heaven, and the quest itself for the discovery and fulfillment of such within the way of man, point to a movement toward self-transcendence that has always given the tradition an unusual inner vitality and dynamism.

Throughout history, Confucianism has served a secular as well as a religious (and ritual) function. However, with the end of the cult of Heaven and the gradual disappearance of an exterior cult offered to ancestors, Confucianism has little more to offer in ritual terms. Still, it remains religious at its core on account of its spiritual teachings of sagehood or self-transcendence, so strongly affirmed and developed by the Neo-Confucian thinkers. It is, besides, a teaching directed to every human person and, as such, has served as well to strengthen a basic belief in human equality.

But it is not to be denied that the influence of Confucianism is growing more and more diffused and, at times, almost elusive. With the gradual disappearance of the ancestral cult, today—but only today—Confucianism seems more a philosophy than a religion. Yet to the extent that it is not only a philosophy of life, but also a *living* one that exerts a real influence and directs those who hear its call to the goal of self-transcendence, it may still be called a religion.

The Confucian tradition has lost ground in modern times, but it is not dead. Like Christianity, it has had to confront the challenges of science and technology. Like Christianity, it has also had to respond to the political and social challenges of a Marxist regime. And recent indications point to an increasing recognition, on the part of this regime itself, of the vitality of Confucianism. The encounter between Marxism and Christianity began only a short while ago. The encounter between Christianity and Confucianism is not yet over.

A Marxist China should be, by strength of its name, a "Westernized" China. But today's Marxist China finds itself still distant from achieving the goal of modernization. Many Chinese intellectuals are asking for *more* Westernization, meaning by it the intellectual pluralism and individual freedom that were called for during and after the May Fourth Movement of 1919. China's leading intellectuals today, such as Li Zhehou and Tang Yijie, no longer are debunkers of the Confucian tradition as were many in 1919, but offer a vision of the future where tradition and modernity are integrated in the best interests of humanity.

Is Confucianism still relevant? If we mean by Confucianism a backward-looking ideology, sterile textual studies, a society of hierarchical relationships excluding reciprocity, the permanent dominance of parents over children and of men over women, and a social order interested only in the past and not in the future, then Confucianism is not relevant and may as well be dead.

But if we mean by it a dynamic discovery of the worth of the human person, of the possibilities of moral greatness and even sagehood, of one's fundamental relationship to others in a society based on ethical values, of an interpretation of reality and a metaphysics of the self that remain open to the transcendent—all this, of course, the basis for a true sense of human dignity, freedom, and equality—then Confucianism is very relevant and can remain so, both for China and for the world.

However, to be in this sense relevant, Confucianism will have to take into account the recent events of history in China and in the world. It will have to be satisfied with itself remaining a system of diffused values, and independent of state support. It will have to perceive itself once more, as at the time of its origins, as one school among many, in a world of many states. It will have to be open to other schools of thought while it develops its own central message in loyalty both to its own inspiration and to the spirit of growth in freedom. And it will have to push the concerns of ethical humanism and self-transcendence for their own sakes—over and above the concerns of its own survival or revival.

In this way, even the universalism residing at the heart of ethical humanism may find its fulfillment in a world divided over self-interest, in a world where the human being risks losing himself or herself through the dissipation of his or her mind and heart. Confucian humanism calls one back to oneself—at the deepest level as well as in the realization of one's ethical relationships with others. Mencius has said, "Humanity is man's mind; righteousness is man's path. Alas, how this path is neglected and not followed, and this mind is lost and not sought for. . . . The way of learning is nothing other than looking for the lost mind" *(Mencius* 6A:11).

And to conclude with a few lines of poetry from Wang Yang-ming:

> The sages' teachings have come down a thousand
>   years:
> "Knowing the good"*(liang-chih)* is their pass-
>   word.
> Compasses give circles and quadrants squares.
> Look for the first unity, but wield no axe,
> Leave not the common realm of actions—
> Go straight to the first [formless] moment,
>   without the pictures.*

* Reference to "diagrams," such as the eleventh century Chou Tun-i's *T'ai-chi,* or Great Ultimate, that seek to explain the cosmos. The English translation is by Julia Ching. Consult her book, *To Acquire Wisdom: the Way of Wang Yang-ming* (New York, 1976).

2. *Hans Küng:* A Christian Response

In this response, I want to take up the question where Julia Ching left it: with the effects of Confucianism on society until today. For my part, I want to reinforce all the analyses that have been presented. It is, after all, no secret that the *Muslim countries* of this earth from Morocco to Pakistan seem to be losing their historic chance to catch up scientifically and technologically with the industrialized countries of the West. In spite of a relatively early start to modernization (in Egypt, already in the nineteenth century) and the massive influx of petrodollars, the transition from merchant capitalism to industrial society has been largely unsuccessful. Indeed, in the light of accelerated processes of innovation in today's world economy, these countries seem to be falling increasingly behind. Internationally oriented economists have been watching this with concern for a long time already.

What is missing? It can hardly be capital, of which there is enough available. It seems more likely that the "human factor" is lacking. Could the problem be the people—their basic attitudes and values, their ability to learn, their sense of responsibility, and their social discipline? And as we know, these factors are, for their part, determined jointly by the religio-cultural infrastructures of both the Muslim and the Christian or East Asian cultures. The Near East specialist Dieter Weiss has delivered a penetrating anal-

ysis of the situation: "In Muslim societies, the processing of Western or secularized Christian concepts of a scientific worldview in
the sense of an integration into indigenous value patterns, has in
their [the Muslims'] own view often not been satisfactorily
achieved. This is in contrast to the East Asian cultures" *(Zur wis-
senschaftlichen Kooperation mit den Ländern des vorderen Orients,* Europa-Archiv Series 22 [1982], p. 681).

Indeed, "in contrast to the East Asian cultures." It is really
amazing: in contrast to Muslim countries, but also in contrast to
the *Hindu-influenced* countries of South and Southeast Asia, the
Latin American nations, and especially the *black African* states,
one particular group of countries has had astonishing success in the
last two decades. Their portion of world production has risen from
8.3 percent in 1960, to 15.9 percent in 1981; and there are predictions that by the year 2000, with around 20 percent, they may well
reach the level of North America (United States and Canada; compared to Western Europe with around 23 percent, the USSR and
Eastern Europe with around 17 percent). These are the so-called
Sinicized countries, characterized by Chinese writing, culture,
and religion. Under the economic leadership of Japan, they include the "big dragon," China (according to the International
Fund for Agricultural Development, agricultural production between 1978 and 1986 exploded by 56 percent and average income
by almost 70 percent during the same period), and the "four little
dragons"—Taiwan, South Korea, Hong Kong, and Singapore (only
the special case of Vietnam is different). Together they are responsible for a growing shift of geopolitical importance from the Atlan-
tic (which has been dominant throughout the European modern
age) to the Pacific.

In a nuanced synthesis entitled *Le Nouveau Monde Sinisé* (Paris,
1986), the French Sinologist Léon Vandermeersch has analyzed
the economic, political, and cultural dimensions of this group of
countries which has arisen between the Western and the Eastern
blocs. (The statistics quoted earlier were taken from this book.)
However different these countries may be from each other, they
are bound together by the *same Chinese writing system:* the ideo-
grams that can be understood in all the different languages, even
though they are read differently. Vandermeersch stresses the fact

that, unlike alphabetic scripts, the Chinese written characters express meanings and reflect common basic attitudes and values that, in all these countries, are essentially determined by the more than two thousand year old *Confucian tradition.* Julia Ching has, for her part, already demonstrated that this tradition belongs to all of East Asia. Moreover, the old Confucian virtues in particular seem to be especially important in such an age of high technology as our own. And why? Because, unlike earlier times, the present day no longer demands only technical and mechanical competence, but also soberness of mind, impartiality, adaptability, flexibility, creativity, and foresight—all typically Confucian qualities that can easily be blended with Taoist and Buddhist beliefs.

In their confrontation with modernity, all the Sinicized countries have undergone the greatest upheavals of their long histories. First, there was Japan, with the Meiji Restoration in the nineteenth century and then the American occupation after the Second World War. But then came China as well, with the Nationalist, followed by the Communist, and finally the Cultural Revolution. Is it any wonder, then, that everywhere there are signs of a *renewed appreciation of the traditional culture?* This common culture in East Asia is thoroughly influenced by Confucianism—right up to the extraordinary importance of, for instance, education or thrift. (For example, from 1965 to 1978, the Japanese saved between 15.3 percent and 19.8 percent of their gross national product. It was the same with China, Korea, and Taiwan, compared to between 7.8 percent and 8.6 percent in the United States.) Even Buddhism has to a large extent adopted the Confucian ethic in practice. Although fundamental Confucian institutions such as the family, rites, and officialdom were drawn into the great crisis, it is certain that the spirit of Confucianism will nevertheless be preserved in that wonderful fabric, the Chinese writing system with its semantic texture that is the texture of Confucianism itself. Since all the languages spoken from Peking to Tokyo and from Seoul to Taipei communicate meaning that is expressed in the same written characters, the new patterns of behavior in these rapidly modernizing societies are undergoing modifications that can only be understood with reference to the ancient Confucian heritage.

According to Vandermeersch, the Confucian legacy differs from Western individualism on three points in particular:

1. *Family Structure:* although urbanization may to a large extent be dissolving traditional family structure in the Sinicized countries as well, it is only "with reference to the old model of a society structured by familial relationships that one can discover the meaning of a very contemporary social style which can only be characterized as *communitarian [gemeinschaftlich]."*

2. *Rites:* although the typical Confucian rites may have disappeared completely with the old order, it is only "with reference to the Confucian understanding of these rites that one can discover the meaning of what makes contemporary Sinicized societies ones that are still very much imbued with *ritualism."*

3. *Officialdom:* although the old forms of authority may have disappeared, it is only "with reference, finally, to the old system of the Mandarin state that one can discover the meaning of a conception of the state that is largely based on what can be called a *functional,* as opposed to a 'political,' conception of the state" (see Vandermeersch, *Le Nouveau Monde Sinisé,* pp. 161–203).

Published at the same time as that of Vandermeersch, studies on the *psychology* of the Chinese people have gone in the same direction. Now as ever, Chinese social psychology is characterized by the Confucian legacy as follows: "Man exists through and is defined by his relationships to others; these relationships are hierarchically structured; social order is ensured through party's honouring the requirements in the role-relationships. . . . Many aspects of Chinese social relationships can be linked to this distillate of Confucianism" (M. H. Bond, ed., *The Psychology of the Chinese People* [Hong Kong and Oxford, 1986], p. 216).

For the Christian theologian this all means that Confucianism is in no way a religion of the past, but rather a living, *contemporary spiritual power* that influences people directly or indirectly. Its massive influence has had a corrective effect even on folk religion (discussed in the previous response), transforming it from a purely utilitarian religion into a specifically moral *religion* that more clearly exhibits a transcendent dimension. And what about this transcendent dimension?

THE TRANSCENDENT DIMENSION

With respect to Vandermeersch's conclusions, I would debate with him on two points. It seems to me questionable that *individualism* (in contrast to Far Eastern communitarianism) is a typically Western product (it is, I submit, only characteristic of European modernity after the Reformation). It is also questionable that Chinese religion, for its part, either lost its *transcendent and godly dimension* in the time of Confucius or dissolved it into purely cosmological and anthropological relationships. We heard otherwise in Julia Ching's exposition. There is the ancient ancestral cult that still endures in many places today, testifying to belief in a life after death. There is also the cult of Heaven that was commonplace long before the time of Confucius, and is in many respects the principal hallmark of Chinese religion, a witness to a genuine belief in God. Finally, even today, there is the widespread popular belief in a "higher power."

In fact, since time immemorial, the Chinese have believed in a supreme divinity or in a moral power that rules the world and takes a personal interest in human destiny. They have particularly believed in the divine sanction of the political order. Human thinking, feeling, action, and volition were thus associated with the transcendent; and ethics, ancestral cult, and rituals have all been conditioned by it. In Confucius' time, many Chinese thinkers centered their reflections on the heavy responsibility of especially the ruler for the whole—not only in relation to his subjects, but also in relation to Heaven. How must the ruler behave if, unlike earlier fallen dynasties, he is not to lose the favor and protection of Heaven? It was not least with this central concern in mind that Confucius and his successors reinterpreted all of the old literature, including divination texts, ritual prescriptions, chronicles, and folk songs. Historically, however, all too often this high morality and religiosity of an empire existing "by the grace of Heaven"—comparable in legitimacy to the Christian Holy Roman Empire existing "by the grace of God"—sank to a pure ideology of power, often enough making a mockery of concrete social reality. Eventually, such discrepancy contributed decisively to the ruin of the empire—in China as in the West.

Yet the Chinese Communists still polemicized against the evidently still living *religious* dimension of Confucianism, condemning it as "metaphysical idealism," as "scholasticism," indeed, as "theology." And during the Cultural Revolution, they damaged, destroyed, or converted to profane uses not only many churches and mosques, but also many Confucian (and Taoist) temples. All this shows only too clearly how far away from Chinese reality were those Western analysts who, from the limited perspective of European modernity, believed that they could disregard the religious dimension or reduce it to a purely social dimension when studying the entire Sinicized world!

The current revival of religion even on the Chinese mainland confirms the enduring significance of the transcendent dimension. Many Chinese intellectuals close to the Confucian tradition have, moreover, not ceased to reflect on fundamental ethical and religious questions. Already in 1958, Chinese scholars in Taipei published "A Manifesto for the Reappraisal of Sinology and Reconstruction of Chinese Culture." Although politically one-sided and not always completely fair where Christianity was concerned, it was nevertheless definitely to be taken seriously. Had we in the West done so, subsequent events in China—first negative, then positive—would have taken us less by surprise. In this manifesto, the signatories emphasized the harmony between the "way of Heaven" *(T'ien-tao)* and the "way of man" *(jen-tao)* as the central legacy of Confucianism (cf. Carsun Chang, *The Development of Neo-Confucian Thought* [New York, 1963], vol. 2, appendix). At the same time they challenged Western Sinologists to pay closer attention to Confucian spirituality as the core of Chinese culture.

According to these scholars, this core of Chinese thought has been particularly "neglected and misunderstood" by Sinologists. It exists especially in what "was called the 'conformity of heaven and man in virtue,' and this is the traditional doctrine of *hsin-hsin[g]*. If we realize that this doctrine is the core of Chinese culture, then we must not allow the misunderstanding that Chinese culture limits itself to external relations between people,

with neither inner spiritual life nor religious or metaphysical sentiment" (pp. 461, 464). In order to understand this core, we must
once again return to the origins of Chinese religion and to the
historical developments, especially as regards the strictly philosophical and theological problem, that is, the question of God and
man.

THE DUALITY OF GOD'S NAMES IN ANCIENT CHINESE AND ISRAELITE RELIGIONS

We can take it as a given that none of the great religious traditions in human history, whether of Semitic, Indian, or Chinese
origin, has a single and uniform understanding of the ultimate,
supreme, and most real reality—of Heaven, the Tao, the Absolute,
the Godhead, God. The difference in names already indicates that
the term God is often not simply understood in the same way even
within a single tradition. To be sure, it is also not simply understood as something else. Rather, as will become clear in the course
of our reflections, it is understood in a related or analogous way:
always as a first or last, a highest or deepest, that determines all of
reality, whether as a ruling or immanent person or as a paramount
or dominating principle.

Within our framework, this allows us to take a closer look at the
parallels and differences between the Judeo-Christian tradition
and the Chinese tradition in particular. We will thus gain a better
understanding of the development of the Chinese tradition. Parallels between the ancient Chinese and the ancient Israelite religions become apparent with the names for God. These are enlightening for an assessment of today's questions.

As we heard, in very early *Chinese* religion, in the second millennium before Christ, there were already two different names for
God owing to two cultural traditions that can be traced to two
ethnic groups, the Shang and the Chou.

• On the one hand, there was the Lord *(Ti)* or Lord-on-high
(Shang-ti), the supreme Lord over all the nature deities and spirits. He was understood more anthropomorphically and was particularly associated with the ruling house.

• On the other hand, there was Heaven *(T'ien)*, understood origi-nally in a personal sense, but then increasingly less anthropomor-phically as a cosmic and moral power (order, being) that possesses intelligence and will and impartially directs the fate of all human beings.

• The two names were *joined* together during the Chou dynasty to designate the one supreme being, the all-embracing power.

Similarly, in early *Israelite* religion, there were also two different names for God which, as we know, were what initially made possi-ble a distinction in the Five Books of Moses (that is, the Penta-teuch) between the Yahwist and the Elohist sources.

• On the one hand, then, there was Yahweh (the Hebrew word YHWH). This name was explained to Moses in the burning bush scene with *'ehjeh ăser 'ehjeh,* rendered as "I am who I am" by the Greek translators, the Church Fathers, and the scholastics. Long misunderstood in Christian theology as a static ontological declara-tion of God's essence (God = Being itself), today this phrase is more adequately rendered by Martin Buber (and modern exegesis in general) as "I shall be what I shall be." It is a word that must be understood as a declaration of God's historical and dynamic will: "I shall be there, present, and effective," liberating, helping, and strengthening (cf. Ex. 6:6f.).

• On the other hand, there was the term Elohim (originally plural from El, meaning God), designating a plurality of gods but used in the Old Testament (with the singular verb) for one God—indeed, most often for the one true God. The concept of God was then extended: "As abstract plural this word calls forth our idea of the 'Godhead' and tends to signify the notion of divine might in a personal unity" (Walther Eichrodt, *Theology of the Old Testament* [London, 1961], vol. 1, p. 115).

• *Both* words were also *fused,* later on in the Old Testament: "that you might know the Lord (Yahweh) is God (Elohim); there is no other besides him" (Dt. 4:35) expresses such a process, although, in contrast to *T'ien* and especially *Tao,* even "Elohim" retains a thor-oughly personal character.

It is sufficient here to have pointed to the duality of the names for God. In connection with Taoism, we will examine further this Chinese understanding of God that is also found in Confucianism and Neo-Confucianism; although, in contrast to Judaism, Christianity, and Islam, it is not as central in the Chinese case. At the moment, the fundamental question before us is, how is a Christian theologian even to approach this Confucianism which has become an inseparable part of the society and thought of the Chinese nation? First, we shall draw attention to a further important parallel—this time in Christianity, where, not as in Judaism but more as in Confucianism, a normative leading figure—together with the canonized Five Classics—occupies center stage.

THE QUEST FOR THE HISTORICAL CONFUCIUS

Just as *Roman Catholicism* has for centuries led its followers to believe that everything in the Catholic church—from liturgy to dogma to discipline—has remained unchanged from the beginning, so is it in a very similar way with *Chinese Confucianism*. Many of its adherents were for a long time convinced that everything in China had always been the same: religious doctrines, morals, rites, state, and society. And it was only in the last century, as modern critical thinking from Europe and North America made its way into China as well, that more and more intellectuals there took account of what enormous changes China and its religions had undergone during four thousand years or so of history.

No, neither Christianity nor Confucianism has always been the same. Both Christianity and Confucianism have experienced extremely *complex histories* with profound and epochal ruptures. It is certain that just as *Jesus Christ* has been variously perceived in the primitive Jewish community, in Hellenistic Byzantium, in medieval Rome, in the German Reformation, and in European modernity, so too have different "total constellations of convictions, values, and modes of behavior" (that is, paradigms) determined the varying images of the wise *Master K'ung* (K'ung Fu-tzu), who has influenced the life and thought of his people more than any other figure in Chinese history (cf. Fung Yu-lan, *A Short History of Chinese Philosophy* [New York, 1962], pp. 47f.).

• The total constellation was different in feudal China at the end of the Chou dynasty, when Confucius lived as one teacher among others, than in the bureaucratic Han state, when Confucius became *the* teacher (indeed, nearly a god) and Confucianism the state orthodoxy.

• After a long period of Buddhist dominance, the constellation was again different in the Sung Neo-Confucianism that was influenced by Buddhism and Taoism: Confucius was no longer regarded as divine.

• After the Mongol rule, the constellation was different in the restoration period of the Ming dynasty, when the first Jesuit missionaries came to China. And finally, it was different during the Ch'ing dynasty, when four Jesuit fathers caused such a furor in Enlightenment Europe with their translation of three Confucian writings under the title *Confucius Sinarum Philosophus.*

Yet it was only on the basis of research into Chinese language, literature, history, and culture undertaken in modern Sinology (first chair in Paris in 1814; Germany followed only with Hamburg in 1909) that a *critical assessment of the Confucian legacy* gradually took place in late nineteenth-century China itself. This needs to be continued in the late twentieth century with determination and in a constructively critical way that goes beyond modern European and Chinese Marxist critique.

Like Indian and Hebrew religion, Chinese religion has an uninterrupted history of around four thousand years that extends into the present day. But while people in India were more fascinated with the eternal world of religious belief, people in China and Israel demonstrated an explicit historical consciousness from early on: not a cyclical conception such as in India, but a linear and progressive understanding of history! With regard to the *beginning* of *Chinese history,* one may assume that, just as the Biblical accounts of an original earthly paradise cannot be taken as historical, neither can the Chinese myths of a Golden Age be understood as fact. And, as in the case of the stories of the Old Testament Patriarchs—Abraham, Isaac, and Jacob—one can similarly not expect to verify the legends of the Three Sovereigns and Five Emperors (culture-heroes, primitive inventors) in their historical details. In contrast to India with its rich mythology that is by nature not overly interested in the historical authenticity of people and events, the interest that the Chinese show in historical verification is truly striking. In this respect, China is much more like the Semitic-prophetic tradition than the Indian-mystic. Both the classical Chinese and the Biblical traditions extend history back into antiquity by reconstructing genealogies. They thereby place emphasis on having a chronology from the beginning. In comparison with the world around them, they therefore reveal a high degree of implicit demythologization and historicization. Indeed, in China as well, mythology exists only in fragments and has largely lost its place as a subject of literature.

This means that, just as it is possible to have a relatively reliable picture of pre-Christian *Jewish* religion, so too, as Julia Ching's first presentation has shown, can the same be said about pre-Confucian *Chinese* religion. And just as it is possible to discover the *historical Jesus* of Nazareth behind the picture of Christ presented by the later church, so too can the *historical Master K'ung* be discovered behind the picture of Confucius presented by traditional Chinese folk piety. Moreover—and this is decisive—for the Chinese, Confucius is evidently not a mythical, but an entirely historical personality. Therefore, given the current reopening of China, I would ask that Chinese research once again take up the question of the historical Confucius which was initiated in the twenties and thirties by Ku Chieh-kang and Ch'ien Hsüan-t'ung, only to be interrupted by the Sino-Japanese War. The question should be pursued through the different changes of paradigm throughout Chinese history right up to present times.

Indeed, it was a long and varied path that led from Master K'ung, a philosopher among many others who was little esteemed during his lifetime, to that Confucius who became *the* sage par excellence; to whom more and more writings were attributed and ever more temples were dedicated; who, on December 30, 1906, shortly before the fall of the Ch'ing dynasty, was declared on a level with the gods of heaven and earth by imperial edict; and who was then just as vehemently attacked and vilified during the Communist Cultural Revolution. For this very reason, however, the way back, the quest for the historical figure, is long, difficult, and delicate. As the preceding exposition already showed, such a quest will not, any more than will the research into the historical Jesus, yield a historically precise and verifiable "Life of Confucius." It will not give us an exact biographical chronology, geography, and psychology of this man who lived twenty-five hundred years ago, or even a "closed" picture of Confucius. But we can expect to discover the *characteristic tendencies and outlines of K'ung's teachings, his attitudes, and his destiny.* And, from the religious point of view, is this not precisely what is both sufficient and decisive for the believer? More important than the historically verified authenticity of particular words, deeds, and stories of K'ung are, even for today, the characteristic tendencies, the specific behavior, the basic character, and the unambiguous essentials. In short, it is the "open" overall picture of Master K'ung that is important and not what fits into schemata and models.

As the exposition demonstrated, classical Confucian thought encompasses much more than what is contained in the *Analects.* Confucianism went through a deadly crisis under the Communist regime, especially during the anti-Confucius campaign that reached its climax in 1973–74. Now, within certain limits at least, it is celebrating its resurrection; and since 1984, Confucius' birthday —long a day of celebration in Taiwan and South Korea—has been permitted in the People's Republic of China as well. In the light of these events, Confucianism in particular may be more interested than before in such historical-critical research. Why? Not because such historical and critical research into Confucius could ever directly create (or destroy) religious conviction, belief, and certainty. It is rather because such research, if carried out with the courage to think critically and with respect for the facts, is commensurate with the basic Confucian attitude itself: *the rational review and scrutiny of the tradition.* And to what end? In order to answer to oneself and to others for one's religious faith, specifically in the face of both modern hypercritical unbelief and still existing, premodern, uncritical credulity. What is at issue, therefore, is not a blind, authoritarian Confucianism, but rather one that understands—one that, in good Confucian fashion, is *reasonable and responsible.* "Where all praise, we must examine; where all blame, we must examine," said Confucius himself *(Analects* 15:27).

No, neither the "neutral" historian, nor the unbelieving Communist, nor the believing Confucian himself can be indifferent to such a historically possible, scientifically legitimate, and practically necessary questioning when understood in its entirety.

• The *historian* cannot be indifferent: how else is he or she going to be able to explain the emergence of a Confucianism that, more than anything else, has determined the Chinese way of life for the last two thousand years?

• The *anti-Confucian Communist* cannot be indifferent: how else is he or she (or even the Western positivist) to know what the conflict is ultimately all about? Is he or she fighting real opponents or phantoms? Has he or she hit upon the matter itself, the heart of Confucianism, or merely the political or social consequences of Confucianism?

• The *convinced Confucian* cannot be indifferent: how else is his or her religion, as a comprehending, responsible religion, to be purified from both naive superstition and the ideologies of vested interests? How else are the obstacles to religion removed and how else is the willingness to believe awakened?

In sum, a comparison between Confucianism and Christianity must be historically grounded and cannot begin arbitrarily somewhere on the surface. It must fundamentally begin with the Confucius of history and compare him with the Jesus of history. What then, let us now ask, are the similarities and differences between Confucius and Jesus of Nazareth?

SIMILARITIES BETWEEN CONFUCIUS AND JESUS
OF NAZARETH

No comparison is possible without considering the very *different sources.* For the way to the historical Confucius is even more difficult than finding the historical Jesus. Whereas the first Pauline epistles (the oldest documents of the New Testament) were written a good twenty years after the death of Jesus, and the first

Gospel (of Mark) around forty years after that event, the *Analects*
(Lun-yü: principal source of the teachings of Master K'ung) were
compiled at least one hundred years (probably more) after Confucius' lifetime, and the first biography of Confucius (by Ssu-ma
Ch'ien) was written almost four hundred years after that lifetime.
A minimum of solid historical evidence has called forth an abundance of *legendary materials,* although the *Analects* exhibit less
"kerygma" and editing than the Gospels.

• Like Jesus' *year of birth,* that of Confucius is not certain, and his
birth is also entwined with legends.

• Like Jesus, Master K'ung was allegedly born of noble ancestry
(David, the Shang royal house), even though he actually came
from *humble circumstances* and an unimportant *family.*

• Like the boy Jesus, the boy K'ung was said to be marvelously
precocious, even though we know nothing certain about either
boyhood.

• Like Jesus, Confucius died after *years of arduous wandering*
without apparently having achieved his goal. In the light of their
great hope for a coming kingdom of peace, they both suffered
disappointment and *failure.*

• Like Jesus' work, that of Confucius became *historically influential only after his death.*

Yet, for both Jesus of Nazareth and Confucius, the *public teaching*
is significant. The followers of both of them held on to that which
was for them decisive in the teachings of the masters. The following is conspicuous in this regard:

Just as the *Analects* of Confucius present a collection of isolated
sayings, anecdotes, and conversations (20 chapters and 497
verses), so too are the *Gospels* (of course against the background of
a very particular history of suffering) a comparatively short collection of words, parables, and conversations.

And like Jesus, K'ung developed *no systematic* and structured
teaching in which manners, morals, law, philosophy, and theology
were clearly distinguished. In the case of Confucius, his teachings

were systematized to a certain extent only with Mencius (c. 371–289) and Hsün-tzu (c. 298–238).

And as with the preaching of Jesus, so too the application of *modern hermeneutics* and differentiated methods—developed two hundred years ago for examination of the New Testament—to the teachings of Confucius may well allow the discovery of much more that is historically reliable.

Even on the basis of contemporary historical knowledge, however, quite a few *parallels* between the self-understanding and the practice of Jesus and Confucius become apparent:

• Both lived in *a time of social crisis* among their people and, as wandering "teachers" and "masters" ("Rabbi," "Fu-tzu"), tried *to respond to this crisis with their message.*

• Without their own families' playing a role, they both attracted *disciples or students* (without regard to social background) who were to spread their message.

• Neither of them was an *ascetic* (hermit, monk) wishing to withdraw from the world. Instead, both worked in the midst of this life, ate, drank, and were criticized for this by the "pious."

• Neither of them was a *mystic* practicing psychological self-analysis, teaching the steps of meditation, and in search of ecstasy or Nirvana.

• Neither of them was a *metaphysician* speculating about God, the ground of being, and ultimate questions in general; neither of them called himself God at all. Both of them were rather more concerned with the practical following of their message.

• Conversely, neither the one nor the other was a *sceptic* or a *rationalist* bent on reducing all thought to the rational and all religion to morality without taking cognizance of a transcendent reality (God, Heaven).

• Moreover, both shared *traditional religious ideas* that are to some degree foreign to us today (messianic expectancy in the case of Jesus; sacrifice, belief in spirits and omens in the case of Confucius).

• Both were very practically confronted with the *established order* (the "law" or Torah, the "rites" or *li)* and criticized outer conformism and hypocrisy in this order in favor of an inner attitude.

• Both lived what they preached and presented a highly individual and personal *ethic* that expressed itself in clear moral demands.

It is, of course, precisely at this point that the decisive differences emerge. For the sake of the particular profiles of Confucius and Jesus, these must be elaborated just as sharply.

THE PERSONAL PROFILES OF CONFUCIUS AND OF JESUS OF NAZARETH

If one wants to describe the *basic differences* between Jesus of Nazareth and Confucius in historical perspective and without value judgments, then the following profiles emerge. As much as both are after renewal and in actual fact lay the spiritual foundations for a new era:

• *Confucius,* even when looking forward, oriented himself *backward*—to a better *past,* to the *early empire* of the ancient kings.

That is, K'ung's clear guiding vision for the future was that of an idealized *antiquity* with its moral-political ethos grounded entirely in the family, and with its sociopolitical order.

From this vantage point, questions of external forms were unusually important: the internally motivated *observance of the old rites,* and the original religious and civil mores, social customs, and ritual decrees (of the Chou dynasty). "I am a transmitter, not an innovator; I believe in antiquity and love the ancients" (7:1). Human beings were not to concern themselves anxiously about gods and spirits. They were rather to bow before the great tradition of the ancients.

• *Jesus of Nazareth,* on the other hand, while being rooted in the faith of the Fathers, oriented himself *forward*—to a better *future,* to the *coming Kingdom* of God the Father: "Thy Kingdom come!" (Mt. 6:10 [RSV]).

That is, Jesus' challenging guiding vision was the *Kingdom of God*, its grace and promise.

External forms, practices, ritual purity, and Sabbath prescriptions were therefore unimportant to him. The inner attitude was what mattered. The individual was called to decision; the family had to step back.

Although he fundamentally presupposed the *keeping of the commandments* to the extent that they are the commandments of God, Jesus concentrated them all into one great commandment: "You shall love the Lord your God and your neighbor as yourself" (Mk. 12:30f. [RSV]). Human beings were not to bow before the tradition of the Fathers. They were rather to bow before the will of God which, in certain concrete cases, might permit the commandments to be put aside for the sake of a human being.

From the outset, therefore, there is a clear difference between the *religious horizons* as well as the *central messages* of Confucius and Jesus of Nazareth, both of which were to serve as models for the immediate disciples and the later admirers:

• The religious *horizon* for Confucius was Heaven *(T'ien,* understood as effective power, order, law, or being). It had displaced the original lively gods of ancient China and is only named Shang-ti (Lord-on-high) once in the *Analects.* It was supreme above all, and human beings (and especially the ruler) were to hear and obey it: "He who sins against Heaven has no one to whom he may pray" (3:13). The word T'ien is found eighteen times in the *Analects,* and always in connection with will, action, and emotion.

But *central* to the interests of Confucius was the *human person* with his or her natural and basic family (and thus also social) relationships. The human person was not to be a holy person, but rather one who was always open to everything good, true, and beautiful (music!), a noble person (not a nobleman, but rather a moral noble), one who was to become a politically committed sage.

On the whole, then, this vision is *anthropocentric,* albeit with an entirely religious emphasis.

• The religious *horizon* for Jesus of Nazareth was the coming Kingdom of Heaven, identical with the Kingdom of God. The Kingdom of God was understood as the fulfillment of the old promises and salvation from all evil. It was that into which human beings were to enter in response to the gracious call of God.

Central to Jesus' thought, action, and prayer was thus *God* himself (to be addressed as a personal other), the merciful Father whose will is completely oriented toward the salvation of humanity: "Thy will be done on earth as it is in heaven!" (Mt. 6:10 [RSV].)

On the whole, then, this vision is *theocentric,* albeit with an entirely human orientation.

It is perhaps already apparent how the figure of Confucius, from a global historical view, fits into the single "religious history of humankind" and its outstanding figures.

A THIRD BASIC TYPE OF RELIGIOSITY

In the preface to this book, I pointed out that, next to the two great religious river systems of the Semitic-prophetic and Indian-mystic traditions, there exists in the history of humanity a third one: the Chinese-sagely tradition that, as we saw in our first chapter, already began to appear in outlines during Chinese antiquity. We can now be a little bit more concrete while leaving the further clarification of what we will now say until later. Next to Jesus Christ (in the line of the Hebrew prophets and then, following Jesus, the prophet Muhammad) on the one hand, and Gautama Buddha (and all the Indian mystics) on the other, *Confucius* personifies a third basic type of religiosity that can and must be distinguished from the other two—without thereby ranking them.

It is of little help for the clarity of things if certain concepts such as prophet (or shaman) are expanded so as to deprive them of their sharp outlines—something that H. H. Rowley does in his well-known book, *Prophecy and Religion in Ancient China and Israel.* He uses basically secondary ("reformer") or even alien ("statesman") points of view so that he can subsume Confucius and the great Israelite prophets such as Amos, Isaiah, and Jeremiah under the same conceptual heading of prophet. He does this in spite of the fact that, at the end of his book, he has to admit that Master K'ung does not have what is most distinctive about the great prophets of Israel. Not only do the prophets have a different intimate and personal understanding of and relation to God. They also have a specific mission through the one true God—by which the prophet becomes the direct representative of God, making known the word and will of God: "Thus says the Lord." "This is the word of the Lord!" Rowley after all also says about Confucius: "His confidence in the power of Heaven to preserve him, and his sense of a mission to men appointed by Heaven, is as strong as that of the prophets of Israel. Where he falls short of them is in the remoteness of God, and in the small place that God had in his teaching. While for him God was real and His purpose was clear, his unwillingness to talk about Him meant that he did little to make Him real for his followers. There might be a will of God for him, but he said nothing to make men feel that there was a will of God for them, and worship was but the offering of reverence and not the receiving of grace. Hence, in effect, his teaching was reduced to ethics, instead of the communication of the religion which he himself had" (Rowley, *Prophecy and Religion,* pp. 125–26).

Rowley had to develop a skewed perspective because he did not seriously take into account the religious type and the literary genre that had little to do with the Israelite prophets, but a great deal to do with Confucius and even the ancient Chinese tradition: this is the religious type of the *sage* and the literary genre of *wisdom literature.* As we shall see in connection with Lao-tzu and Taoism, this type and genre are to be found in the later strata of the Hebrew tradition as well (more in Chapter III). It is not without reason that Confucius received the title of "greatest sage and first teacher"; that his grave and temple in Ch'ü-fu (Qufu), Shantung, became a pilgrimage site for Chinese scholars; that his birthday is today still celebrated as Teacher's Day (Taiwan). The sage K'ung has been the ideal and model of the Chinese tradition throughout the centuries!

For my part, without subordinating one type to the other in this historical comparison, I want at this point to sketch briefly the differences by characterizing the different figures, the different messages, and the consequent different actions of Jesus Christ, Gautama Buddha, and Master K'ung.

1. To what extent are we dealing here with three typical *figures?* Briefly:

• Jesus Christ was an impassioned *messenger and thus a guide for others in the Semitic-prophetic spirit.* To many during his lifetime already he was the *Anointed* (Messiah, Christ), pure and simple.

• Gautama Buddha was a person who turned his back on the world, an innerly peaceful and harmonious *Enlightened One and thus a guide for others in the Indian-mystic spirit.*

• Master K'ung, by contrast, was a man of sober reflection on ethics and politics, the comprehensively learned *teacher and thus a guide for others in the spirit of Far Eastern, humanistic wisdom.* He only became influential long after his death. In response to the question "What is wisdom?" Master K'ung replied, "To be devoted to one's duties regarding others, to honor the gods and spirits and remain far from them, this may be called wisdom" (6:20).

2. To what extent do their *messages* also show different characteristics? In a short formula:

• Jesus Christ, sent by God, called men and women to conversion with a view to salvation from guilt and all evil in the *Kingdom of God.* He asked people to will to do the will of God in practical service to their fellows.

• Gautama Buddha, sent by no one, preached the *release from suffering* in Nirvana, specifically by ceasing to will. Accordingly, he exhorted his followers to turn away from the world and to turn inward unto themselves. He advocated methodical meditation in stages of concentration with the ultimate goal of enlightenment.

• Master K'ung, by contrast, listened to the voice of the ancients rather than divine revelation. He demanded the renewal of the outer constitution of the state as well as the inner constitution of every individual; both were to be done in reverence for the will of Heaven. Accordingly, he called for the moral and political reestablishment and consolidation of a benevolent government, a *social order, and harmony in the family and the state:* "When one rules through decrees and punishments, the people will seek to avoid the transgressions but have no sense of shame. When one rules through virtue and propriety, the people will have a sense of shame and become good" (2:3).

3. To what extent are the consequent *actions* different? Even though they have a great many of the elementary moral laws in common, one can still say that:

• Jesus Christ proclaimed a personally involved love. This love includes those who suffer and those who are oppressed, the sick and the guilty, but also the opponent, the enemy. It is a universal *love* and an entirely active *doing of the good.*

• Gautama Buddha brought to every sentient creature, whether human or animal, patience, sympathy, kindness, and friendliness. He did this with equanimity and without any personal involvement that binds the heart to earthly things. This is a universal *compassion* and caring *goodwill.*

• Master K'ung, by contrast, wanted to strengthen the sense of human autonomy and responsibility through sober, rational reflection. Human destiny was to be mastered in reverence for Heaven but without anxiety about ghosts and spirits. A harmonious relationship between human beings and nature was to be sought. All people were to be shown *humanity (jen),* human goodness, kindness, benevolence; evil ones were, however, to be given *justice* instead of love. "What can rites do for a person lacking in the virtue of humanity? What can music do for a person lacking in the virtue of humanity?" *(Analects* 3:3).

In the light of these comparisons, is it so incomprehensible that the Jesuit missionaries of the sixteenth and seventeenth centuries saw in ancient Confucianism, much more than in Buddhism, something like a natural religion on a philosophical plane? They saw a religion that, somewhat like the Greek philosophy of a Plato, an Aristotle, or the Stoics, represented a *praeparatio evangelii,* a *preparation for the Gospel.* It could therefore definitely be used critically and integrated positively for their contemporary presentation of the Christian message. To be sure, their approach to this undertaking was in many cases naive, both with respect to Confucianism and with respect to Christian teaching. The two are not so easily harmonized and express very different religious systems, something that John D. Young emphasized in his study of the failure of the Christian mission in the seventeenth century *(Confucianism and Christianity: The First Encounter* [Hong Kong, 1983]). And yet, in the context of today's dialogue between the world religions, is it not worth considering whether the *humanum (jen)* of Confucianism might not be something like the foundation for a common ethic of humanity?

THE *HUMANUM* AS THE BASIC NORM FOR AN ETHIC OF WORLD RELIGIONS

The *humanum (jen)* is both what is given and what it is given to do: it is both *the essence and the task* of humanity. A human being is not an animal, an instinctual being. A human being must be truly human. Being human is the measure of the human being! On the other hand—and this is, according to Confucius, a perpetual task of lifelong learning—the human being must *become* human. He or she must realize *humanity:* humanity not as a particular, but as a universal virtue; not as one virtue among others, but as the soul of all virtues. It is a virtue that is not given once and for all. Like all virtues, it can be taught and learned. It is to be appropriated to oneself as an attitude in daily self-education. As a Western reader, one is astonished to find so much of the *Book of Rites (Li-chi)* devoted particularly to pedagogical instructions: humanity varies according to the different familial and social relationships. According to Confucius, as we heard, these relationships involve especially loyalty *(chung)* to one's own heart and conscience, and reciprocity *(shu),* that is, mutual respect and consideration between people.

On this basis, would Confucians perhaps agree if a Christian theologian formulates (as I have already suggested in the context of folk religion) the general and fundamental ethical criterion for every religion as follows: The *good* is that which helps a human being to be truly human! Accordingly, a basic ethical norm is that the human being should not be inhuman, antihuman, but should rather live an entirely humane life. Humanness must be realized in all its dimensions! What is morally good is therefore that which brings lasting success and happiness to human life in its individual and social dimensions. It is what makes possible the optimal unfolding of the human being at all levels and in all dimensions. It is accordingly this humanity, at every level (including the level of impulse and feeling) and in every dimension (including its relation to society and nature), that human beings must realize as individuals and as a community.

In the 1980s, several younger authors in the People's Republic of China raised the *call for more humanity*— for understanding, reconciliation, and the overcoming of class antagonisms. While this call may be unexpected, after the misanthropic excesses of the Cultural Revolution it is certainly understandable. A famous and much criticized article by Wang Ruoshui, entitled "In Defense of Humanism," begins with the words "A spook is going around in China's intellectual circles—the spook of humanism!" What is striking here is that outspokenly humanistic authors such as Zhang Xiaotian ("Luxuriant the Grass on the Plain," "Publicly Private Material") and Li Ping ("At the Twilight Hour") are again taking up in bold fashion the long-taboo theme of religion—indeed, even Christianity. (For this development, see Karl-Heinz Pohl, "Chinesische Literatur der achtziger Jahre: Zeugnisse einer 'Glaubenskrise' der Jugend," *Stimmen der Zeit* 204 [1986], pp. 397–407.)

Indeed, something would be missing at the core of human existence itself if the dimension of "Heaven," of the "transhuman," of the unconditioned, encompassing, highest ultimate were to be denied or ignored. Being human without this dimension would be stunted. Western interpreters have often misunderstood as atheistic naturalism what Neo-Confucians have understood under "human nature" *(hsing)*. "Whoever acts also conscientiously and knows nature, knows also Heaven; whoever regulates his emotions serves also Heaven. Human nature reflects the nature of heaven; the morality of man is also that of heaven. What man does to perfect his own nature is also what gives praise to the manifold manifestations of the universe" (Manifesto, p. 464). The Heaven that is spoken of here is impartial. Its mandate falls on the worthy and the virtuous. And this mandate is not permanent, as we heard: if a dynasty fails, it goes.

This basic norm of true humanity therefore allows one to distinguish *good and evil,* true and false. It also allows one to distinguish what is fundamentally good and what bad, what is true and what false *in a religion,* whether Christianity, Confucianism, or another. But now the question arises, is human nature good?

HUMAN NATURE: GOOD OR EVIL?

This question, which Julia Ching raised, has to be considered in its proper context. As we heard, one can agree with the optimist Mencius (and with the Jesuit Ricci) and regard human nature as good; *or* one can follow Hsün-tzu (and some Christian theologians following Augustine) and regard it as evil. But this is a primarily abstract and theoretical way of posing a line of reasoning that neither Confucius nor Jesus of Nazareth is reported to have followed. Yet, the question of whether education through *li* (customs, rites) restores the human being to his or her original goodness, or only produces the good in the (as such evil) human being in the first place, is not, for the Chinese, a question of ontology (of human nature as such) or even of theology (of salvation or its opposite), but rather, in typically Chinese fashion, a question of *pedagogy.* It basically refers to two different theories of education. The inductive-developmental theory of Mencius wants to bring out the good in the human being; the formal-regulative theory of Hsün-tzu, however, seeks to tame the evil inclinations and impulses.

As a result, *Confucian scholars* after the time of Mencius and Hsün-tzu, all convinced of the perfectibility and educability of the human being as well as of his or her responsibility and ability to do evil, tried to harmonize the two teachings. At first, they made a temporal distinction between a nature that has only a rudimentary goodness that must be transformed by the power of education and that same nature as it exists later. Subsequently, especially Neo-Confucians asserted the existence of two fundamental sides to human nature, a heavenly essential nature that is good, and a physical or existential nature that can be either good or evil.

In the history of *Christian theology* we encounter similar distinctions between essence and existence, between being and action. Taking the Biblical creation story as our point of departure, the human being as such, according to his or her essence, was created good, in the image of God. Concretely, however, he or she could be misled to evil and was in fact capable of doing evil. Yet Genesis 1–3 should not be regarded as literal accounts of the beginning of humanity, of an ideal and sinless state in paradise and a historical Fall into sin. These are rather statements of faith about the fundamental nature of the human being as such ("Adam" = "human being"), of every human being. They are therefore a description of the *basic situation of the human being* between the ideal and the real, between being and nonbeing.

The Chinese, especially the Confucian tradition, have correctly criticized Christian anthropology for the traditional doctrine of *original sin.* Catholic and Protestant doctrines of original sin have been based on the idea of a first sin that is transmitted in the sex act to all human beings. This original sin results in a weakening, if not also a corruption, of human nature, reason, and freedom. This focus on sexuality cannot be traced to the Old or New Testament, but goes back to Augustine, who had his own problems with sexuality. Contemporary Christian theology on sin no longer sets store in such derivations, which are laughable in the light of the theory of evolution. Rather, they understand original sin as an interpretation of the profoundly ambivalent basic human situation between good and evil in the individual as well as social domains. Today's Christian theological anthropology puts the accent on the image of God in human persons and not on original sin.

Today, Christians and Confucians can in general agree on the diachronic as well as synchronic *interrelatedness of human responsibility and culpability.* We should seek a consensus in this direction:

• For both sides, the human being is neither simply good nor simply evil. Although the good creation of God or Heaven, the human being is nevertheless capable of either humanity or inhumanity in his or her concrete behavior.

• For both sides, however, the human being is neither entirely preprogrammed by heredity nor completely conditioned by his or her environment. Within limits, within the limits of heredity and environment, the human being is free: free as opposed to dependent on power and compulsion; free in the sense of self-determination, autonomy; free for ethical responsibility.

This is an important point in Christian-Confucian dialogue. The *elementary ethical requirements* of humanity are common to both Christians and Confucians. Thou shalt not kill, lie, steal; you should be good, acting in a truly human and humane way. Here Christians and Confucians share a fundamental human ethos (more on this in the Epilogue). But how far does this agreement go? What about the primary ethical assertions?

LOVE OF OTHERS/LOVE OF NEIGHBOR/LOVE OF ENEMY

In both Confucianism and Christianity, the ethic of humanity culminates in the *love of the fellow human being*. A half century before the Sermon on the Mount (and the great Rabbi Hillel, who lived twenty years before Christ), the *Analects* of Confucius already gives that famous Golden Rule: "What you do not wish others to do to you, do not do to others" (15:23). Jesus was to accent this positively as "Whatever you wish that men would do to you, do so to them" (Mt. 7:12 [RSV]).

In Confucianism, the love of others remains oriented entirely to natural feeling and to familial and national ties. For Confucius, the neighbor is first of all the family member. Confucius had no reservations about the domination of the Chinese (that is, Chou) over the "barbarian" tribes, permitting these only the Chinese way of life. Some of his later followers appeared to follow in these footsteps with respect to the Vietnamese and the Tibetans. . . . To be sure, in Confucianism *love of neighbor* extends beyond the family in the narrower sense, from one's own to other's parents, children, and elders. And yet there is a graduated distinction between the two.

With Jesus, by contrast, *every* human being—as in the parable of the Good Samaritan—can become the neighbor, can become *my* neighbor. Jesus wants to overcome flesh-and-blood distinctions between family and strangers, adherents to one's own religion and those of another, comrades and noncomrades. Love is naturally not understood as feeling emotion, as conquering passion, as permanent possession, but rather as selfless, active goodwill, respectful of the other. Such love is owing to the neighbor, whom we can encounter in every human being.

In every human being: indeed, even in the personal, political, or religious opponent—in the rival, the adversary, the *enemy*. The social-critical explosiveness of this message for a Confucian or Marxist society in China or a bourgeois or socialist society in the West is obvious. It is striking how the anthropocentrism of Confucius allows narrower limits to the love of neighbor than the theocentrism of Jesus of Nazareth. *Love of enemy?* "Someone asked, 'What about returning kindness for injury?' The Master said, 'What then will you return kindness with? Injury should be returned with correctness; kindness should be returned with kindness'" (14:36). Jesus is very different here: "Do good to those who hate you, bless those who curse you, pray for those who abuse you"! (Lk. 6:26f.; cf. Mt. 5:43ff. [RSV].)

Is this asking too much? Isn't this all vastly overdone and exaggerated, particularly for the average person? Ought one to go this far? Go two miles instead of one, give the shirt as well as the coat, and even turn the other cheek? It is not just the Confucian who will ask such questions. The answer is that the human being *can* and *may* go this far—not as a general rule, but as the case may be! The love of the enemy is not a purely utopian law, but a great realistic possibility, an opportunity. But why?

• It is certainly not from some philosophical universalism, on the basis of a universal humanity, for the sake of an abstract, human nature common to all. That doesn't obligate me to anything like this.

• It is also certainly not from some universal compassion for all suffering beings. Such compassion is without personal involvement: in the face of the endless suffering in this world, it wants to show peaceful benevolence.

• Rather (with Jesus, who is here similar to the Chinese sage Mo-tzu), it is because God *himself loves all* human beings—because, as Father, he makes no distinction between friend and foe, but rather lets the sun shine and the rain fall on good and evil alike. His also gives his love to the unworthy (and who is not?)!

Here we have reached the decisive point of theological controversy between Christianity and Confucianism. It is the understanding of God to which corresponds an understanding of the human person. This love makes it possible for people to feel that they are the sons and daughters of God, not only within the confines of the family, the clan, or the nation, but in the world in general. Enemies can become brothers and sisters! For the Christian, *God's* love for every human being is the basis for every *human being's* love for every other human being, for everyone who may need me. Love of neighbor is love for the person who happens to be beside me. In the same way, God's own love for the enemy is the basis for people to love their enemies.

In a world that has become polycentric, transcultural, and multireligious, such a practical attitude of love of the enemy can be of the greatest significance for peace between the enemy nations, regions, and religions. Who would contest this? It is precisely here that we can say, no peace among the nations without peace among the religions! But both Christianity and Confucianism are challenged to extend their ethical reflections beyond the individual and his or her individual relations, and pay closer attention to the social dimension of action as well. Just as, for the sake of coping with complex social problems, many enlightened Chinese thinkers, especially in Taiwan, welcome the addition of a sixth relationship (the public, society) to the five basic Confucian relationships, so too many Christians today see the need for a sociopolitical reassessment of the ethical appeals of the Sermon on the Mount.

A FUTURE FOR CONFUCIANISM?

Currently, Confucianism finds itself once again in a historically decisive situation, especially since the political pressure has abated. The question that was raised at the end of the exposition is exciting enough: does Confucianism have any chance at all to come to terms with modernity and find a way to postmodernity?

At first, it did not look that way in our century. We heard that, in its glorious and problem-filled history all the way to Korea and Japan, Confucianism did not always spread the teaching of humanity with the desired clarity. A well-known puzzle about all world religions is symptomatic of this: the inferior position of *women* in Confucianism. Confucius, in total contrast to Jesus, ignored women or denigrated them with pejorative comments such as "Women and servants are to be treated severely. If you are familiar with them, they become impudent; if you ignore them, they are offended" (17:25).

Yet with Confucius, it was not only the relation between man and woman that was governed by *patriarchalism and authoritarianism,* but the other basic human relationships as well. Even though all of these were conceived as being reciprocal, they could easily be used to justify the domination of the father over the wife and children and above all of the princes over their subjects. Right into the nineteenth and twentieth centuries, all sorts of things were regarded as *li,* as more or less obligatory rites or manners: from cradle to grave, from morning until evening, from forms of greeting to feasts and burials; for administration, work, and war; for officials, ladies of the court, and fathers of families. This whole world of Chinese ritual was put into serious question, first by the confrontation with European modernity, then by the nationalist reformers of the May Fourth Movement at the beginning of this century, and finally, especially by the Communist revolutionaries in the thirties and forties. The Maoist Cultural Revolution of 1966–76 was hopefully the last such storm. In this whole process, an enormous burden from the patriarchal clan system of feudal times and from the hierarchical officialdom of the Middle Ages was thrown out. It was rejected as an utterly *premodern,* ossified, reactionary, futureless, religious *ideology* in the service of a decadent sociopolitical establishment. It was beyond salvation.

Thus, in the revolutionary storms of our century, many of the now empty old forms and formulas, rules and regulations—indeed, much of the age-old legalistic Chinese way of life—collapsed as the expression of the *ancien régime.* This happened not only in the People's Republic of China, but to a large extent also in Taiwan and Hong Kong, in Southeast Asia and North America. In the final analysis, *modernity* could not be stopped. Indeed, in China it was delayed longer than in Japan, ultimately only to burst through in a storm that took the form of a typically modern, antireligious, totalitarian ideology of European import.

The study that I mentioned earlier on the psychology of the Chinese people shows statistically that "post-Confucian" values are evolving under the impact of societal modernization. The preferences for inner development, for collective relations, for social self-effacement and self-control are on the wane—as are authoritarian modes of behavior and especially religious values. In their place, preferences for performance, for individual relations, for the pleasures of the senses, for aesthetic values, and for democratic modes of behavior are on the increase. All in all, these are not exactly the traditional Confucian virtues (cf. *The Psychology of the Chinese People*, pp. 160f.).

Have Confucianism and its humanism then come to an end? Certainly not if, now freed of all the unnecessary premodern, ideological, and institutional ballast, it emerges from its impotence to concentrate on its original essence. This presupposes a reorientation to the *original and central impulses of Confucius himself!* Not to his hierarchical and static worldview, to patriarchalism and immobility, but rather to his great ethos of true humanity and of moderation between the extremes. This is an ethos of the median between a Buddhist-Taoist emigration out of the world and an unbridled absorption in this world (in the spirit of Mo-tzu and the Legalists)—all according to the Golden Rule. As we heard in the exposition, Confucianism has a future not as an ideology of human domination, but as philanthropic truth. But what about the spirit of the modern age?

If current indicators in China do not deceive, Confucianism, like other religions, has demonstrated a high degree of flexibility and adaptability to modernity. In the future, modernization, as we discussed it earlier, does not necessarily have to mean simply the Westernization of the Sinicized countries. On the contrary, given that modernity has broken over these countries with such elemental force over the last decades, the question will be whether they can avoid the sometimes catastrophic side effects of modernity that have come to light in Europe, in North America, and also in the Soviet Union. The future of the Sinicized world will be determined not only by its ability to shake off modern colonialism and imperialism—something that it has largely done—but also by its ability to, if not avoid, then at least limit the negative effects of modern science, technology, industry, and democracy. In other words, their future depends on being able to find a way not only toward a postcolonial and postimperialistic constellation, but rather toward a *postmodern constellation* in general. In such a constellation

• science will not be irresponsible, but will be tied to ethical norms;

• technology will not enslave human beings, but will make them its masters;

• industry will not destroy the natural foundations of human existence, but will preserve them;

• democracy will not neglect social justice in favor of individual freedom, but will, in the spirit of freedom, allow justice to be realized;

• and finally, the transcendent dimension will again come to be valued—for the sake of the humanity of humankind.

Master K'ung was not recognized in his own time, but his witness has endured in China like no other. "Alas, there is no one who knows me!" said the Master. "I do not murmur against Heaven: I do not complain against other men. I strive to know the things below, but reach up to those that are above. There is Heaven that knows me!" (14:37.) The decisive alternative is as follows: will Confucianism be reduced to a purely secular communitarianism, ritualism, and functionalism, or will it be able once again to satisfy the metaempirical, the truly religious needs of human beings? In his sympathetic presentation of Confucius, the existential philosopher Karl Jaspers pointed out that, where "metaphysical indifference" reigns (something that he felt was not the case with Confucius), either scepticism takes over or uncontrolled superstition fills the void of agnosticism, and palpable magic and illusionary expectations find a place. (Karl Jaspers, *The Great Philosophers.*)

But this does not have to be. We already know about the profound "crisis of faith" of the "lost generation" of the Cultural Revolution, their disillusionment with the Communist economy of privilege and the bureaucracy. It is precisely the systematic and often brutal suppression of the transcendent dimension that may lead to a renewed orientation.

"THEY ARE 5000-YEAR-OLD PICTOGRAMS"

In conclusion, we shall present a most impressive testimony of such a reorientation. This is the poem "Answer," by *Bei Dao*, pseudonym of the young Chinese writer Zhao Zhenkai, who was born in Peking in the year of destiny, 1949, and first came on the scene as a storyteller. He expresses the feelings of a whole generation that no longer believes in the alleged happiness promised by official policy, countering it with a hope that breaks with the here-and-now of materialistic politics. According to its German translator, Wolfgang Kubin, a "new concept of hope" has been brought to bear here: "The much criticized exposure of human existence, which is conceived to be one of crime, serves to destroy a new mythology which has contributed to the transfiguration of the human person instead of to his or her enlightenment. Hope is not understood as a part of unfulfilled or unfulfillable promises, but as the common awakening of the entire generation born after 1949, a generation that wants reality instead of consolation" (in *Das neue China* 2 [1985], p. 29). Thus, the "confession of unbelief" in the first part of the poem expresses a devastating critique of the promises of happiness and the articles of faith of the official policy:

> Disgust is the password of the disgusting
> Nobleness is the epitaph of the noble
> Look! All across the gilded sky
> Sway the distorted shadows of the dead.

> The ice age is now over;
> Why are there icicles everywhere?

The Cape of Good Hope has been found;
Why are a thousand sails racing in the Dead Sea?

When I came into this world,
I had but paper, rope, and shadow,
To proclaim, before the judgment hour,
With the voice of the damned:

I say to you, world,
I—do—not—believe!
If a thousand challengers stand before your feet,
Count me as the thousand-and-first.

I don't believe that heaven is blue,
I don't believe in thunder's echo.*

But the poem continues in an unexpected fashion. Unexpected is not only the return to the religious dimension, but also the poem's criticism of the official strangling of religion. Also unexpected is the return to the ancient Chinese, indeed the Confucian legacy, evoked in the image of the "5000-year-old pictograms," the "turning-points" especially for "future humanity." Thus the poem continues:

I don't believe that dreams are unreal,
I don't believe that death is all.

If the sea should break the dikes,
Then let its bitter waters fill my heart.
If the firm ground should rise,
Then let mankind choose a new peak of being.

New turning-points and the glittering stars
Deck the undisguised firmament:
They are 5000-year-old pictograms,
They are the clearly seeing eyes of future humanity.

The poet, Bei Dao, moves in this double direction of a confession of unbelief vis-à-vis party dicta on the one hand and a simultaneous turning toward Chinese tradition on the other. He does not

* This poem is translated directly from the Chinese, with help of Julia Ching.

stand alone. One of the most important young lyric poets is *Yang Lian,* who likewise experienced the ravages of the Cultural Revolution on his own body. He distanced himself from this revolution's tendency to paint everything black and white, and gave renewed expression in his poetry to the individual dimension, to the long-closed world of personal feeling. In Yang Lian's poetry *(Pilgerfahrt: Gedichte* [Würzburg, 1987], as well, a "search for the origins" can be recognized. His German editor, Karl-Heinz Pohl, has demonstrated this convincingly. He sees "a turning to the tradition, a search for the spiritual values of the Chinese tradition that have been buried since the beginning of the 20th century" (p. 12). Religious traditions belong to these origins as well. Yang Lian has dedicated a cycle of six poems to the site of Dunhuang. This place "represents a rediscovered Buddhist cultic center from the sixth to the twelfth centuries. Many other aspects play a role: Dunhuang was one of the most important stations along the Silk Road that, during Chinese antiquity and its Middle Ages, joined together China and the West. This was the route by which intellectual currents and religious teachings—Buddhism, Islam, the teachings of the Nestorians and Manichaeans—reached China. It was the path taken by the famous Buddhist pilgrimages to India" (p. 15). It is in this tradition that the young poet Yang Lian places himself. He is "a religiously motivated poet." He is concerned "with spiritual knowledge, with the rediscovery of the buried spiritual sources of humanity—with a spiritual rebirth" (p. 18). The most impressive testimony to this is his poem "Pilgrimage," with which we shall conclude this chapter on Confucianism and its future. The poem ends with the lines:

You, Thrice-Dangerous Mountain, going nowhere:
A huge bronze mirror
Higher than human measure.

You eye yourself with time's cruelty.
The holy has always been the peaceful.

Look, how the wind levels the graves that shatter our line of
     vision;

Listen to the choir of hearts that each generation devotes to
    dreams;
Think deeply, lift up your head
And just count the stars that cannot bear to shine alone.
This is the best comfort:
The holy remains forever the peaceful. (pp. 49f.)*

Was the poet aware that, along with the Buddhist texts, the
theological writings of Nestorian Christians were also found in the
caves of Dunhuang? Witnesses to the first Christianity in China?

* Translated directly from the Chinese.

III.
Taoist Naturalism–
Philosophy and Religion

1. *Julia Ching:* Chinese Perspectives

INTRODUCTION: WHAT IS TAOISM?

What Is Taoism? asked Herrlee G. Creel in the book (Chicago, 1970) which bears this as a title. He explains that it is foolish to try to propound a single, sovereign definition of Taoism, since the term denotes not one school but a whole congeries of doctrines. The problem is all the more complex because the word *Tao* (the Way) is used by every school of Chinese thought or religion, and because the English word *Taoism* is used to refer to both Taoist philosophy *(Tao-chia)* and Taoist religion *(Tao-chiao)*. Besides, there has always been a certain shroud of secrecy surrounding Taoism, which, as a philosophy of recluses and for recluses, prefers anonymity, chooses to articulate its teachings in riddles, and, as an esoteric religion, discloses many of its secrets only to the initiated.

Chinese thought has manifested a certain rhythm: a moment of activity, its *yang* side, in Confucian moral and social philosophy—usually dominant during the periods of political unity and social order—and a moment of passivity, its contemplative, *yin* side, in Taoist "naturalism" and quietism. Taoism tends to be a tradition of the recluses, of persons who prefer to keep their distance from political involvement. This is a characteristic of both Taoist philosophy and Taoist religion; however, since Taoism is a complex movement, there are always exceptions, both in theory and in practice. The legendary Lao-tzu (literally, "old master") was first an archivist before he retired from the civilized world that was China by going west. The small book he has allegedly left behind contains unmistakably political statements. Taoist alchemists have won political favor at court, and Taoist masters are known to have resisted and combated politically both Confucianism and Buddhism. However, the reclusive character of many Taoists has led to their remaining basically mysterious and anonymous—which is probably what they preferred.

TAOISM AS PHILOSOPHY

Taoist philosophy is especially found in the two texts of *Lao-tzu* and *Chuang-tzu,* bearing the names of their alleged authors, of whom we possess only legendary information. The former is a brief but cryptic text, containing a little more than five thousand words presented in parallel verses and poetic stanzas.

The text *Lao-tzu* is also called *Tao-te ching,* or the Classic of the Way and Its Power. The concept of the Tao is what has given the school its name, Taoism. *Lao-tzu* begins with the famous line "The Way *(Tao)* that can be spoken of, is not the constant Way *(Tao)."* There is a double play on words here, since the term *tao* is also a verb, *"to speak."* It is really saying, "The Tao that can be *tao*-ed, is not the constant Tao." I mention this because the Chinese word Tao is an equivalent of *both* the Greek word *logos,* the Word, and the Greek word *hodos,* the Way. It has been used in translations of St. John's Prologue—"In the beginning was the Tao"—and contains therefore echoes of the line "I am the Way, the Truth and the Life."

To mention this is to do a kind of Christian appropriation of Taoist philosophy. The above quotation, however, serves also to show the dialectical method in Taoist thinking and the effort to point to the nameless Tao as the first principle—indeterminate, and yet that from which all things proceed to become determinate. Besides, "Deep, it is like the ancestor of the myriad creatures" (4:11). "It images the forefather of the Lord *(Ti)*" (4:13). And also:

> There is a thing confusedly formed,
> Born before Heaven and Earth.
> Silent and void
> It stands alone and does not change,
> Goes round and does not weary. (25:56.)

The Tao is thus described as existing before the universe came to be, an unchanging first principle, even as the ancestor of all things, that by which all things come to be. It appears to be a philosophical attempt to conceptualize an earlier, religious belief. In the Confucian classics, Lord-on-high has referred to a supreme deity, while Heaven has sometimes been given a progenitor's or creator's role, as that which gives birth to all things. The term Heaven did not completely disappear from Taoist philosophical writings, appearing especially in *Chuang-tzu* alongside the term Tao, but "Tao" has obviously taken over "Heaven" in *Lao-tzu*, as the natural Way as well as the human way, even the political way. If the Tao is no longer a personal deity, it remains as a model for human behavior.

For the Taoists, contemplation of the universe has led to the discovery of the nameless first principle, and of the disposition that should accompany such contemplation, and indeed the whole of life. This disposition is expressed by the term *wu-wei*, literally, "nonaction." It does not signify the absence of action, but rather acting without artificiality, without overaction, without attachment to action itself. Here we come already to the practical part of *Lao-tzu*, to the *way* of living according to the Way. I refer here to the "power" *(te)*—by which the universal Tao becomes particular. It is the power of the natural, of simplicity, even of weakness. Yet it teaches the lesson of survival, of how to keep one's own integrity in a time of disorder. This is possibly the most important practical lesson of Taoist philosophy, and it has had immense importance in the development of Taoist religion.

Lao-tzu suggests a measure of asceticism, of withdrawal from the world—its pleasures, and even its cherished values. For the person seeking the knowledge of the Tao, the senses and passions are in need of purification or moderation, since:

The five colors blind man's eyes.
The five notes deafen his ears.
The five tastes deaden his palate.
Riding and hunting make his mind go wild (ch. 12).

Civilization marks a departure from the Tao. The virtues preached by the Confucians, such as humanity and righteousness, are relativized; instead, one is to follow nature, and nature only.

But *Lao-tzu* also offers political teachings, ostensibly to the ruler, and these are the most controversial. The work appears to advocate a small, pacifist, village state, where the sage-ruler seeks to undo the cause of troubles coming from too many prohibitions and prescriptions, too many philosophical contentions, including the ethical teachings of Confucianism. Rather, by a government of nonaction, he is to keep the people healthy but ignorant, protecting them from the excesses of knowledge. These lines evoke a sense of "back to nature" romanticism but have also been interpreted as political authoritarianism.

Chuang-tzu shares with *Lao-tzu* the central concept of the Tao as the principle underlying and governing the universe, while showing a complete eremitical distaste for politics. The text, which is ascribed to a thinker presumably of the fourth or third century B.C., resembles a collection of essays and makes abundant use of parable and allegory, of paradox and fanciful imagery. It makes an ardent plea for spiritual freedom: not so much the freedom of the individual from social conventions and restraints, but rather a self-transcending liberation from the limitations of one's own mind— from one's self-interested tendencies and prejudices. According to the text, such freedom can only be discovered in nature itself, and ultimately, in the Tao.

Chuang-tzu's central concern may be described as the finding of absolute happiness, which the author believes comes with transcending the distinctions between one's self and the universe by perfect union with the Tao. This involves a higher level of knowledge—the knowledge of wisdom, which goes beyond the distinctions of things, including that of life and death. This may be called mystical knowledge, since it is not acquired by ordinary means. Indeed, it comes only with "forgetting" the knowledge of all things—especially that of the self. There is mention in the text of "sitting and forgetting" *(tso-wang),* as well as of a "fasting of the mind, which is different from fasting of the body. This requires the emptying of the senses and of the mind itself. Let your ears and your eyes communicate with what is inside. . . . Then even gods and spirits will come to dwell. . . ." *(Chuang-tzu,* ch. 4.)

Occasionally, Chuang-tzu uses Confucius as his own mouth-piece, to give expression to Taoist teachings and ideals. The practice of "sitting and forgetting" as well as of "fasting of the mind" is thus explained in a feigned conversation between Confucius and his favorite disciple, Yen Hui:

> [Yen Hui said:] "May I ask what the fasting of the mind is?"
>
> Confucius said: "Make your will one! Don't listen with your ears, listen with your mind. No, don't listen with your mind, but listen with your spirit. Listening stops with the ears, the mind stops with recognition, but spirit is empty and waits on all things. The Way gathers in emptiness alone. Emptiness is the fasting of the mind." *

Another time, Chuang-tzu has Yen Hui and Confucius exchange the following conversation:

> Yen Hui said, "I'm improving!"
> Confucius said, "What do you mean by that?"
> "I've forgotten benevolence and righteousness."
> "That's good. But you still haven't got it."
> Another day, the two met again and Yen Hui said, "I'm improving!"
> "What do you mean by that?"
> "I've forgotten rites and music!"
> "That's good. But you still haven't got it!"

* *Chuang-tzu,* ch. 4; English translation in Burton Watson, *The Complete Works of Chuang Tzu* [New York, 1968], pp. 57–58.

> Another day, the two met again and Yen Hui said, "I'm
>   improving!"
> "What do you mean by that?"
> "I can sit down and forget everything!"
> Confucius looked very startled and said, "What do you
>   mean, sit down and forget everything?"
> Yen Hui said, "I smash up my limbs and body, drive out
>   perception and intellect, cast off form, do away with
>   understanding, and make myself identical with the
>   Great Thoroughfare. This is what I mean by sitting
>   down and forgetting everything."
> Confucius said, ". . . So you really are a worthy man
>   after all! With your permission, I'd like to become
>   your follower."*

To live according to nature is to respect its laws, including that
of dying. By a superior wisdom, the sage is no longer affected
emotionally by the changes of this world. He has not lost his sensi-
bility, but he has risen above it. Such acceptance of the natural
indicates an attitude of equanimity regarding life and death,
rather than a sole desire to prolong one's life. Nevertheless, there
are other passages in *Chuang-tzu* that could be interpreted otherwise. For example, *Chuang-tzu*'s lyrical descriptions of the perfect
man, the sage, have especially led to the development of the
religious belief that there are immortals who have conquered
death and are able to help others to overcome sickness and other
evils. I refer to such lines as these: "There is a Holy Man living on
the distant Ku-she Mountain, with skin like ice or snow. . . . He
does not eat the five grains, but sucks the wind, drinks the dew,
mounts the clouds and mist, rides a flying dragon, and wanders
beyond the four seas. By concentrating his spirit, he can protect
creatures from sickness and plague and make the harvest plenti-
ful" (ch. 1).

Taoist philosophy has left behind an interesting if ambiguous
legacy. This may be discerned if we look at the commentaries on
Lao-tzu and *Chuang-tzu*. For example, is *Chuang-tzu*'s Tao the

* *Chuang-tzu*, ch. 6; English translation in Watson, *The Complete Works*, pp. 90–91.

same as *Lao-tzu*'s? This question has been asked, and the answers can be diametrically opposite, depending, actually, on whether one focuses on some or other of the chapters of *Chuang-tzu* and on whether one agrees or disagrees with some of his chief commentators, especially Kuo Hsiang (d. *circa* A.D. 312). Kuo claims that *Chuang-tzu*'s Tao is really nothing, and his teaching is therefore, in Western terms, nominalistic. For the sake of a pun, we may say that the unnamed Tao is then understood as a name only, representing nothing in reality. But this interpretation has not remained unchallenged. Whereas Wang Pi (226–49) has interpreted *Lao-tzu*'s Tao in a philosophically realist sense and has been accepted by posterity as correct, Kuo Hsiang's commentary has remained controversial. According to Kuo's understanding, there is no creator or progenitor God, not even an impersonal or transpersonal one; instead, all things produce themselves according to a law of natural "self-transformation" *(tu-hua)*. In this light, the universe is in constant flux, as are social and moral institutions.

But Taoist philosophy has also exercised a profound influence on many aspects of culture—inspiring creativity in art and poetry, and eventually contributing to a Chinese appropriation of Indian Buddhism. Mention can be made of the romantic spirit of Taoist spontaneity, as expressed by the term *feng-liu* (wind and stream). In traditional China, this term represents an *aesthetic* attitude toward life and the universe rather than a sexual one. Mention can also be made of the political use of Taoism, especially in various forms of protest and rebellion. Taoism tends to be the philosophy of individuals; it is frequently, by that token, a protest philosophy, often antiestablishment. Perhaps this explains its attractiveness to many young people in the West.

TAOISM AS RELIGION

As a religious tradition Taoism came down from very early times. Indeed, one may say it came from the times of oracle bones and divination, in a society where the diviners and shamans *(wu)* were venerated for their ability to communicate with the spiritual world—the world of the Lord-on-high, and of the other gods, including the ancestral spirits—to bring down rain to the dry earth and to heal the sick. This does not mean Taoism is identical to ancient religion. But this highlights its difference from the philosophical Taoism of *Lao-tzu* and *Chuang-tzu,* through which the ancient religion was partially eclipsed by rationalization and philosophical speculation. Although the Taoist religion that reappeared afterward would revere Lao-tzu (both the man and his text), it would radically reinterpret his teachings as well as those of Chuang-tzu. Indeed, the religion accumulated a huge body of scriptures called the *Tao-tsang* (Taoist canon), which includes over a thousand volumes compiled over fifteen centuries. This collection has a very eclectic character, since it comprises as well certain Buddhist, Manichaean, and even Christian works, which religious Taoism has simply appropriated and called its own. The principal books are alleged to be divine revelations made to Taoist adepts during a state of trance. None bears the name of the author or the date of composition; many are written in a coded, esoteric language which can only be understood by the initiated. Philosophical treatises such as *Lao-tzu* and *Chuang-tzu* have been incorporated into the Taoist canon and given their own interpretations; the *Book of Changes,* a Confucian classic *and* a divination manual, is also part of this canon.

Philosophical Taoism is only one of several strands that converged to make up religious Taoism. The others include ideas from the *yin-yang* school, which understands the natural order under the two complementary yet antithetical aspects of the Tao, and the school of the Five Elements or Agents (metal, wood, water, fire, earth), a group of physical substances which also represent cosmic forces. Both of these schools exercised a formative influence in early attempts to understand the universe, penetrated both Confucian and Taoist philosophy, and became even more prominent in Taoist religion. During the fourth to the third centuries B.C. the legendary Yellow Emperor and Lao-tzu were worshiped as one (Huang-Lao) in an alchemical cult that involved changing base metal into gold as well as finding immortality. There was also a cult of hygiene, which taught yoga exercises and gymnastics as well as the quest of elixirs, through alchemy or from the so-called "isles of the immortals." Taoist philosophy was actually reinterpreted in the light of such cults, which had as their goal the prolonging of life. These strands came together roughly in the second century B.C. to influence both the Ch'in and the Han courts. Indeed, it is characteristic of the Taoist religion that it draws adherents from among both the aristocracy and the commoners. The quest for the elixir can be quite costly, and it serves especially those who can afford it—who happen also to be satisfied with life's lot. On the other hand, Taoist adepts are usually recruited from the less educated, and most of them serve the religious and temporal needs of the simple populace, whether in curing the sick, in burying the dead, or as spiritual counselors and yoga instructors.

THE HEAVENLY MASTERS SECT

In later Han times (second century A.D.), a significant religious movement developed in Szechuan under Chang Lin (also called Chang Tao-lin)—a movement which is frequently considered the beginning of the institutional Taoist religion. Allegedly, Lao-tzu appeared to this hermit (A.D. 142) in a mountain cave complaining of the world's lack of respect for the true and the correct, and of people's honoring rather the pernicious demons. In this revelation, Chang was made the Heavenly Master, with the order to abolish the things of the demons, and to install true orthodoxy.

This new Heavenly Masters sect opposed the bloody sacrifices which were being offered to the spirits of the deceased at that time, and caused offerings of cooked vegetables to be substituted for them. For healing sicknesses, it instituted the confession of sins in "secluded rooms," where the priests prayed for the sick, who wrote down their sins. The document was then offered to heaven (on mountaintops), to earth (by burial), and to the rivers (by drowning). For services rendered, the sect levied and collected a tax of five pecks of rice from the members of its congregation.

Chang organized his followers into "parishes," with male and female priests or "libationers" who served as representatives of the Tao on earth and, as such, were opposed to the numerous spirit-mediums and shamans of the folk religion. Through the teachings of this sect, the invisible world beyond this life came to be represented as that of a systematic spiritual bureaucracy, with officials to whom prayers were made for cures of specific sicknesses. In other ways as well, the Taoist religion represented by this sect gradually served as a superstructure to the many local cults which it had sought in vain to replace.

Eventually, the institution of Heavenly Master became a hereditary one. The line also moved its traditional base from Szechuan to the Dragon-Tiger Mountain of Kiangsi. The sect has been especially popular in southern China. After the Communist takeover (1949), the base was moved to Taiwan. With hereditary instructors, assisted by what resembles parish councils of Taoist notables, including men and women who take part in various ceremonies, as well as secular patrons of the organization, it has always been known for its good organization. (Taoism includes women in its clergy but excludes them from certain rituals.)

Liturgy, the central part of Taoist religious life, was further transformed especially after the alleged revelations received by a family in Mao-shan (Kiangsu) in the later fourth century. Visions and inspired writings crystallized in a Buddhist-influenced ecstatic literature which give assurances of salvation to the initiated during coming cataclysms. New hymns were introduced, together with Buddhist customs such as circumambulation and the chanting of sacred texts called *ling-pao* (sacred treasures). We find here the beginning of the *Tao-tsang's* use as a response of the religion to Buddhist challenges and stimulus, and giving expression to eschatological hopes based on Lao-tzu's new advent, which would establish a reign of peace and equality for the elect, the very "pure." (See Kristofer Schipper, *Le Corps Taoïste* [Paris, 1982], pp. 22–25.)

THE CULT OF IMMORTALITY

The Taoist religion would become especially identified with the quest for immortality, including physical immortality, through the search for elixirs in alchemy and yoga. Physical immortality may appear to be such a chimerical quest, as death has always been a fact of life. But the belief evolved that the Taoist adept only appeared to die, that what was buried in the tomb was not his true body, but only a resemblance. The immortals are alleged to have gone either to one of the paradises, or to the isles of bliss, beyond the boundaries of China.

The belief in immortals goes back very early, at least to the third century B.C., and was elaborated after the founding of an institutional religion. We hear of heavenly immortals who have ascended to the celestial regions, and of earthly immortals who roam about in the sacred forests and mountains. After these come those human beings who appear to die but actually only leave behind their physical frames *(shih-chieh)*. Such fanciful ideas about deathlessness have left their imprint on literature as well as religion. We can discern this in a poem written by Mao Tse-tung (1957) and addressed to a woman who had lost her husband, surnamed Liu (literally, "willow"), in battle. The party chairman reminisces concerning the loss of his own wife, née Yang (literally, "poplar"), killed by the Nationalist government in 1933:

> Long have I lost my Yang, the brave poplar tree
> And Liu, your spreading willow, is now cut down.
> But silken haired poplar seeds and willow wisps
> Float up, as did they, to the ninth heaven.
> Passing the moon, they tarried, and . . .
> Were given to drink of gold cassia wine.
> And the goddess of the moon honoured these
> Loyal souls, with her sleeves spread, dancing for
>   them
> All through the boundless spaces of the sky. . . .*

The wistful allusions to immortal deities, and to drinking of immortality, disclose the fundamental human desire to imagine one's beloved deceased as continuing to live somehow in the hereafter. (It is interesting to note that the beginning of the Cultural Revolution [1966–76] was marked by Mao's displeasure with a play which he considered to have criticized him for, among other things, seeking to "live forever." I refer to the historical drama

* English translation adapted from Joseph Needham, *Science and Civilisation in China* (Cambridge, U.K., 1954–86), vol. 5, pt. 2, p. 113. Consult also Jerome Ch'en, *Mao and the Chinese Revolution* (Oxford, 1965), p. 347.

Hai-jui pa-kuan, in which a Ming official sought to deter the emperor from favoring alchemists and elixirs.)

Such a belief that men and women could become immortals *(hsien)* led historically to the practice of alchemical experiments, such as that of transmuting cinnabar. This is especially given in such early treatises, as the *Ts'an-t'ung-ch'i* of Wei Po-yang (second century A.D.) and the *Pao-p'u-tzu,* written by Ko Hung (253–333?). Taoists have described this effort as the attempt to "steal the secret of Heaven and Earth," that is, to wrest from nature the mystery of life. In so doing, they might not have succeeded in finding the elixir of immortality, but they became, like the medieval European alchemists, the pioneers of scientific experimentation, and they made certain discoveries of lasting value to various fields, including especially chemistry, medicine, and pharmacology.

Elixir mixtures frequently contained dangerous compounds derived from mercury, lead, sulfur, and the like, certain to cause arsenic poisoning. A Taoist text acknowledges the terrifying consequences of such but urges fortitude. "After taking an elixir, if your face and body itch as though insects were crawling over them, if your hands and feet swell dropsically, if you cannot stand the smell of food . . . , if you experience weakness in the limbs . . . or if you feel violent aches in the head or stomach—do not be alarmed or disturbed. All these effects are merely proofs that the elixir . . . is successfully dispelling your latent disorders."*

If metallic poisoning might bring death, there was also the hope that such death was *temporary,* and a necessary phase in the quest for eternal life. A story in another Taoist text helps to explain the faith and perseverance of Taoist adepts in the face of disturbing symptoms and commonsense evidence. I am referring here to the well-known tale in the fourth-century *Shen-hsien chuan (Biographies of Immortals)* recounting the legend of Wei Po-yang. Allegedly, he had made an elixir in the mountains and decided to try it first on his dog, which died instantly. He turned then to his disciples and said, "I have abandoned worldly ways and forsaken family

---

* *T'ai-ch'ing shih-pi chi, Tao-tsang,* no. 874, ch. 2, p. 7a. The English translation is adapted from that by Ho Ping-yü, given in Needham, *Science and Civilisation in China,* vol. 5, pt. 2, p. 283.

and friends . . . I should be ashamed to return without having found the Tao of the Immortals. To die of the elixir is no worse than living without having found it." And so he too took the elixir and fell dead. On seeing this, one disciple commented, "Our teacher is no ordinary person. He must have done this with some reason." So he followed the master's example and also died. The other two disciples said to each other, "People prepare elixirs for the sake of gaining longevity. But this elixir has brought on death. It would be better not to take it, but live a few more decades in the world." So they left the mountains to procure coffins for the burial of their master and fellow disciple. After they were gone, however, both Wei Po-yang and the loyal disciple, together with the dog, revived, became real immortals, and went away! They left behind a message for the other two, who were then filled with remorse.

If physical immortality was not always attained, it would appear that alchemical information and experimentation contributed to the preservation of the physical body. While metallic components such as mercury and lead can be fatal when swallowed, they are also known to have preservative powers. "Mercury rivers" were designed and installed in the tomb of the founder of the Ch'in dynasty (second century B.C.), and bodies from Ming times have been discovered well preserved, with perfumed mercury in the abdomen. Perhaps the knowledge of such was taken by the Taoists as evidence of an apparent rather than real death. Possibly also, Chinese aristocrats made sure that their physical bodies would be immunized from corruption, so that their souls would remain with their bodies, and eventually attain immortality together. In 1972, archaeologists discovered in Mawangtui, near Ch'ang-sha, Hunan, the incorrupt body of an approximately fifty year old noblewoman (second century B.C.), in a state like that of someone who had died only a week or two before. The body had been immersed in a liquid containing mercuric sulfide. Could it be that she had died of elixir poisoning as well, in an effort to gain immortality?*

* Together with the body, archaeologists found various talismans designed to conduct the deceased to her eternal destination after burial, into the presence of the Lord-on-high. See Michael Loewe, *Ways to Paradise* (London, 1979), chs. 1–2.

TAOIST MEDITATION

The Taoist religion also used the human body itself as a kind of "furnace" in which to make the elixir of immortality. Possibly, this was the natural development associated with a recognition of the dangers associated with an outer elixir, and with the failure to find a "final" pill of immortality. We are now referring to methods of inner alchemy, associated with Taoist yoga and meditation. According to the theory behind these methods, the human body is divided into three "cinnabar fields"—head, chest, and abdomen— each of which is inhabited by a large number of gods, who keep it in life and sustenance, but under the supervision of each of the members of the Taoist trinity.* The practitioner usually embraces an ascetic regimen, refraining from such foods as cereals, meat, and wine, until, in theory, he or she could exist only on breath and saliva. The motive, however, was health and longevity. This indicates the extremes of asceticism such a quest for physical immortality entails. For the adept, it appears that life is desirable for its own sake, rather than for the pleasures it brings.

Through yoga and meditation, especially by emptying the heart of all distractions and attachments, and by visualization of an inner light (as, for example, that of the heavenly or astral bodies entering the human body), the Taoist practitioner seeks an interior, ecstatic vision which would enable a vision of and a visit with the gods within the body—and there are thousands of them. Through such contact, the adept may obtain help to cure sicknesses by driving away evil spirits, and even acquire an inner elixir through spiritual illumination, eventually to produce within oneself an ethereal and immortal body.

Methods of meditation included the focusing of the mind on the inner organs of the body or on the gods residing therein, who were regarded as direct emanations of primordial energy (ch'i) in the human organism. Ko Hung has left behind a formula for visualization of the god called the Great One (T'ai-i), present at the same time in his celestial palace and in one's own body.

* See below.

Visualize the One in the center of the Northern
    Culmen and in the deepest abyss of yourself:
In front—the hall of light (in the head);
    behind—the scarlet palace (in the heart).
Imposing: the Flowery Canopy (the lungs); lofty:
    the Golden Pavilion (the kidneys?)
Left—the *Gang* Star; right—the *Kui* (of the
    Northern Dipper). Rising like a wave, sinking
    like the void itself.

         . . .

Guard the One and visualize the True One; then the
    spirit world will be yours to peruse!
Lessen desires, restrain your appetite—the One
    will remain at rest!
Like a bare blade coming toward your neck—realize
    you live through the One alone!
Knowing the One is easy—keeping it forever is
    hard.
Guard the One and never lose it—the limitations
    of man will not be for you!
On land you will be free from beasts, in water
    from fierce dragons.
No fear of evil spirits or phantoms,
No demon will approach, nor blade attain!*

An advanced stage of Taoist yoga involved what is called "embryonic respiration" through the conscious imitation of the life of the fetus in the mother's womb. Scientifically, it was a recognition of important metabolic processes within the human organism. Psychologically, it involved as well the quest for inner peace and the integration of the human personality. Besides, in the many methods associated with inner alchemy, which developed especially in the T'ang and Sung times, the theory behind outer alchemy is reinterpreted in the light of the nourishing of the *yin* and

* See *Pao-p'u-tzu*, ch. 18. Consult the English translation by James Ware, *Alchemy, Medicine and Religion in the China of A.D. 320: the Nei-p'ien of Ko Hung* (New York, 1966), pp. 303–4.

the *yang* of the human body, the fusing and uniting of the two in an effort to recover the primordial energy, *ch'i*, which permeates and sustains all life. The Taoist speaks also of finding the "True Self" within and, by doing so, of achieving as well greater harmony with the rhythm of the cosmos outside. This "True Self" is sometimes envisaged in terms of a new birth within, of the gestation of a new life coming to be.

Although the Taoists developed many techniques of breath circulation, and even of gymnastics and dietetics, it would be a mistake to think that knowledge of such techniques alone could make the gods accessible or bring about the birth of a new self. There is need of a moral life, of good works as well as of ritual penance for wrongdoing. For these reasons, and on account of the belief in the gods, Taoism is more than an immortality cult, more than the sum of magical and ecstatic techniques; it is really a religion.

Indeed, with Buddhist influence, the Taoist religion further developed its own doctrines of meditation and of spirituality, while often using the language of "guarding the One" *(shou-i)*. According to the T'ang dynasty texts, true immortality can only be attained upon physical death, when the spirit-self ascends to heaven and takes up its place in the otherworldly bureaucracy. However, while on earth, an aspiring immortal should strive to make progress in meditation and also in daily living. Worldly necessities such as food and clothing should be treated as means to an end: to be used for a while and abandoned afterward. One is to detach oneself from sensual attractions and eliminate all feelings of enmity and hatred, which do injury to oneself. And death is to be regarded as a change of residence: the aging body is like a house with rotten walls, and it must be exchanged for a better one. The T'ang dynasty Taoist mystic Ssu-ma Ch'eng-chen even says, "How is it possible to desire eternal life in this body?" (Consult Livia Knaul Köhn, "Taoist Insight Meditation: The T'ang Practice of neiguan," in *Taoist Meditation and Longevity Techniques*, ed. Livia Knaul Köhn [unpublished manuscript version].)

Such an attitude implies an utter equanimity toward life and death, sickness and health, gain and loss, wealth and poverty—that is, going beyond all the values usually held by people. If it contributes to the creation of the immortal embryo, that truly immortal body the production of which is the goal of inner alchemy, it is also more than this. It is at the same time the transcending of all desires for immortality as well as their fulfillment. It represents, indeed, the apex of "sitting and forgetting," an expression which became a technical term to refer to certain methods of meditation in a higher mystical tradition, as well as to a stage where all the symbolic images of the alchemical transformation are abandoned. We speak here of a gradual process toward union with the mystical Tao—involving the preparatory steps of fasting, abstinence, and a secluded life, leading to the emptying of body and mind, and enabling an improved practice of inner visualization, of "sitting in oblivion," of the in dwelling of the Tao, and of "spirit liberation." (Livia Köhn, *Seven Steps to the Tao: Sima Chengzhen's Zuowanlun*, Monumenta Serica Monograph Series, no. 20 [1987].)

THE TAOIST CANON

The structure of the Taoist canon, which came down from the fifth century A.D., can actually shed light on its sectarian character. The canon is composed of seven sections placed under the tripartite division of the so-called Three Caverns, each of which originally grew up around a particular scripture or group of scriptures:

The Three Caverns (each of which is divided into twelve subsections):

   i. The first Cavern (Tung-chen) has as its nucleus the Shang-ch'ing scriptures; is built around a liturgical poem with secret names of gods and spirits; is associated with the Mao-shan movement; originated near Nanking in southern China.
  ii. The second (Tung-hsüan) has as its nucleus the Ling-pao scriptures; emanated also from the South; contains talismans and added texts; discloses a strong Buddhist flavor; is associated with the Ling-pao sect.
 iii. The third (Tung-shen) has as its nucleus the San-huang (Three Sovereigns) scriptures. Their origins are less clear; they might have come from the circles of Tao-

ist masters serving at court, and contain at their core, talismans and ancillary exorcism texts. They have been connected with the Heavenly Masters sect.

The Four Supplements:

i. the T'ai-hsüan is ancillary to the First Cavern. Its central text is actually *Lao-tzu* itself (which shows the curiously subordinate place of this treatise).

ii. the T'ai-p'ing is ancillary to the Second Cavern. Its central text is the well-known *T'ai-p'ing ching* (*Classic of the Great Peace*), a utopian and messianic text.

iii. the T'ai-ch'ing is ancillary to the Third Cavern. Its central texts deal more directly with alchemy.

iv. the Cheng-i is a supplement to all three. Its texts are made up of the canonical texts of the Heavenly Masters sect.

The term "cavern" *(tung)* is used presumably because of the claim that the principal texts were allegedly revealed, or discovered by hermits, in caves. Each of the Three Caverns is placed under the protection of one of the three members of the Taoist trinity. In fact, however, *all* of the central texts in the Supplements are older than the texts around which the Three Caverns are created. Perhaps the Four Supplements were added to the Three Caverns during a reform movement seeking to resist Buddhist infiltrations into Taoism.

THE PERFECT TRUTH SECT

The Taoist religious movement produced many sects and subsects. However, sectarian differences were not doctrinal, but practical. The sects and subsects placed varying emphases on outer and inner alchemy, sexual hygiene and meditative exercises. For example, the Ling-pao tradition gave special attention to rituals at court, while the Mao-shan tradition is better known for its meditative preferences. Although the appearance of the Taoist canon itself signifies the union of these groups into one large, eclectic tradition, sectarian distinctions have persisted until today, on the basis of style and performance of rituals.

In more recent times, Taoism has known a steady decline, especially since the seventeenth century. The two sects that have survived well are its southern school, as represented by the Heavenly Masters sect (sometimes called the Cheng-i), and its northern school, known under the name of the Perfect Truth (Ch'üan-chen) sect, which developed especially during the Yüan (Mongol) dynasty. The Perfect Truth sect discloses the most Buddhist influence, with monasteries of celibate monks who are required to practice frequent fasts, abstain from alcohol, and pursue the techniques of inner alchemy and meditation. Its best-known monastery is the White Cloud Monastery in Peking, which has been restored, with visits permitted to the public, since 1981. The headquarters of the Chinese Taoist Association, which oversees the religious activities in the country today, is located there. The Heavenly Masters sect has kept a married and often hereditary priesthood and few food taboos. It is active in the use of charms and talismans, whereas the others are more concerned with personal cultivation (including cultivation of longevity), and more difficult exercises of healing and exorcism.

TAOISM AS A SALVATION RELIGION

The Taoist religion may be called a religion of salvation. The word "salvation" is derived from Greek. The Greek word *soter* refers to a savior or healer. Salvation implies a kind of fallen state from which one is to become whole again—with the help of a savior, or, in the case of some non-Western religions, through one's own striving.

Does Taoism know of any longing for salvation? The quest for immortality may seem rather earthly. It appears naive and even smacks of hubris. Yet the wish for deathlessness hides within itself a quest for transcendence. *Eritis sicut deus:* "to be godlike" has always been the deepest of human longings.

Unlike Confucianism, Taoism is a salvation religion. It seeks to guide its believers beyond this transitory life to a happy eternity. There is a belief in an original state of bliss, followed by the present human condition, that is, the fallen state. And there is reliance on supernatural powers for help and protection. Possibly some of these features represent greater Buddhist influence.

Salvation also refers to wholeness. As we have seen, religious Taoism tends to associate human weakness and sickness with sin, that is, offense against both the conscience and the deity, and Taoists also associate the healing of such ills with the confession of sin, and the forgiveness and help of higher powers. On the other hand, their attention to physiology as well as to pharmacology has led to many contributions in the area of Chinese medicine.

But Taoists do not conceive of eternal life in terms of spiritual immortality alone. Since there is no strict separation of spirit and matter in Chinese thought, they look forward to the survival of the whole person, including the body. This is the authentically Chinese core of the Taoist religion. In order to achieve this, they have developed the doctrine of the Three Life-principles—of breath *(ch'i)*, vital essence or semen *(ching)*, and spirit *(shen)*, each of which has two dimensions, being present at the same time in the human being as microcosm and in the cosmos as macrocosm. For their proper cultivation, techniques are developed—of breath circulation, sexual hygiene (a blending of sex and yoga), and meditative exercises. Much of this teaching is esoteric and is transmitted in secret from master to disciple. I presume that the esoteric concern for such matters as sorcery and sex within the "native" Taoist religion can explain why esoteric or Tantric Buddhism—the religion of the Mongols and Tibetans, which has parallel concerns —has never taken root among the majority population in China. Besides, the fact that such concerns surfaced very early in Taoism has led some scholars to speculate even regarding a Chinese origin for Indian Tantrism, with Taoist influence on what became eventually Tibetan-Mongolian Buddhism.

THE TAOIST PANTHEON AND POLITICAL MESSIANISM

The Taoist religion has maintained a belief in the supernatural, not only as *powers*, but also as *beings*. I refer to the belief in a hierarchy of gods (including mythical figures, as well as many who were divinized human beings) under the supremacy of the highest. During the second century B.C., this highest was the T'ai-i (Great One). Soon afterward, a triad of Gods was worshiped; they assumed different names in different periods. In early Han times, these triadic Gods were known as the T'ien-i (Heavenly One), the Ti-i (Earthly One), and the T'ai-i (Great One). They are sometimes interpreted as the supreme deity (a direct emanation of the Tao itself); his disciple, the Lord Tao (the Tao personified); and *his* disciple, the Lord Lao (Lao-tzu deified). While Lao-tzu appears in this way as only the third in a hierarchy of Gods, the cult honoring him is very old, and many in the T'ang dynasty and later considered him as having revealed all the principal texts in the Taoist canon.

Still later, the Taoist trinity would receive other names, including especially that of the Three Pure Ones *(San-ch'ing),* who were the Lords of the Three Life-principles. Their names were the Primal Celestial One *(Yüan-shih t'ien-tsun),* the Precious Celestial One *(Lin-pao t'ien-tsun),* and the Way-and-Its-Power Celestial One *(Tao-te t'ien-tsun).* Metaphysically, they each represented some aspect of the ineffable Tao, transcendent and yet capable of becoming "incarnate" especially through Lao-tzu's revelation.

But why is deity worshiped as a trinity? Has there been any Western influence? A Gnostic connection has been suggested; but the very ancient origin (second century B.C.) of the Taoist trinity has made this hypothesis difficult to accept. Perhaps, some light may be found in Chapter 42 of the *Tao-te ching* itself:

> The Tao gives birth to One;
> One gives birth to Two;
> Two gives birth to Three;
> Three gives birth to the myriad things.

By T'ang times, the Taoist trinity had become well established. By then, of course, Nestorian Christianity was also active and well known in China. Certainly, there was contact and interaction between the two religions, and it is no surprise that the Taoist trinity should have been likened by scholars to the Christian trinity: the Primal Celestial One, controlling the past, has been likened to God the Father; the Precious Celestial One, controlling the present, has been compared to God the Son; and the Way-and-Its-

Power Celestial One, controlling the future, has been compared to God the Holy Spirit. (See Needham, *Science and Civilisation in China,* vol. 2, p. 160.)

Taoist extravagance is manifest also in the evolution of a pantheon of innumerable spiritual beings—gods (or celestials) and immortals, as well as deified heroes and forces of nature. They make up a divine hierarchy, resembling in its functions a state bureaucracy. There are books devoted to establishing the ranks in this hierarchy of transcendent beings, but these efforts actually augment the confusion.

Taoist messianism is especially given in the *T'ai-p'ing ching,* which looks forward to a future epoch of great peace. Even in an incomplete and partially restored version (seventh century A.D.), it is sometimes regarded as the most important text in religious Taoism after the *Lao-tzu,* although it later yielded its importance to the principal texts of the Three Caverns. The text teaches a doctrine of salvation, with a savior, a "divine man," in possession of a "celestial book," which teaches the return to ideal government while awaiting the arrival of the fullness of time, the Great Peace. The divine man has the mandate of passing the revealed words on to the "true man" *(chen-jen),* a prophet figure who is to transmit the texts to a ruler of high virtue. This prince is to rule by the Tao and its power. He is to be a benevolent ruler, governing with the help of his ministers and the people at large, careful to maintain harmony within the realm but slow to punish.

Possibly, the text originated in the circle of those individuals who attempted to influence the ruler in the direction of reform during the Han dynasty. Their lack of success led then to the Yellow Turbans revolt (184–215), involving hundreds of thousands of Taoists (wearing yellow kerchiefs) and a large part of the country. While the revolt failed, Taoist messianism became the inspiration for successive movements of political protest, organized by secret societies throughout history, and the reason why the religion has always been regarded until today with suspicion by the various governments.

RITUALS AND PRIESTHOOD

The Taoist religion gives much attention to ritual expressions. Its complex systems include a quasi-sacramental regard for ritual initiation, for purification and renewal in the life cycle and development of the human person. Taoist priests are actually *licensed* to do rituals of particular traditions, even though, since the Sung dynasty, and in return for a fee, the authorization has come usually from the Heavenly Master, with a decision made after examination of the individual's ritual knowledge. Exorcism rituals are often carried out in cases of sickness, with the exorcist struggling for a victory over the evil spirits. Many other rituals are regularly performed around the lunar year and its festivals. The best-known ones surround the lunar New Year, with dragon dances and firecrackers to chase away the demons, and prayers to the kitchen god —a very important Taoist deity, known already in ancient religion. There is besides the rite of cosmic renewal, celebrated at the time of winter solstice and symbolizing the cosmic rebirth. And there are more soteriological rituals, bearing Buddhist influence; these include the *p'u-t'u* (general amnesty) ritual, celebrated with lantern processions just before the autumn harvest by both Chinese and Japanese inhabitants in today's Hawaii. This is done for the purpose of freeing all the souls of the deceased who have not yet been released from a "hell" that resembles more a purgatory. Food (cooked or raw, depending on the ritual), wine and fruit, and incense and fire are regularly used.

Incense is indeed central to Taoist ritual, together with the sacrificial offering of sacred writings, such as the burning of paper talismans. Sometimes, the papers sacrificed bear the prayers of the faithful, giving their names and the intentions for which the service is being performed. While ritual expertise on the part of the religious leaders is important, the faithful participating in such rituals are usually urged to prepare for them by fasting and by a spirit of forgiveness and reconciliation. Some of the priests who lead the rituals and say the prayers are also shamans, soothsayers, or spirit-mediums, who can assist the faithful with their counsels and fortune-telling, explain the baleful influence of the stars, and assist communication with the spirits of the beloved dead. Within the religion itself, those priests who practice ritual as an expression of meditation or inner alchemy usually earn more respect than those who do "external" exercises of exorcisms and healing for the sake of making a living.

IS TAOISM ALSO FOLK RELIGION?

Is there any distinction between Taoism and folk religion, or are they one and the same? To this question, my answer is that Chinese religion has many manifestations, and that Taoism represents manifestations that are found on the folk level. Yet this is not to mean that Taoism *is* Chinese folk religion—only that it represents the most influential strand unifying many diverse manifestations of folk religion, without being everything that folk religion stands for.

The Taoist religion is not the whole of folk religion, because the latter includes also many Buddhist beliefs and practices, some of which (but not all) have been incorporated into the Taoist system. Neither should the Taoist religion be identified with the ancestral cult, which can be traced to the earliest times, but which, while being an ancient tradition, shares bonds with both Confucianism and Taoism.

It is difficult to separate Taoist beliefs and practices from Confucian and Buddhist influences. Perhaps it is best to say that the "Taoist religion" I refer to is a pragmatic designation, useful for the purposes of discussion, since in actuality it is almost impossible to separate Taoist religion from folk Confucianism (in its moral teachings) and folk Buddhism (in its religious beliefs and in some of its rituals).

Another difficulty in distinguishing between Taoism and folk religion regards the role of the practicing sorcerer, the fortune-teller or physiognomist, the geomancer who offers advice on "wind and water" *(feng-shui)* or on where to locate proper sites for burials, buildings, residences. And these persons remain useful today, not only in East and Southeast Asia, but also in the West, where they have followed the Chinese migrations and have also gained respect among certain Westerners. Are all these practitioners Taoists? It is hard to say. In some but not all cases, they appear to have proper "ecclesiastical" accreditation.

Taoism is a tradition which, in many ways, rivals Christianity with the belief in a supreme being governing over a spiritual universe of deities and immortals, many of whom were historical persons. Taoism's pantheon offers certain resemblances especially to the Catholic religious universe, peopled as it is by God, the Virgin Mary, and a multitude of saints. For those who desire more theological sophistication, the Taoist religion offers its doctrine of the cosmos and of cosmic process and harmony, tracing all back to the Great Ultimate *(T'ai-chi)* and to the interactions of the two modes of *yin* and *yang*. But the T'ai-chi is not just an abstract principle, as it is in Taoist or Neo-Confucian philosophy. Indeed, the T'ai-chi emblem, in a circle with a curved line in the middle, separating a darker side from a brighter side, representing *yin* and *yang* surrounded by the trigrams of the *Book of Changes,* can be found over the house doors of many homes in Taiwan and elsewhere, and it is also found on the South Korean national flag. As the great East Asian symbol, the T'ai-chi is alleged to have the power of protecting those who live under its emblem. Taoist ritual action, moreover, discloses certain parallels to Christian—especially Catholic—liturgical action, with their common functions of offering expiation and giving thanks. (John Lagerwey, *Taoist Ritual in Chinese Society and History* [New York, 1987].)

KOREA AND JAPAN

The Taoist religion, probably the most visible heir to ancient Chinese religion, is still alive and vibrant today after all the historical vicissitudes, in those regions where the Chinese live (Taiwan, Hong Kong, Singapore) and has reemerged even in mainland China during the recent liberalization. Besides, it resembles in many ways the folk religion still found in Korea and Japan, which is dominated by shamanic beliefs and practices.

Where Korea is concerned, Taoism has been known there since the seventh century, with its use of talismans, its practice of exorcisms, and its quest for immortality, in each of the three medieval kingdoms of Koguryo, Paekche, and Silla. Thence it spread also to seventh-century Japan, when that country opened itself to Chinese influences. Even with the unification of Korea under the Yi dynasty (fourteenth century), which preferred Confucianism, Taoism suffered less than Buddhism; its deities continued to receive worship, and it retained its influence especially among the common people. Korean Taoism tends to have more in common with the Heavenly Masters sect, with its married clergy, although the Korean priests wear white whereas their Chinese counterparts prefer dark blue. On account of its amalgamation with popular shamanism, Taoism continues its presence in Korea today, exercising an influence on many newer cults that emerged during the last two centuries.

In spite of protestations to the contrary on the part of scholars who prefer to believe in a Japan with an uncontaminated native Shinto tradition, Chinese ideas of *yin* and *yang* and the Five Agents are already reflected in such early Japanese works as the *Kojiki* and the *Nihongi* with their myths and legends. Taoist influences can be discerned in the Shinto veneration of such sacred objects in its temples as the sword and the bronze mirror, both used in Taoist rituals. In comparison with Korea, Taoist influences appear more diffused in Japan, and less distinguishable from native shamanism. In comparison with Confucian influences, Taoist influences are more implicit than explicit, and are usually not recognized by the Japanese as having an alien origin. This does not mean that Japanese scholars have escaped from its influences. Among others, Nakae Tōju (1608–48) is known to have worshiped a personal deity whom he called the Daiotsu sonshin who was no other than the T'ai-i of early Chinese Taoism.

ANY IMPORTANCE TODAY?

Whereas philosophical Taoism has contributed to the transformation of Buddhism, religious Taoism has actually been transformed by Buddhism, accepting such doctrinal presuppositions from the latter as rebirth or transmigration, and a system of heavens and hells where the deceased find final—or semifinal—retribution, and even incorporating into its pantheon various Buddhist deities and bodhisattvas. All this took place in a popular synthesis on the level of folk consciousness, without Taoist acceptance of the basic Buddhist starting point: that all existence is "suffering" (Sanskrit *duḥkha*). Indeed, the quest for physical immortality presupposes a contentment with life in this world, which is diametrically opposite to the preoccupation with suffering. Taoism has no universal response to suffering, although it deals with it on a piecemeal basis—for example, through its practices of faith healing.

In some ways, Taoism appears the diametrical opposite of Confucianism. In Taoism, we can find those formally religious features that are lacking in Confucianism, including the clearly enunciated belief in a hierarchy of gods and in their saving power, the acceptance of man's sinful condition *(ch'eng-fu),* and the attempt to bridge the gap between the human and the divine through ritual practices of prayer and penance. Yet the Taoist religion has been at times an uneasy ally of Confucianism, particularly when the two joined strength against Buddhist competition. Confucian rationalism is basically incompatible with Taoist fantasy and what may also be called superstition. But Confucian rationalism is also a weakness, in a system which does not provide for consolation in distress, while Taoism offers a different option as personal religion. Many individual scholars are known to have followed particular Taoist practices or rituals. More often, these were literary men, rather than speculative thinkers. Besides, the annual calendrical festivals are attractive to all, whether intellectual or illiterate, so that it is difficult to draw a clear line between practices considered Taoist and those that are not. This is but another testimony to the ambiguity surrounding the character of Chinese religion as a fundamentally singular reality; it is inseparable from culture itself, but has plural manifestations to which we can associate the identities of particular religious traditions.

With the growing rate of higher education, Taoism is beginning to lose its adherents among the more educated and urbane. This does not necessarily mean that a scientifically educated individual would automatically abandon his or her religious tradition. On the contrary, there are many, even among the greatest scientists, who are content with a few simple, religious answers to life in this world and perhaps even the beyond. Not only has science failed to answer many important questions of life, but science itself has its

bonds with the occult—having been born, one might say, of alchemy and magic, and frequently offering possibilities that were
once associated only with the magical.

To what, then, will the young and disillusioned turn—to secular
materialism or humanism, or to Christianity? Probably to both.
But at the same time, it looks as though the Taoist religion will
continue to thrive for a long time. With the present liberalization
of policy on China's mainland, the Taoist religion, which was considered dead there, has once more reemerged. The *forms* of Taoism may be, to some extent, different, depending on the geo-
graphic regions, but its strength and tenacity is the same. And this
is tribute enough to a tradition which has evolved during centuries, even millennia, to respond to and fulfill the human needs to
relate not only to a natural environment, but also to the universe
of spirits, combining a belief in a supreme deity with that in a
multitude of intermediary spirits who may be more accessible to
prayer and who are interested in the temporary as well as eternal
welfare of their devotees. For Taoism is a tradition which offers
people the possibility of communicating with the gods as well as
that of *becoming* gods—either experientially in a brief trance, or
in the hereafter. It affirms mystical experience, while encouraging
a moral life. It gives consolation in distress, while offering the hope
of the fulfillment of temporary needs and desires, including those
of communal action and political protest. With all its theoretical
defects, Taoism served generations of followers well, and may
continue to do so for many more generations to come.

2. *Hans Küng:* A Christian Response

A Multilayered Salvation Religion

In her exposition, Julia Ching discussed the question of the relation between Confucianism and Taoism. I want to start with this and develop a few further perspectives. I will then move on to a matter that is also known in the West, the question of Taoistically influenced Chinese medicine. Thereafter, I will turn to the central theological problems. What applied to the previous "Christian responses" applies here even more: they cannot proceed in the same descriptive-phenomenological way, but must follow their own systematic-theological path. It is therefore impossible to address, whether materially or methodologically, the many individual questions raised by all the different Taoist sects, movements, and canonical books. Particularly as regards the Taoist canon, there is much that remains to be discovered and made accessible to the scholarly discussion on religion. And as, in my response to Confucianism, the comparison of Jesus and Confucius was central, so here the question will essentially be the problem of wisdom and the understanding of God.

Is Confucianism, as is sometimes asserted, the religion of the successful (or at least of those striving for success) while Taoism is that of the unsuccessful (or at least of those who despair of success)? This seems to me just as tendentious as the idea that Confucianism is oriented toward the social whereas Taoism is oriented

toward the individual. No, both are *specifically Chinese wisdom.*
For Lao-tzu, the universally valid model for social order is also
antiquity, not of course in the sense of civilization and customs,
but in the sense of the proximity to nature of the early peoples.
The scholarly controversy about whether Confucianism or Taoism
is *the* Chinese religion par excellence therefore seems to me to be
futile.

To be sure, Confucianism is in the first order a humanistic religion concerned with moral and political organization. By contrast,
Taoism is, as we heard, primarily a naturalistic *salvation religion*
concerned with redemption from guilt and sin, with prayer and
consolation, with long life, indeed, with immortality. It is a kind of
mystery religion, at first for the initiated, but then also for the
masses. It is not without reason that Taoism was regarded with
bureaucratic distrust first by imperial Confucian China, then later
by Communist Maoist China, and also by Taiwan. As an originally
esoteric, secretive, magical, and syncretistic religion of hermits,
Taoism was so often the religion of the quietistic dropout, but also
the religion of rebels, revolutionaries, and apocalyptic visionaries,
of protest movements and secret societies.

Taoism today is a popular religion that thrives on the periphery.
In Taiwan it is especially strong among the indigenous Taiwanese
as a sign of their ethnic identity. But even on the mainland it has
resurfaced as some temples have been reopened. As we heard, this
Taoism has developed into a richly amorphous and complex structure of clerical ritualism, profound religious thought, contemporary folk religion, and audacious alchemy. It is difficult to define
this syncretistic salvation mysticism for the masses, associated as it
is with every imaginable ritual (partially taken over from Buddhism) and institution (monasticism), with superstition, magic, and
elixirs of eternal life.

As a theologian, one cannot and does not have to "respond" to
everything. For the moment, it is enough to learn to differentiate;
and this is anything but easy. Why? Because official Chinese historiography, often the history of the dominant written by the dominant, has been almost completely silent about Taoism. Even today,
there is not a single book (in spite or because of the enormous
canon of Taoist scriptures) that traces the history of Taoism

through the centuries, a fact lamented by Kristofer Schipper, a leading authority on Taoism, following Max Kaltenmark and Henri Maspéro (the latter having been killed at Buchenwald). Of course, a more systematic distinction between the different *layers* of Taoism, as was presented in the foregoing exposition, would go some way to removing the seemingly contradictory appearance of this religion. This would also reveal some parallels to developments in Christianity in general and to Roman Catholicism in particular.

The first layer would be elements of the *archaic religion* that have been preserved in Taoism, even though recent research (for example, Michel Strickmann) has shown that they were at first opposed in early Taoism (third and fourth centuries). These include shamanism and ancestor worship, divination, sacrifices, and other rituals. Enough was said about these earlier.

There is, however, a second layer, as we heard. This is the fascinating *religious spirituality,* for which the term "Taoist philosophy" is hardly an entirely adequate expression. The Tao is and remains a religious concept. And the *Tao-te ching,* the "classic *(ching)* of the Tao and the *te,"* is after all anything but a philosophical treatise. This most translated work of Far Eastern literature is responsible for the harmony of the different Taoist currents. The experiences and findings contained in its aphorisms can be appropriated by each reader in his or her own way, since there are no philosophical arguments. A distinction is therefore made between Taoism as philosophy and Taoism as religion, perhaps as a terminological solution to an embarrassing problem regarding philosophical content. For Taoist philosophy is profoundly religious, and even neo-Taoist religion always appealed to the "philosophical" teachings of Lao-tzu.

It is only in the most recent historical and textual research that a third level has been discovered: *Taoist mysticism.* There are two forms:

• The old *shamanic ecstatic* mysticism which arose from the innumerable legends about immortals. These immortals continue to live in this world through the centuries, go up to heaven on white cranes, and nibble on the mushrooms of immortality. This mysticism is practiced in the form of visualizing meditations in which the human spirit is freed for such adventures (cf. Isabelle Robinet, *Méditation Taoïste* [Paris, 1979]; Michel Strickmann, *Le Taoïsme de Mao Chan: Chronique d'une révélation* [Paris, 1980]).

• Then there is the higher, *methodical, quietistic* mysticism, based on the classical Taoist works of Lao-tzu, Chuang-tzu, and their commentators. It developed during the early T'ang period under the influence of Buddhism with its predilection for mental techniques. Here the systematic purification and perfection of both body and spirit are accomplished by progressive steps along a mystical path: a mystical ladder of either five or seven steps representing the three levels of the body, the spirit, and finally the Tao, where physical immortality or transcendence of such becomes possible (cf. Köhn, *Seven Steps to the Tao*). A comparison between Buddhist and Christian forms of meditation that cannot be repeated here (cf. Küng et al., *Christianity and the World Religions,* pt. C, ch. 4, p. 2) could be supplemented by a confrontation between the ascent to the Tao and the results of empirical psychological research into meditation (cf. Deane H. Shapiro and Roger N. Walsh, eds., *Meditation: Classic and Contemporary Perspectives* [New York, 1984]).

Finally, there is a fourth layer, the elements of a *later folk religion* similar to what can still be found today in Roman Catholic areas. This is a kind of Taoist church with, of course, married priests (exorcists, sorcerers, geomancers, diviners), and celibate monks who strive for perfection as hermits or in cloisters. For the people, there are such things as spectacular cults and feasts tied to the rhythm of the seasons, holy water, confession and penance, fasting and legends of the saints. Here on earth, at the pinnacle of this "church," there is a Taoist pope: the Heavenly Master as representative of the supreme God. In heaven, however, there are countless divine or quasi-divine figures, even a kind of Madonna (the goddess Ma-tsu). Connected with this is the absolute deification of the human founder figure ("Supreme Lord Lao") as the third person in a trinitarian doctrine that is actually equivalent to a belief in three Gods (the "Three Pure Ones"). These features lead to the assumption that the Taoist trinitarian belief has been influenced by Nestorian Christianity (or Gnosticism), something that can of course hardly be verified. But enough of this: folk religion and its ambivalence was dealt with in the first and also (as concerns the critical reexamination of history) in the second response.

Something else is more important. More than with anything else, Taoism was identified in the popular mind with the quest for immortality. Yet here is not the place to repeat what has been said on these questions from a Christian perspective in previous theological publications (cf. Hans Küng, *Does God Exist?* [Garden City, N.Y., 1980]; Hans Küng, *Eternal Life?* [Garden City, N.Y., 1984]). Instead, specific Taoist theories and practices will be discussed.

SALVATION/HEALING/HEALING ARTS

For the people, what in fact became more important than anything else in Taoism were the Taoist theories and practices for the maintenance and increase of life, from breathing techniques to sexual life. For this salvation religion was from the beginning also a *religion of healing.* Already in the earliest Taoist sources, healing was of extraordinary importance, evidently in relation to confessions of guilt and acts of contrition vis-à-vis the priests as representatives of the Tao on earth. In the case of Taoism, however, healing was from the beginning also connected with its particular organic cosmology and anthropology. The holistic attitude of Taoism in China, which also included precise observation of nature, meant that it contributed not only to the rise of poetry and the interpretative arts, but also to *science.* In his monumental work, *Science and Civilisation in China,* Joseph Needham amassed a mountain of material to show that the Taoists, although sceptical about reason and logic and little interested in experimentation and systematization, nevertheless used their sensitivity to transformation and change to lay the foundations for the beginnings of chemistry, mineralogy, botany, zoology, and pharmacology in East Asia. This would be comparable to what, for instance, the pre-Socratics and Epicureans did in Greece (cf. Needham, *Science and Civilisation in China,* vol. 2, pp. 33–164).

It was, of course, a quite specific Chinese science that, more than any other, also created a sensation in the West, namely, *Chinese medicine and healing arts.* These can be regarded as a kind of by-product of Taoist salvation-and-healing religion. Today we are less interested in the fact that Taoist alchemists had been working with cinnabar and experimenting with the artificial production of gold since the Han period, using both in the search for long life, indeed immortality. What is more important for us today than this outer alchemy is what Taoists contributed to inner alchemy—to breathing techniques and meditation, and especially to the early development of Chinese medicine and healing arts. All this happened long before Taoism even became an organized religion in the second century.

It is important to keep in mind that the significant development of Chinese medicine is also associated with the great Chinese classical period from 300 B.C. to A.D. 300. It would be interesting to discuss here the various medical paradigms (change *and* persistence!), from oracular and demonic medicine, to religious and therapeutic drug medicine, to Buddhist, correlative, and finally modern medicine (cf. Paul U. Unschuld, *Medizin in China. Eine Ideengeschichte* [Munich, 1980]). At any rate, in Sinicized countries there has existed until today, beside Western-oriented medicine, an empirical medicine that considers itself to be the heir of *traditional Taoist medicine.* This folk medicine, without which the medical care of especially the rural population could not be assured, has recently increasingly awakened the interest of Western doctors as well (cf. the work of Pierre Huard and Ming Wong, *Chinese Medicine* [New York, 1968]; J. Lavier, "Médecine Chinoise," in *Encyclopedia Universalis* [Paris, 1984], vol. 4, pp. 885–89).

The *specific approach* of this medicine from Taoist tradition is *holistic.* The illness is not merely to be localized as the disease of an organ in need of repair, but rather is to be understood as a disturbance of the overall balance of forces in the human organism: a result of disharmony and imbalance. At issue, at any rate, are not merely diseases that a person *has,* but rather a person who *is* sick, who is embedded in a universal system of relations, correspondences, and vital energy currents between organs, their components, the body surface, and the environment. In the background stand the law of the analogy of macrocosm and microcosm, and the law of that rhythm of passive *yin* and active *yang* which determines everything in the world from the rhythm of day and night to the rhythm of breathing. What is sought is the harmony between the conduct of individual life and the laws of the macrocosm.

Many of the anatomical and physiological conceptions on which this is based (Five Elements or dynamic states and "meridians" of bodily energy) are considered to be purely speculative by modern Western anatomy; the corresponding etiology (theory of causes) is considered irrational. This is certainly not without justification. And yet, the indisputable *successes of this medicine* have in the last few years captured the attention of many doctors and patients. We refer to its highly differentiated nosology (classification of diseases) and its comprehensive diagnostics, including palpation and pulse diagnosis, but also its extensive stock of medicines, its dietetics sensitive to climate and milieu, and, above all, therapeutic methods that are in part already thousands of years old. These include acupuncture (a Latin nomenclature of the Peking Jesuits during the seventeenth century), certain breathing techniques and yogalike practices, massage and physiotherapy. In the light of a widespread uneasiness with some of Taoist medicine's manifestations, all these things make an *integration into modern Western medicine* seem meaningful and desirable. Accordingly, the World Health Organization (WHO, *The Promotion and Development of Traditional Medicine,* Technical Report Series, no. 622 [Geneva, 1978]) has recently been working closely with indigenous healers, with "holistic" health care in the Third World as its aim. The idea is to incorporate them into today's health care as has been done successfully in China since the Communist revolution (at that time, there were around five hundred thousand traditional healers and around seventy thousand modern doctors).

In other words, the challenge of this medicine for the West does not lie simply in a few "more natural" diagnostic and therapeutic techniques, but in this "alternative," holistic-synthetic approach, one that still shows the spiritual-ethical-religious roots of medical science and is now often the goal in the West as well. The challenge is to take seriously once again (in a postmodern paradigm) the inseparable *connection in medical sciences between healing and wholeness,* including psychology, psychiatry, and psychotherapy. The linguistic roots of "being whole" already point to both "healthy" and "holy." Physical and moral hygiene have something to do with each other. One cannot separate physical, spiritual, and social well-being; nature, the individual, and society.

There is no question that we are living in a time when modern medicine in the West is recording tremendous success in bringing many historical diseases and epidemics under control. In the last hundred years the average life expectancy in many countries has almost doubled. But it is also a time when civilizational diseases—from malnutrition to work-related stress, from poisonous drugs to environmental poisoning—are steadily spreading. In this context, many doctors in the West are now also becoming increasingly aware of the need to regard and treat both the sick and the healthy person as a *whole,* inclusive of his or her spiritual-ethical-religious forces:

• The individual must be treated (as is not the case in Cartesian dualism) as a *unity* of body and soul, as a person who exists neither idealistically as a flesh-conquering spirit nor materialistically as a "machine" merely in need of repair.

• The individual must be seen as a being in an *environment,* a being that should live in unison with nature and in harmony with its familial and social world.

• The individual must be regarded as a moral and "hopelessly religious" being who is characterized by a transcendent dimension even if he or she denies, suppresses, or rejects it—of course, often with pathological consequences.

Food for thought: the earliest Chinese manual of medicine and acupuncture, the *Nei-ching* (Inner Classic)—attributed to the legendary Yellow Emperor, Huang-ti—was first compiled at least five hundred years before Christ. This book not only already tried to locate, delimit, and define precisely the rhythmic disharmony that seems to be the source of each illness. In Chapter 25, one also finds the different therapeutic interventions listed in clear priority sequence: *before* acupuncture comes medication; before medication comes proper nutrition; before proper nutrition, however, comes the treatment of the *spirit!*

It is precisely Taoist salvation-and-healing religion that therefore leads us to the heart of a discussion on the "Chinese wisdom" complex. This, after all, not only consists of Confucian ethics, but is also concerned with the Tao, that primal law of the human individual and the cosmos according to which each person must live. But "Chinese wisdom" is also concerned with *yin* and *yang,* that opposition of forces in the human person and in nature which the individual must keep in balance. All this is to be seen in the overall context of the specifically Chinese tradition which, as with the ancient sages (wise kings), also liked to see the sages K'ung and Lao together, to the point of fashioning legends to this effect. In order to gain some historical perspective, we now turn to a comparison of the Chinese wisdom tradition with the development of an externally inspired wisdom tradition in Israel.

EXPERIENTIAL KNOWLEDGE IN CHINESE AND ISRAELITE PROVERBIAL WISDOM

The development in Chinese religion of a humanistic and world-oriented *wisdom literature* is discernible since the sixth century before Christ. For us, the most famous example of this literature is the *Analects* of Confucius. It is an entirely practical, experience-dominated, ethical wisdom. In complete contrast to, for instance, Greek philosophy (which developed around the same time), it does not aspire to a speculative explanation of the world. It also does not recount the constant miraculous intervention of God in world affairs, as Old Testament writings do. Rather, it seeks in astonishingly rational fashion to instruct in the proper valuation of things and in the correct behavior for everyday life. In spite of and in all its worldliness, it retains the notion of Heaven, that is, a transcendent horizon. Indeed, the express purpose is to understand the will of Heaven and to follow it.

And what about Israel? Ever since the early kingdom, the Israelite religious communities also had a *wisdom literature* with a similarly entirely practical orientation. Such literature was quite common in the Near East; the Israelite one got its inspiration and even borrowed from the Sumerian-Babylonian-Assyrian and especially the Egyptian domains. Next to the king and his court, the priests and prophets, the group of sages is expressly mentioned (Jer. 18:18). Individual sayings may well have actually stemmed from King Solomon, the son of David.

At any rate, God and his historical actions are really not the central focus in this Israelite wisdom either. These matters are hardly ever mentioned. Instead, everything revolves around the human person: how his or her behavior can reasonably be integrated into the great order of nature and interpersonal relations (the five basic Confucian relations can also be found here). The outstanding example of Israelite wisdom literature is the Proverbs of Solomon, a succinct summary of life experiences, as the simplest means of orientation, that concentrates on the mastering of everyday life. Nevertheless, much as in the Chinese example, the religious dimension is not excluded. On the contrary, the "fear of the Lord" is called the "beginning of knowledge" (Pr. 1:7), and wisdom is regarded as the gift of God.

It was doubtless at the beginning of the fifth century B.C. that Master K'ung founded the first Chinese wisdom school and laid the foundations of Chinese ethics and politics for more than two thousand years. Yet, as both China and Israel demonstrate, even wisdom can become an all too trivial doctrine (no master is spared his unimaginative retinue) in which everything is harmonious and capable of being resolved through rational action. No wonder, then, that in the last centuries before Christ—in China it was the time of the Warring States (fifth through third centuries), in Israel the time after the Babylonian exile—a crisis of wisdom occurred. Unbelievable as it seems, wisdom became the object of protest!

THE PROTEST AGAINST WISDOM IN CHINA AND IN ISRAEL

Who was it that in *China*, already during the lifetime of Master K'ung or shortly thereafter, dared to level a severe *critique* against this kind of wisdom?

• There was, first of all, *Mo-tzu*. He criticized the exaggerated ritual observance of the Confucians, their rigid conservatism and passivity in politics and war. He preached justice, heroic virtue, and (guided by practical considerations), universal love that was not limited to family members and countrymen.

• There was, in total contrast, *Yang Chu*. He represented a doctrine of complete individual freedom and naked egoism. Moral laws and duties are illusions. Everyone is his or her own neighbor! The true sage savors this sorrowful life as far as possible.

• There were, above all, the *Legalists*. They put their faith in law, power, *Realpolitik*, and the unitary state, as opposed to all the moral motivations and argumentations of the Confucians.

Two and a half centuries after Confucius, the Legalists assisted the first emperor of the Ch'in dynasty in the political unification of feudal China. They did this after the emperor, in 213 B.C., ordered the *burning of all books*—excepting only those on medicine, agronomy, and divination—and ostensibly also had four hundred scholars critical of his regime buried alive. These probably included above all Confucian scholars. Until very recently, orthodox Marxist historiography has seen the history of China as one of class conflict between the ("materialist") Legalists and the ("idealist") Confucians (cf. Bernd Eberstein, "China's History in Chinese Dress," *Oriens Extremus* 24 [1977], pp. 145–66).

And how was it in Israel? Did wisdom in *Israelite* religion not also undergo an epochal *crisis?* As everybody knows, yes: specifically after the Babylonian exile, perhaps even in the same fourth and third centuries before Christ as in China. The realities of life and suffering as they were then experienced could now no longer be met with an appeal to wisdom. The burden of suffering crushed everything. A didactically ossified wisdom tradition that had an optimistic view of a moral world order, that asserted a correspondence between (good or bad) human action and (good or bad) human circumstances, indeed, that evidently took a just God for granted—such a tradition could no longer keep pace with people's experience. Let us look at two witnesses to this critique.

Protest was registered by that "preacher" ("Kohelet") of Ecclesiastes whose cool, detached observations were recorded in more philosophical than theological aphorisms. He greatly impressed upon the consciousness the dubiousness of the world and the vanity of human existence, its being unto death. In sum, God (he avoids the name Yahweh) is unpredictable, reality is impenetrable, its order unrecognizable. One should therefore seek the good and endure evil—in the fear of God, to be sure, but not with an excess of piety or even of wisdom. In short, one should enjoy life while there is still time.

• The didactic story of *Job* in particular has a critical function. Job is a faultless man who loses his possessions, his children, and finally his health. In a series of debates with his three wise, moralizing friends, he calls the current wisdom with its retributive theology radically into question. As if there were a divinely guaranteed connection between piety and good fortune, between fault and suffering! As if his enormous suffering could thus be accounted for in a wisdom conception of order! Rebelliously, Job confronts first his friends, then God with his suffering. Ultimately he even appeals to God against God: he demands a judgment that obviously gives him neither an explanation for his suffering nor God's justification. Instead, in a remarkable reversal, it transforms him from one who asks God to one whom God asks.

Should one, can one, may one therefore appeal to God against God? Is there perhaps a tension or polarity in God himself, just as in Chinese thought there is a polarity that permeates everything? We now have to examine the *Taoist* opposition to the Confucian wisdom doctrine more closely. Taoism, itself a wisdom doctrine, predates Confucianism in many of its ideas, as we heard in the exposition; but later it constantly serves as something like Confucianism's opposite pole. The Taoists rejected political involvement, ridiculed the Confucian ideals of wisdom, ritual, and government, and countered Confucian activism by advocating a return to nature, a passive and escapist "doing nothing." They built their own characteristic wisdom school in critical contrast to that of the Confucians, even if in later centuries the former grew more and more to be a supplement to Confucianism. Faced with these two significant forms of expression of the Chinese spirit, the other directions—the Mo-tzus, Yang Chus, and Legalists—could not last very long.

We have therefore come to the core of the problem. The greatest challenge of Taoism to Christianity is the mysterious word Tao itself. Is this something entirely unprecedented, without analogy, or does it have parallels in the Occidental Christian tradition?

WHAT IS THE TAO: WAY OR BEING?

One could say that, in Chinese, there is a *Tao,* a Way (law, teaching, principle of order), for everything: a Tao of nature, of culture, of spirit; a Tao of the beginning, the middle, and the end. All this already demonstrates the incomprehensible and at the same time all-pervasive quality of the Tao. In pre-Confucian China, Tao was still a symbol for human ideals. Even Confucius did not use it in a comprehensive sense. It was always concretely the Tao of something, the way of something. Yet later it was considered *universal:* Tao was the *all*-inclusive Way.

This, at any rate, is the way Tao is understood in the *Tao-te ching,* that piece of classical wisdom literature attributed to a now unknown Lao-tzu. It is the all-encompassing first and last principle, indefinable, inexpressible, and indescribable, the ground of all worlds before all worlds, that existed before heaven and earth. The mother of all things, it calls all things into being, without action and in stillness. And it is *te,* the "power" of Tao that is at work in all generation, unfolding, and preservation of the world. It is the power of Tao that is in all appearances and makes them what they are. And yet, the Tao with its power is nowhere tangible and available. It is a "not-being" in the sense of "not-being-thus": it is "empty," without characteristics perceptible to the senses. And it is only when the human person, in "emptiness" and freed of passions and desires, allows the Tao to rule his or her life; only when he or she lets himself or herself be filled by the Tao and quietly abides in purposeless action or "doing nothing" *(wu-wei)*—only then will he or she attain unity with the Tao. It is his or her goal according to the universal law of return to the origin *(fu).* All things originate from the Tao and return to that in which all opposites, while preserved, are transcended.

The Tao is certainly not an anthropomorphic, personal divinity: one does not pray to the Tao. And yet, from the Judaic-Christian-

Islamic tradition, the question is unavoidable: is this Tao—this one imperceptible, incomprehensible, unfathomable reality, from which the world and humankind originate and to which they return, the incessantly and forever cyclic one that nevertheless remains fixed and unchanged—perhaps that first and last reality that, in less anthropomorphic than philosophical terms, can be described as God? Some parallels do indeed seem amazing. For example, in the *Tao-te ching*, the Tao is spoken of as an inexpressible, immeasurable, unceasing reality whose face one does not see, which one only finds if one loses oneself, and which one only attains in ceasing to strive. Would it not be possible to talk like this about God and his grace in the Judaic-Christian-Islamic tradition?

Perhaps, but one must above all keep in mind that Tao essentially means *Way*. This Way must of course be conceived quite comprehensively, something to which no one less than *Martin Heidegger*, the philosopher of being, drew renewed attention in our century. For him, the Tao is "the way that gives all ways, the very source of our power to think what reason, mind, meaning, *logos* properly mean to say—properly, by their proper nature. Perhaps the mystery of mysteries of thoughtful Saying conceals itself in the word 'way,' *Tao*, if only we will let these names return to what they leave unspoken, if only we are capable of this. . . . All is way" *(On the Way to Language* [New York, 1971], p. 92).

If, however, all that is is Way, then is the Tao not identical with *being?* At least if being is not understood in the static Greek sense but instead in the dynamic modern sense: the way in which Martin Heidegger just tried to think and express it, without formulating it precisely. Being, in this sense, would have to be described by way of ever renewed approaches and evoked by way of suggestion:

• "Being" understood as *history of being*, indeed, as the power of history that delivers to the human person his or her temporal, historical, transient existence.

• "Being" understood as *destiny of being* which in every case is beyond the disposal of the human person.

• "Being" understood no longer as isolated from time, as a static state, but as *event in time*. It is not rigidity or abstraction, let alone a formula of emptiness. It is rather a happening, grounding, presiding, unavailably availing fullness and life that reveals and conceals itself, manifests and withdraws itself.

Is being therefore, understood in its various epochs, the encompassing and illuminating *fundamental event* whose power and meaning flow from itself and do not depend on human beings? In brief, "being" understood as "being in becoming." Or, as we could now say, *being as the Way*, the *Way as being. . . .* One might therefore ask, are Taoism and the modern Western philosophy of being then reconciled at the highest level of speculative philosophy? Are East and West united in the philosophical harmonious heights?

And yet, there is a question that remains open here. If Tao is everything, if it can be understood as "being in becoming," would it not then ultimately be identical with God? Naturally, this would not be in the primitive anthropological or even in the ontological, pantheistic sense. Rather it would be understood in the differentiated way of the great Occidental philosophical and theological tradition from Augustine to Thomas to Nicholas of Cusa: as "being itself" to which the being of the existent refers.

Tao = God?

In his tiny, barely seven page long meditation about the "path in the field" *(Feldweg* [Frankfurt, 1962]), Heidegger wrote: "The breadth of all things that arise and linger along the path in the field bestows world. It is only in what is unspoken in their speech that, as the old master of living and learning, Eckhart, says, God is God. —But the promise of the field-path speaks only as long as there are people who, born in its air, can hear it" (p. 4). The promise of the field-path thus "awakens a sense that loves what is free and open, and hurdles adversity at the right spot into final serenity" (p. 5). After this, the question at the end is not surprising: "What is always the Same alienates and releases. The promise of the field-path is now perfectly clear. Does the soul speak? Does the world speak?

Does God speak?" (p. 7). Heidegger's cryptic reply: "Everything speaks renunciation into the Same. Renunciation does not take. Renunciation gives. It gives the inexhaustible power of the simple. The promise makes one at home in a long ancestry" (p. 7).

We can hardly be satisfied with this sort of direction and evasion. No, the question has to be focused theologically. If one can speak like this about being, as something that forever reveals itself anew in the world through nothingness; if, as in Heidegger, being can, in the end, be adorned with almost mythical words and images, with divine attributes and metaphors; then what is there left to distinguish it from the concept of *God?*

The human person is always a wanderer on the way to being, and its history makes his or her destiny. I ask myself, if *nothingness* is the *veil of being* through which being reveals itself, then could the *being* in which humanity participates not also be understood as the *veil of God?* In a word, the answer is that the being of what exists in becoming covers over the "being itself" that can rightly be called God. Using Heidegger's formulation, for the Christian theologian, God himself is also the " 'Way', Tao, the mystery of mysteries of thoughtful Saying." And conversely, the Tao can be identified with the original and final reality: "It can be identified with ultimate transcendent reality (Maspéro)" (G. H. Dunstheimer, *Histoire des religions,* ed. H. C. Puech [Paris, 1976], vol. 3, p. 389). There is in my view, therefore, a possible structural parallel in the concepts of Tao, being, and God, a parallel that could be of the greatest significance for an understanding of the absolute that bridges the cultures and religions.

This does not yet solve the conceptual problems, however. Tao, being, God? All positive? How then do we approach the problem of *negativity* in life: finitude, suffering, evil? This is the acid test for every religion. If God is not simply to be negated in the face of negativity, can one, should one, may one not *appeal to God against God?* We heard it with Job. Is it not possible that there is after all a polarity, a tension, even a contradiction in God himself, and therefore also a contradiction in the Tao? A contradiction that could explain the contradictoriness of immanent reality, all the suffering and misery of this world?

POLARITY IN GOD: LIGHT AND DARKNESS?

In the *Western tradition,* it was the seventeenth-century Silesian shoemaker and theosophist Jakob Boehme who completely redis-covered the sun's reflection on a dark pewter vessel and whose foundational experience was that pure light only shines if it en-counters darkness—and, therefore, that God must incorporate both light and darkness, love and hate, yes and no. That which is against God is in God himself! *Georg Wilhelm Friedrich Hegel,* in his *Lectures on the History of Philosophy* (Suhrkamp edition of collected works, vol. 20, p. 97 [English translation, New York, 1955]) remarks, "Thus he struggled to conceive and grasp the negative, evil, the devil in God."

"Nemo contra Deum nisi Deus ipse": no one against God aside from God himself. No one less than *Goethe* used this enigmatic saying of previous, unknown origin as the motto to head the fourth part of his autobiography (1830, two years before his death). He himself calls it a "singular, but tremendous saying"; it implies a battle within God, and was then often misused by theologians as the foundation for a speculative trinitarian doctrine that bore scant relation to the New Testament. Is it therefore—as Goethe's congenial interpreter, Eduard Spranger, thinks—only a matter of an "act of final trust and the most valiant overcoming of all temp-tations if it can, in the final analysis and with pious certainty, be said of these impenetrable forces: Nihil contra Deum nisi Deus ipse: even this mystery was born *in* God" *(Gesammelte Schriften* [Tübingen, 1974], vol. 9, p. 327)?

The clear affirmation of this polarity of light and darkness, in-deed, this contradiction in God, was reserved for *C. G. Jung,* the psychologist, psychotherapist, and mythologist who was also famil-iar with Eastern wisdom. Referring specifically to Job, he writes in one of his last works, *Answer to Job* (Cleveland, 1954): "This is perhaps the greatest thing about Job, that, faced with this diffi-culty, he does not doubt the unity of God. He clearly sees that God is at odds with himself—so totally at odds that he, Job, is quite certain of finding in God a helper and an 'advocate' against God. As certain as he is of the evil in Yahweh, he is equally certain of the good. In a human being who renders us evil we cannot expect at the same time to find a helper. But Yahweh is not a human being: he is both a persecutor and a helper in one, and the one aspect is as real as the other. Yahweh is not split but is an *antinomy*—a totality of inner opposites—and this is the indispensable condition for his tremendous dynamism, his omniscience and omnipotence" (English trans., p. 28).

Hegel, Goethe, Boehme, Jung: all in all, weighty witnesses to be sure. Are they not confirmed from the East? After all, *Hermann Hesse* also appeals to Chinese wisdom when he has his Siddhartha find fulfillment at the great river, where everything comes together in the unity of life and opposites stand reconciled beside each other: "And all the voices, all the goals, all the yearnings, all the sorrows, all the pleasures, all the good and evil, all of them together was the world. All of them together was the stream of events, the music of life" *(Siddhartha* [New York, 1951], p. 138).

Now, as regards the *Chinese* tradition, is the central conception from time immemorial not precisely that all of reality consists in opposites of light and darkness, hard and soft, male and female, indeed, *yang* and *yin?* Is there therefore not also a fundamental polarity in the final reality, in the Tao, in God?

POLARITY IN THE TAO: *Yin* AND *Yang?*

In the *Book of Changes (I-ching),* one finds the idea that all things and situations arise out of a combination of primal cosmic potencies, *yin and yang.* The primal powers of *yin* and *yang* are two polar forces whose interplay brings the entire universe into being. *Yin* and *yang* are symbolized in the famous circular symbol with the white and black surfaces and the black and white dots. This symbol indicates that each of the primal forces already begins to transform into its polar counterpart at the height of its formation! Is it then possible that the highest, first reality also has *two* sides, the way that every mountain has two sides (this is presumably the origin of the *yin-yang* terminology)—one northern, shady, cold, gloomy side *(yin),* and one southern, sunny, warm, bright side *(yang)?* Is the Tao then also in tension between light and dark, active and passive, creative and receptive, hard and soft, male and female?

One ought, however, to be careful with such seemingly effortless interpretations. A precise reading of the text is informative. In the *Tao-te ching*, the Tao is *prior* to heaven and earth, that is, before duality. Indeed, the Tao is before the one and the two, is the origin of the world before all worlds, and is thus the origin of the polarity, not the polarity itself. The Tao, for instance, is not itself structured by the two sex-related principles of *yin* and *yang* —in which, by the way, the woman invariably comes off worse as the passive, dark one. Rather, they offer an immanent explanation of the alternation in nature between warm and cold, day and night, summer and winter, as well as between sun and moon or sun and earth. This means that, in the Chinese conception, *the Tao itself is not ambivalent,* double-sided, contradictory. Rather, in the Tao itself, all opposites are dissolved and reconciled. The Chinese tradition, therefore, also does not provide a simple answer to the problem of the negative in the world: namely, that our own evident contradictoriness allows us to hold ultimate reality to be contradictory as well!

What is important here is that, on this point, Chinese thought and the *great Western tradition* are in total agreement. With due respect to Jakob Boehme, how could Plato have understood the idea of the good to be the same as the idea of the bad, Aristotle the *actus purus* to be the same as the *actus impurus,* Plato the primal one to be the same as the primal not-one? Inconceivable! Equally inconceivable would have been for Augustine to describe, for instance, the highest good, the *summum bonum,* as at the same time the *summum malum;* or for Thomas Aquinas to talk about being itself in the same breath as not-being itself! Even a pantheist such as Spinoza, to whom Goethe constantly referred, was too good a logician to be able to conceive the antidivine as a second principle in God. Such a principle could have acted against God with a certain independence, a Manichaeanism *ad intra,* Satan in God himself! No, an ultimate reality that is both double-sided and contradictory is part of neither the great Chinese nor the great Western tradition. Only penultimate reality is double-sided and contradictory. The consoling thing about this thought is of course that the final word has not yet been spoken about this reality since, in the end, it must return to the ultimate.

What must also be kept in mind is that, for both Taoist and Christian thought, the *innermost essence of the Tao, like that of God,* remains *hidden* to human beings. Whoever thinks he or she can sneak inside the mystery of God to get a kind of inside view of God suffers from the greatest self-delusion. Whoever thinks he or she has comprehended God has already misapprehended him. Whoever thinks he or she has God in hand comes up empty-handed! His or her grasp extends literally into nothingness. On the basis of mystical theology and negative theology, Christians can therefore also understand completely why Taoists refuse all definitions, all naming of the Tao, whether positive or negative. Even Thomas Aquinas asserts that God's proper essence remains inaccessible to human reason and affirms what the mystic Pseudo-Dionysius says: "Wherefore man reaches the highest point of his knowledge about God when he knows that he knows him not, inasmuch as he knows that that which is God transcends whatever he conceives of him." (Thomas Aquinas, *De Potentia,* q. 7, art. 5. English translation: *On the Power of God* [London, 1934], vol. 3, p. 33.)

In the *Tao-te ching,* this fundamental idea is expressed in Chapter 14 as follows: "I search with my eyes but see nothing; I call that the Indistinct *[i]*. I listen but hear nothing; I call that the Silent *[hsi]*. I grope but find nothing; I call that the Subtle *[wei]*. None of these three experiences brings an answer; I find only an undifferentiated Unity. Its upper part has no light; its lower part has no darkness. Indiscernible, it cannot be named, for it has already returned to the domain of the imperceptible" (quoted in Max Kaltenmark, *Lao Tzu and Taoism* [Stanford, Cal., 1969], p. 36).

Max Kaltenmark remarks on this passage, "What we have here, surely, is an indication of one of the phases in the experience of the mystic, who, in order to encounter the absolute, must first experience absence" (p. 36). Indeed, *Meister Eckhart,* for instance, comments on the verse "Saul arose from the ground; and when his eyes were opened, he could see nothing" (Acts 9:8 [RSV]) as follows: "I cannot see what is one. He saw nothing; that was God. God is a nothing, and God is a something. What is something is also nothing. What God is, this he is entirely. Therefore, whenever he writes of God, the enlightened Dionysius says, He is (a) Super-Being, He is (a) Super-Life, He is (a) Super-Light. He attributes neither 'this' nor 'that' to him; and he (thereby) indicates that he is I do not know what, that which lies quite far beyond. If anyone sees something or if something comes to mind, this is not God precisely because he is neither 'this' nor 'that.' Whoever says, God is here or there, do not believe him" (Sermon 71, "Surrexit").

Indeed, even though it carried independent reflection and speculation about God quite far, the great Christian theological tradition always knew how to put a limit to thought in the light of negative theology. And, as far as philosophy is concerned, Immanuel Kant demonstrated for all to see that a "religion within the limits of reason alone" does not get very far. God? According to Wilhelm Weischedel, the "God of the philosophers" is "the source of questionableness" and nothing more *(Der Gott der Philosophen* [Darmstadt, 1972], vol. 2, p. 206). But can people live with this? Hardly. "Man can neither pray nor sacrifice to this god, . . . can neither fall to his knees in awe nor can he play music and dance before this god" (Martin Heidegger, *Identity and Difference* [New York, 1969], p. 72). In sum, even if Taoist (and mystical) thought can never be regulative for Christian theology, it must in any case act as a definite corrective. The question of the negativity of reality, however, has not yet been answered.

In pursuing the central systematic question, we must therefore continue our historical reflections with China and Christianity in view. In the process, we will discuss some developments up to Neo-Confucianism that Julia Ching already addressed in her second exposition.

THE CLASSIC SYNTHESIS: HAN ORTHODOXY AND PATRISTICS

In the religion of China, a gradual yet distinct *paradigm change* began early, with Mencius, the most significant interpreter of Confucius in classical times. Very much later, Christianity underwent a comparable change with the primarily Platonist Church Fathers of classical patristics. These changes represented the transition from a naive anthropomorphic understanding of God (as set forth by the Chinese classicists and the Old and New Testaments) to a more philosophical and reflective interpretation of ultimate reality. The belief in a personal God was of course not simply abandoned.

With the *Han dynasty* (206 B.C.–A.D. 220; contemporary with the Roman Empire), Chinese civilization entered upon the world stage for the first time. Over the Silk and Burma roads as well as by sea, it became known from Southeast Asia to the Mediterranean. And it was precisely during this time that Taoism and Confucianism, though at first opposed, became associated by way of that *yin-yang thinking* which had hardly played any role at all in the thought of Confucius himself. Religious *yin-yang Taoism* had been cultivated privately and became largely normative for the spiritual life of the individual and particular groups. But *yin-yang Confucianism,* having taken up much from Taoist naturalism, ruled the state ideology, the educated bureaucracy, official morality, and public life. This means that both Taoism and Confucianism responded to distinct human needs. Each was emphasized at different times and in different ways, for the history of China alternated between periods of order and disorder. Confucianism, primarily the religion of the intellectual upper class, stood for action and dominated, above all, in times of "law and order." More the religion of the people, Taoism in its contemplative form was, even for the educated, a sort of "philosophical consolation" in times of social chaos and political division.

The strongly eclectic *yin-yang* Confucianism of the Han period therefore reflected a new, comprehensive synthesis. *Yin* and *yang,* the dark female and the light male primal cosmic forces, are equated with heaven and earth, which latter likewise originated to a large extent in the Taoistically understood ultimate reality, the Great Ultimate *(T'ai-chi).* By interacting, *yin* and *yang* generate all things of this world, both great and small, in endless succession, so that the laws of the macrocosm correspond to those of the microcosm in an entirely natural harmony and hierarchy.

This state ideology of a Confucianism of harmony and morality, in which nature is good and moral, was, however, shaken with the *invasion of the barbarians* in the fourth century A.D. Shaken as well was the romantic escapism of the individualistic Taoists. In

China, *Buddhism* now came to the fore and addressed the question that Confucianism and Taoism had neglected—the question of the negative, of *suffering.* According to Buddhism, nature itself, *saṃsāra,* is bad and implies suffering and nothing but suffering. Only the Buddha-nature of all things is good and pure. In the process, Buddhism—above all in the form of a now developing Zen—also absorbed influences from Taoist nature religion and utilized them in everything from a new emphasis on the "emptiness" of all things to landscape painting. Conversely, under Buddhist influence, Taoism became increasingly ascetic, monastic, and esoteric.

Only after many centuries of barbarian domination and of Buddhism and Taoism did the medieval *renewal of Confucianism* finally occur in the tenth century, during the Sung dynasty. In response to the Buddhist challenge, the old Confucian heritage and especially certain classic texts were now reappraised. We have already heard about this in the second exposition. There was a similar renewal in *Christianity* after the collapse of the Roman Empire and the barbarian migration. In this case, the classical heritage in philosophy and theology was reworked and systematized. In the early Middle Ages this was done with reference to Augustine and in the High Middle Ages in response to the Aristotelian philosophy of the Arabs. A further change of paradigms was due.

MEDIEVAL PARALLELS: NEO-CONFUCIANISM AND SCHOLASTICISM

Scholarly, Taoistically colored Neo-Confucianism can in fact be compared with contemporaneous, equally rational and metaphysical Christian scholasticism—its comprehensive commentaries and summas with their Platonist and Aristotelian orientations. This can easily be demonstrated with two classical representatives, *Chu Hsi* (twelfth century) and *Thomas Aquinas* (thirteenth century).

The *biographical and formal* details show similar characteristics:

• Just as the most important Neo-Confucian thinker, Chu Hsi, consciously took up Taoist (and Buddhist) inspirations for his commentaries and comprehensive synthesis, so the most important scholastic, Thomas Aquinas, programmatically combined traditional Augustinian Platonism and the new Aristotelianism propagated by the Arabs.

• Like the Chinese metaphysician, the Western theologian distinguished himself through his analytic and synthetic powers, comprehensive learning, agile mind, clarity of presentation, and enormous capacity for work.

• And finally, just as that greatest medieval systematizer of Confucianism was rejected during his lifetime, but his system became the official state ideology in China and Korea a century and a half after his death; so Thomas, the greatest systematizer of the Christian Middle Ages, was first solemnly condemned, and was proclaimed centuries later the "universal doctor" *(doctor communis)* of church ideology, and his teaching became binding for all (for Chu Hsi's great influence in Japan, cf. Klaus Kracht, *Studien zur Geschichte des Denkens im Japan des 17. bis 19. Jahrhunderts: Chu-Hsi-konfuzianische Geist-Diskurse* [Wiesbaden, 1986]).

Beyond the biographical and formal details, however, the parallels are also evident in *material content:*

• Chu Hsi investigated the relation of *li*, the law or normative principle of a thing, to *ch'i*, its material aspect. Similarly, Thomas Aquinas examined the relation of act and potency, of form and matter.

• For the Chinese thinker, the highest reality was T'ai-chi, the Great Ultimate (sometimes also called T'ai-i, the Highest Unity). For the Western theologian, it is the *actus purus*, pure actuality, or the *ipsum esse*, being itself.

• For the Confucian, Chu Hsi, each thing contains both its specific *li* or principle and the final-first reality that encompasses the different *li* of heaven and earth. For the Christian, Thomas, every being participates through its own being in being itself.

• And just as all things come forth from the limitless T'ai-chi (already called the ground of all being in the *I-ching*) and return to it in succession, so, according to Thomas, all beings are created by the *actus purus* and return to him as the *finis ultimus*, as the final goal of all endeavor.

To be sure, the great fear of *becoming*—provoked in Greece by the shock of Heraclitus, *panta rhei* ("all things are in flux")—is foreign to Chinese thought. For Greco-Christian understanding, the pure divine first principle of being (for Plato, the self-sufficient, incessantly shining spiritual sun; for Aristotle, the unmoved mover of all things moved; for Plotinus, the divine unity) can bear no shadow of change. Why? Because, in light of the ideas of the philosopher of being, Parmenides, this would imply an unrealized potentiality, that is, a *lack* of being, a deficit of being, something bad!

The Chinese understanding is entirely different. Here, the Great Ultimate or Supreme Unity creates everything in uninterrupted phases that alternate from repose *(yin)* to action *(yang)* and from action to repose. From this dynamic process that revolves in upon itself, the Five Elements emerged: fire, water, wood, metal, and earth. Their infinite combinations and analogies form the foundation of all the things of this world. Does this mean a theodicy problem as in Western Christianity? No, in this world process, that cannot occur; for flow and becoming are not evil as such. The human person, following the Tao, should simply adapt himself or herself to the larger whole in which the polar opposites are resolved! All in all, Chinese thought is ill at ease with the extremes. The fascination with evil is foreign to it and the drama of redemption seems unnecessary.

Yet, even in Western thought, at least the rigidity of the philosophical understanding of God was overcome with time. Already in the fifteenth century, the great humanist *Nicholas of Cusa* demonstrated that, in God—the origin without origin—all opposites merge: as maximum, he is also the minimum and therefore goes beyond minimum and maximum. Everything in the world is an other, distinct from other others. It is finite. God, however, is infinite, is the "non-other" *(non-aliud)*. He is not an object to be investigated, but rather the "middle of the middle, the goal of the goal, the symbol of the symbol, the being of the being, and the non-being of non-being" *(Vom Nichtanderen*, p. 87, thesis 5). He is that which enfolds everything, inasmuch as everything is in him; he is that which unfolds everything, inasmuch as he is in everything.

In China, however, in the same century, the great spiritual heir of Chu Hsi's rival Lu Chiu-yüan—the philosopher, statesman, and general *Wang Yang-ming* (a contemporary of Martin Luther!)—developed a so-to-speak modern, idealistic conception of ultimate reality. Influenced by the Buddhist "Consciousness Only" *(Yogā-cāra)* school, he no longer understood it merely as an objective principle, as had his great forebear. He also understood it subjectively as *spirit* that contains all, outside of which nothing exists, and that is identical with the spirit of the universe. Through innate knowledge, it manifests itself in the human person as the universal moral law, in the human being's innate sense of right and wrong. So human beings only have to remain true to this sense.

In the West, parallel thoughts were only developed in German idealism of the eighteenth century (with Kant and above all Johann Gottlieb Fichte). And it was *Hegel* who subsequently conceived final reality in an all-encompassing and totally comprehensive manner. He understood it as dynamic spirit, as spirit that develops by dialectically generating its own opposite. For Hegel, spirit encompasses the entire world process and becomes conscious of itself in human beings. It is objective (nature), subjective (humanity), and absolute (God). Was this the solution? For Hegel's philosophy as well, the acid test was the problem of negativity.

THE PROVOCATION OF THE NEGATIVE IN THE MODERN AGE

In his *Lectures on the Philosophy of World History (Werke*, ed. von Lasson-Hoffmeister, vol. 8, p. 80 [English translation, New York, 1956]), *Hegel* looked upon "history as the slaughterhouse in which the fortune of peoples, the wisdom of states and the virtue of individuals were sacrificed." Although he looked upon this "with deepest sympathy," he then claims to be able to offer a rational explanation and to transfigure this history. How? "As the cunning of reason," as *the cunning of the divine world-spirit* that survives and preserves itself in all catastrophes. Already in the nineteenth century, many found this abhorrent. Indeed, what would one say especially in the twentieth century, in which reason has to an unprecedented extent turned to unreason—in which science, technology, and industrialization have allowed unparalleled megacrimes of frightening proportions to become reality?

Today, the question of *negativity* would confront two great thinkers of the West, Thomas and Hegel, as well as two great thinkers of the Far East, Chu Hsi and Wang Yang-ming. Do any of their philosophical and theological speculations really take the enormous fact of evil, of the negative as such in the world, seriously? For in our world, in light of the Holocaust, Hiroshima, the Gulag Archipelago, and the possible self-liquidation of humanity, this question imposes itself in an altogether different way than it did before. It brings us back to the protest against the all too facile harmonization of the wisdom doctrine. Already registered very early on, this protest evidently only reached its dramatic zenith in European modernity. Here it was transformed into that militant atheism of Ludwig Feuerbach, Marx, Engels, Lenin, and Stalin, an atheism eventually imported into China where, under Mao, it was declared the new official orthodoxy.

To be sure, traditional *Chinese thought* also recognized negativity, the evil in the world, and lamented it. But it was never a part of Chinese thought to make massive accusations, even though human suffering and misery cried to heaven often enough in China as well. Whereas for the Confucian, human and historical fate were simply subordinated to the decree of Heaven, human fate for the Taoist rested in the hands of the individual. And whereas dispassionate Confucian rationalism offered the human person no solace in suffering, Taoism, which viewed life (in contrast to Buddhism) as good and worth extending, tackled suffering in an entirely practical way with prayers for health, divination, healing techniques, and elixirs of life. In the end, however, Taoism also failed to revolt against the Tao, Heaven, God. That would make no sense. No, only submission makes sense—submission to nature and its laws, to inscrutable fate and unavoidable death. All this must simply be accepted.

Of course, *Western scholasticism* also took theological cognizance of the negative, of evil in the world. However, in order to exonerate God, already Augustine and then Thomas as well defined it entirely negatively: on closer examination, they asserted, evil itself has no proper substance. It is actually only a lack of good and therefore, in the strict sense, does not presuppose an efficient but only a deficient cause. In any case, God is not at fault. For God did not will evil; he is, after all, the infinitely good, just, and holy one. Nevertheless, God did not *not* will evil, or else there would in fact be no badness in the world—otherwise he would not be the Almighty. What then? The omnibenevolent and omnipotent *allows evil (permittit)*. But why? Is evil a way of educating and punishing? Is evil an aspect of a divine world order that always requires a gradation and restriction of perfection? Is evil part of a plan the full meaning of which will only be revealed in the future? Can the rationales of medieval theology still be convincing after the monstrous experiences of the modern age?

Even that universal spirit at the beginning of the *modern age* did not get much further when faced with this dark abyss. *Gottfried Wilhelm Leibniz* was the first European to recognize the pluralistic structure of a humanity with races and cultures of equal worth. He strove for the reconciliation of not only the Christian churches, but also Western and Eastern culture. A few months before his death, he published in French his "Discourse on the Natural Theology of the Chinese" (1716), in which he showed an amazingly sympathetic understanding of the old concepts of Shang-ti, T'ien, and even the more philosophical concept of T'ai-chi (Great Ultimate). These he attempted to harmonize with his European philosophical concept of God. His theodicy, his justification of God in the light of the world's evil, resorted to the most precise distinctions between metaphysical, physical, and moral evil, between finitude, pain, and evil. All these were seen as *de facto* necessary for that *"best* of all *possible* (!) worlds" provided for by God. It did not prove to be persuasive. In Europe, after the great Lisbon earthquake a few years later and Voltaire's ridicule, it was soon called radically into question.

Indeed, in the light of all the natural catastrophes, all the absurdities of life, all the orgies of evil, all the rivers of blood and tears, all the murdered innocents, is complaining enough? Complaints can be found everywhere in China as well. Does it not seem more than justified to go beyond complaint to accusation, an *accusation that cries to heaven* in the face of that divine primal principle that is, after all, responsible for order and harmony in this world? And it does not matter if one calls this Heaven, Tao, Lord-on-high, Great Ultimate, Divinity, or God. It was *Dostoyevsky's* Ivan Karamazov who expressed this accusation and indignation more sharply than anyone, from the tolerant Job to the frivolous Voltaire. Appealing to the torture of innocent children, he gave his "ticket" to this so inharmonious world back to its creator. Period!

And yet, Alyosha replies to his brother Ivan, "You have forgotten *Him.*" Then follows Ivan's splendid tale of the Grand Inquisitor, altogether perhaps the most formidable accusation against the church, but, as Alyosha astutely remarks, a marvelous "praise of Jesus." And so, to conclude our considerations here, and to continue our comparison of Jesus of Nazareth, Confucius, and Gautama Buddha, let us return to a confrontation between Christianity, Confucianism, and Taoism. This will be carried out by looking at the personality profiles of their important figures and incarnations.

DEADLY CONFRONTATION

We have already heard how, within Chinese history, the *discrepancies within the Confucian outlook on life* were exposed by the Taoists:

• They criticized the Confucian lifestyle with its conformity to traditional career models and its bureaucratic mentality.

• They saw through the central Confucian virtues of humanity *(jen)* and uprightness *(i)* as aristocratic categories of a conservative and patriarchal ethic—categories that all too easily faded to mere ideals with little correspondence in real-life behavior.

• They distanced themselves from the prevailing orders, rituals, conventions, and conformity in public institutions that ignored individuality and particularity.

• They rejected the hierarchies and had reservations about the all too masculine political activism. This activism, they felt, was a way of ordering the world through interference, instead of simply living in harmony with nature through noninterference. They advocated ruling through nonaction, imitating the still workings of nature.

• In short, they criticized the heavily bureaucratized Confucian literati who conformed their private and social lives all too much to the political system.

Then there were the ironical polemics of *Chuang-tzu*. This second great representative of Taoism was probably a contemporary of Mencius. He was the author of the classic *From Southern Blossom-land*, in which he presents a humorous and penetrating critique of Confucius, state, and society. As with Lao-tzu, we have very little historically verifiable information about him. One episode, however, seems to characterize him precisely. This is an anecdote out of a historical work from the western Han dynasty which outlines not only Chuang-tzu's original character, but also his distaste for conformity and accommodation: "King Wen of Ch'u, hearing of Chuang Tzu's talents, sent a messenger to him, bearing costly gifts, and inviting him to come to court as his minister. Chuang Tzu laughed and told the messenger from Ch'u: 'A thousand pounds of gold make a handsome sum indeed; ministerhood is indeed very honorable. But have you ever seen the ox being led to the sacrifice? After being fattened up for several years, it is decked out in embroidered trappings and led into the great temple. At this moment it would undoubtedly prefer to be an uncared-for piglet, but it is too late, isn't it? Go away! Do not defile me! I would rather frolic joyously in the mire than be haltered by the ruler of a state. I will never take office. Thus I will remain free to live as I see fit" (quoted in Kaltenmark, *Lao-tzu and Taoism*, p. 71).

This, then, seems to be typically Taoist: whoever sees in nature nothing but the perpetual change of appearances; whoever has seen through the ambivalent character of the world—he will only laugh at the offers of the world. Offices? They enslave. Institutions? They cripple. Involvement? It defiles. No, only not-ruling keeps order in the world. Only this principle of nonintervention *(wu-wei)* guarantees peace.

And what about *Jesus* of Nazareth? Here again, he is distinctly different:

• No wise, "stoic" poise: all the facets of true humanity are manifest in his life. He is a man of deep emotions, of affection and of anger, of joy and of tears, of hope and of despondency.

• No ideal of great age: Jesus was no sage who lived seventy or eighty years like Masters K'ung and Lao. Instead of decades, he was granted at most three years, perhaps not even one, to proclaim his eschatological message. In his thirties, his life was brutally ended hardly before it had begun.

• No definite role expectations or career: he was neither in principle on the side of the establishment and bureaucracy like Confucius, nor did he practice that escapism, that flight from every public involvement, practiced by Lao-tzu or Chuang-tzu.

• Jesus is part of another tradition, the prophetic tradition that takes a critical stance toward the world, the establishment, societal institutions, and traditions—a stance no less critical than that of Chuang-tzu. Yet, at the same time, Jesus' stance does not avoid *public confrontation.* Indeed, Jesus provoked his society with a message that was not his, but that he nevertheless had to proclaim because he saw himself selected for this task by God.

• In contrast to Confucius, Lao-tzu, or Chuang-tzu, this led to what one typically calls the *fate of prophets:* it led to conflict between this as yet still young man and the powers of law and order, a life-and-death struggle in which literally everything was on the line.

It is the *end* of his life here that confirms what we described as the profile of those world-historical, important figures: Jesus was neither a political reformer and educator like K'ung Fu-tzu, nor an

apolitical escapist and quietist like Lao-tzu or Chuang-tzu. He was
the type of the admonishing and threatening prophet. That all of
them stood in opposition to the status quo of their society is beyond question. But only with Jesus did this conflict take a dramatic,
even deadly form. Indeed, he, Jesus, became what Chuang-tzu
wanted at all costs to avoid becoming: a sacrificial victim! Israel's
great prophet Jeremiah had already spoken of such a one: a lamb
that is led to the slaughter (Jer. 11:19). Jeremiah ended his life
forgotten, but not murdered. Now, in a very different way, the
fearlessly consistent young man from Nazareth, who nevertheless
trembled before his violent death, became someone about whom
one would say after his ignominious execution, "As a sheep led to
the slaughter or a lamb before its shearer is dumb, so he opens not
his mouth" (Acts 8:32 [RSV], quoting Isaiah 53:7).

The incontrovertible fact is ultimately this *death.* No matter
how one judges Jesus, his death makes him *unambiguously distinct,* not only from Gautama Buddha and K'ung Fu-tzu, but also
from Lao-tzu and Chuang-tzu. As a result, whether it is understood or not, the *cross* has remained until today the *proprium
christianum* wherever it is found, even in China. No, here I do not
mean the cross as moral sledgehammer and ornament for prelates
(difficult to understand for Confucians, Taoists, and Buddhists). I
mean the cross seen realistically as the warning sign and yet also as
the sign of hope that promises deliverance, freedom, and redemption to all those in this world who, even in suffering, pain, and
death, are crucified. How? In the light of faith, specifically faith in
the deliverance from unfathomable suffering, abandonment, and
death by Jesus through the all-encompassing one himself. It is not
as if Jesus, like a Taoist saint, "went to heaven in the bright of day"
(only Luke, after the crucifixion of Jesus, introduces the legend of
an Ascension). It is rather that he died unto that Great Ultimate
(T'ai-chi or Tao) that Christians, for lack of a better name, call God.

CROSSED-OUT WISDOM

Is God then good *and* evil? On the contrary, it was only now that
the Christian community ventured to understand the Great Ultimate, *God himself,* in a new way. It was only now that, faced with

all the suffering and all the evil, they could understand God's goodness, love, and wisdom in a new way. In the light of Jesus' death and eternal life (the original hope of all Taoists is fulfilled here!), no longer was it possible to speak of the hidden, incomprehensible, indifferent, apathetic God-on-high, who looks down dispassionately from his heaven while allowing humanity to stew in its misery, to fight, to protest and perish, or simply to give up and die. No, now it was possible, justifiably and without theological exaggeration, to speak of *God's com-passion,* of "God's solidarity" not only with this one, but with all the suffering, the humiliated, the exploited, the abandoned unto death. It thus became possible to take the reality of all the negativity in this world completely seriously and yet ultimately take it up positively into the infinite— and this without assuming that there is in God an antinomy, a contradiction, indeed, the devil himself. Doesn't this seem to pass the acid test for any religion?

Indeed, this certainly made it possible to speak in a new kind of dialectic about the *wisdom* of God instead of his contradictoriness. Paul did it in his confrontation with Greek wisdom. *Sophia, philosophia,* wisdom? In Corinth at that time this was a major theme. Was there wisdom for the Christian? Yes, but without the harmonization with which the teachers of wisdom rendered suffering and death harmless. The horrible suffering and death of Jesus in total abandonment had to be taken seriously. And it was precisely this suffering and dying one who revealed to all people the suffering and dying that the wisdom of *God,* without contradicting itself, reaches to an entirely different depth than does *human* wisdom. For, similar to the Tao, God is unlike any human idea about him. The Chinese person may perhaps be reminded here of the line from the *Tao-te ching:* "The soft conquers the hard, the weak conquers the strong" (ch. 36). Indeed, for Christian faith, the weak and powerless Christ, as God's self-attestation, calls all human wisdom radically into question. Why? Because the wisdom of the world is here literally *crossed out* by that wisdom of God which in fact appears in yet another way than it did with Job of the Old Testament. It is no longer arrayed in the splendid attire of the creator, but in the figure of foolishness—the foolishness of the cross, of lowliness and insignificance.

Non-Christians are often better at recognizing what constitutes the challenge, indeed the demand, in the Christian understanding of God. This is particularly so in religious historical comparison. In his *Principle of Hope,* Ernst Bloch found some thought-provoking ways of expressing this challenge: "If, instead of the three wise men, Confucius, Lao-tzu, and the Buddha had come out of the East to the manger, then only Lao-tzu would have noticed the insignificance of the mightiest, although he would not have prayed to him. But even he would not have noticed the *stumbling block* that Christian love represents for the world with its old associations and hierarchies of power. Jesus is precisely the symbol that contradicts the power of domination. It is precisely this symbol that the world contradicted on Calvary: the cross was the world's answer to Christian love, to the love for the last who shall be first, for the rejected. It is in this love that the true light collects. It is the love for that joy which, according to [Gilbert K.] Chesterton's incisive remark, was the great publicity of few heathens and became or will become the little secret of all Christians" *(Gesamtausgabe* [Frankfurt, 1977] vol. 5, p. 1489).

What then is the goal of *Christian* wisdom? This goal is not a harmonious accommodation to the world as with K'ung Fu-tzu. It is also not seeing through the doubtless ambivalent and transitory character of the world and getting off as with Lao-tzu and Chuang-tzu. Its goal is to make it possible to live with an other Great Ultimate, a God who is wholly other and in whom one can put one's unconditional trust. The goal is not the ability to live in harmony with the world (K'ung Fu-tzu) or to let go of the world (Lao-tzu). The goal is to let go of all false ideas of God and implicate oneself with the one God, the one Tao, the one Heaven that lets the rain fall on good and evil alike. This then also means implicating oneself with one's fellow human beings, good and bad. For Christians, the outward symbol is not the strict moral mien of the Confucian, nor the knowing laughter of the Taoist, but rather the realistically involved and quietly trusting in-spite-of-everything of the prophet and apostle: "But we preach Christ crucified, a stumbling block to Jews and folly to Gentiles, but to those who are called, both Jews and Greeks, Christ the power of God and the wisdom of God. For the foolishness of God is wiser than men, and the weakness of God is stronger than men" (1 Cor. 1:23–25 [RSV]). Confucians, Taoists, and Christians must today engage in dialogue about this form of wisdom.

IV.
Buddhism: A Foreign Religion in China

1. *Julia Ching:* Chinese Perspectives

INTRODUCTION: THE ETHNIC AND THE MISSIONARY RELIGIONS

Traditional China represents a cultural and, most of the time as well, a political unity. But the country was not completely ignorant of, or entirely untouched by, outside influences. Such was impossible and would also have been unhealthy. There was knowledge in Han China (206 B.C.–A.D. 212), of the Eastern Roman Empire, and there was contact and exchange with India, the center of another great civilization, especially through the spread of the Buddhist religion. But India, in contrast to China, had been more often politically fragmented than unified. For this reason India never posed a real threat to China and its sense of self-importance. Besides, China had knowledge of, and friendly contact and exchange with, the land and people of Persia, especially during the Sasanian Empire. If Buddhism entered China through India and Central Asia, first Zoroastrianism, Manichaeanism, and Nestorianism, and after these Islam, would enter China through Persia. Western Christianity also came into the country, but only in the thirteenth century, comparatively much later than the other religions.

In discussing the topic of Buddhism as a foreign religion in China, I wish to make a distinction, in the Chinese context, between Islam and Judaism (and, to an extent, Nestorian Christianity) on the one side as "ethnic religions," and Buddhism and Western Christianity on the other side as "missionary religions." Here I am proposing a distinction between religions entering and remaining in China as the cultural heritage of ethnic minorities, and religions that went with missionary and proselytizing intent. Although a proselytizing religion by nature, Islam entered China as the religion of certain ethnic groups, especially groups from Persia and other parts of Central Asia. So too did the earliest Christian group in China, the Nestorians, who had a Syriac liturgy. Even the Catholic Franciscan missionaries of the thirteenth century, who worked in Mongol China, appear to have proselytized relatively little, ministering mainly to those Europeans who were already Christian. But the *later* Christian missionaries, both Catholic and Protestant, were of a different order. They resembled more the Buddhist missionaries of an earlier age who came from South and Central Asia. Thus Islam survived in China as a religion identified with ethnic minorities, without making many inroads into the majority population of the Chinese Han people, who remained Confucian, Taoist, and Buddhist. However, Buddhism and Christianity acted differently, arousing much more attention as well as controversy, as each attempted to make its impact upon the larger society.

I consider this an important point, distinguishing the later Christian missionaries from the earlier Christian (Nestorian) *settlers.* It seems to me that while religions such as Islam and Christianity are by nature proselytizing ones, the missionary movement really began only with the arrival of the Catholic missionaries, especially those of the late sixteenth century and afterward, followed, as they were, by the Protestants (and later Catholics) of the nineteenth century. Whereas Muslim and Christian Nestorian visitors and settlers went into China usually as migratory peoples from neighboring countries, the later missionaries went principally, and often exclusively, for the purpose of converting the natives. This is one reason why Christianity met much stronger opposition than did Islam or Judaism, the followers of which sought merely to *survive* in the midst of an alien culture.

The Jews appear to have been always a small group, incapable of exerting a large influence. Today there are about two hundred families in Kaifeng, Honan, who still remember their Jewish ancestry—which can be traced back at least to the twelfth century—although, for several generations already, they have not followed the Torah. Culturally (and ethnically), they have become assimilated to the majority population, and many are ignorant about the religion of their Semitic ancestors.

The Muslims were and remain numerically strong. The figure given today varies from ten to forty million in the People's Republic, and the higher figure is sometimes favored as opposed to the official tendency to present a lower figure, possibly to forestall any growth in the minority's political self-confidence. While their size is relatively small when compared to the country's total population of one billion, it exceeds very much the number of Chinese Christians. Those Muslims (of mixed origins) living in the large cities and in areas populated mostly by the majority group or "Han" Chinese have become culturally assimilated without always abandoning their faith. Other Muslims inhabiting Chinese Central Asia belong to various groups of Turkic origins, for whom religion is an important hallmark of communal identity. The Chinese Muslims have made great efforts during their long history to maintain their own identity by keeping alive their religious faith. But they have done little to evangelize their non-Muslim compatriots.

And why did the followers of these religions refrain from the proselytizing effort? We may offer certain reasons for this behavior. Their relatively small number is only one of these, and it is not a very good one where the Muslims are concerned. A better explanation is the cultural cohesion of the host country itself. If Islam had won over many steppe peoples of Central Asia, these converts appear to have lacked a high culture of their own at the moment of conversion. Besides, where Islam is concerned, conversion frequently follows war and conquest, involving sometimes the systematic destruction of an earlier religious tradition, such as happened with the Arab conquest of Persia. China has had a long, historic culture, and while the country had been overcome time and again by various steppe peoples (such as Mongols or Manchus) from outside its frontiers, none of these had been Muslims. Indeed, many of them came in time to accept the high culture of China with its three religions of Confucianism, Taoism, and Buddhism.

Against this perspective, we may perceive a certain resemblance between the introduction of Buddhism and that of Christianity into China. In spite of their very basic doctrinal differences, each made immense proselytizing efforts. The Buddhist missionaries came from nearer lands, and frequently, though not always, as invited teachers. Indeed, many Buddhist missionaries were invited to China because of the initial curiosity of the Chinese regarding the Indian religion. The Christian missionaries, however, invited themselves. They proselytized less to satisfy the curiosity of their hosts, and more to follow their own religious imperatives.

BUDDHISM AS A CHINESE RELIGION

Probably a contemporary or near contemporary of Confucius, Gautama, the *historical* Buddha, is reported to have died in 544 B.C.—or, as most modern scholars would have it, about sixty years later. The presence of both in the same century gives some substance to the hypothesis regarding the "axial ages" in human civilization. But given the distance that separated the two countries, Buddhism was introduced into China only sometime before the first century A.D., roughly five or six hundred years after the deaths of the two men.

The introduction of Buddhism to China was an event with important consequences both for the development of Chinese thought and culture and for the evolution of Buddhism itself. By that time (first century A.D. or earlier), this religion of Indian origin had already undergone several centuries of development in both theory and practice. It acted as a harbinger of civilization in many areas, introducing a written script as well as inspiring art, literature, and philosophy. But China was already home to a vigorous civilization with an ancient canon—the Confucian classics—and time-hallowed traditions. The meeting of the Buddhist religion and Chinese culture became the occasion for conflicts and controversies, which were resolved only when Buddhism adjusted itself to the Chinese environment—taking account of Confucian moral values such as filial piety while making use of Taoist ideas and terminology for its own survival and advancement.

The Buddhism that went into China included both the older

Theravada (Shravakayana) and the newer Mahayana branches, although the latter prospered while the former declined. While the first foreign monks presumably preached with the help of doctrinal summaries, many Buddhist texts were eventually translated into Chinese. Indeed, Chinese itself has become an essential language of the Buddhist religious canon, since translations have survived where the originals are no longer complete or even extant. Buddhism turned attention to problems of cosmological theories as well as of suffering in the universe of sentient beings. It introduced the presupposition of rebirth or transmigration, and the practice of monastic life, into a society where ancestors were venerated and descendants desired. But Chinese realism and pragmatism also influenced Buddhism—affirming this life and this world, including the values of family, longevity, and posterity. The big historical question Buddhism has introduced into China remains: has it been the "Buddhist conquest of China," or the "Chinese conquest of Buddhism"? And the historical as well as missiological question that may interest Christians is, would the course of Christianity have been different had it allowed more cultural adaptation, and to what extent could such adaptation have been possible given Christianity's dogmatic presuppositions?

Thus if Buddhism succeeded in gaining a foothold in China, it was after accommodating itself to the Chinese environment to the point that it became one of the Chinese religions. This did not happen overnight, and remains as one of the world's most important cultural encounters, leaving behind profound historical consequences. As such, this can be regarded alongside the meeting of Jewish Christianity and Hellenistic culture. In this light, Chinese Buddhism offers a parallel model to Hellenistic Christianity, provided that we keep in mind the differing geniuses of the peoples concerned. Whereas Greek culture contributed to the speculative legacy of the interpretation of Judeo-Christian doctrines, Chinese culture rendered simpler, and more pragmatic, the highly speculative and analytical doctrines of early Buddhism.

CONFLICTS AND CONFLUENCES

To relate the story that is told by legend, a Chinese emperor, Ming-ti (first century A.D.) of the Han dynasty, had a dream in which he saw a golden giant enter his palace. On asking courtiers for an interpretation of this dream, he was told that the giant represented no other than Gautama, the wise man from the west. Immediately the emperor sent a delegation to India to inquire after this wise man. Buddhist monks from India were also invited to China to preach their religion to the Chinese.*

But this did not mean that Buddhism's introduction was not met with resistance. From the Confucian side, there was incredulity that any wisdom might come from outside of the country, and without being mentioned in the Chinese classical texts. There was revulsion that Buddhist monks did injury to their bodies (which they received from their parents) by shaving their heads, that they even abandoned family and society by embracing celibacy and asceticism, therefore going against the demands of the ancestral cult and of filial piety. And there was much ill ease that the Indian belief in transmigration was incompatible with the Chinese veneration for ancestors as well as with the custom of eating meat. How could one imagine one's ancestors (and one's descendants as well) as anything but human?

From the Taoist side as well, there were misgivings born of rivalry and competition. The claim was made that the Buddha was no other than Lao-tzu, who went west and preached to the barbarians! There was also disappointment that Buddhism had no great contribution to make to the information on elixirs of immortality. But Taoist philosophy was much more compatible to Buddhist teachings, with metaphysical propensities and a language of negation. And the Taoists, with their own preference for solitude, were able to better appreciate Buddhist asceticism and monasticism. Eventually, Taoist ideas and expressions were used in the transla-

* The interpretation of the dream suggests that Buddhism was already known in the country. Scholars believe its introduction was slightly earlier than suggested by the legend.

tion of Buddhist scriptures into Chinese, resulting in a blending of Indian and Chinese thought.

In the course of time, Buddhism prospered in China, especially under the patronage of various rulers. Its rich and elaborate imagery and concepts fascinated many Chinese minds, who generally preferred the Mahayana teachings of universal salvation to the Theravada ideal of monkhood and holiness. Perhaps, this had to do with the character of Chinese society, which was less stratified than that of India. Perhaps also, it had to do with another preference, that which developed within Confucianism for the philosophical belief in human perfectibility and the universal accessibility of the goal of sagehood. Besides, the practical nature of the Chinese also influenced the development of this religion in their country. Certain practices were favored, especially that of mindfulness and meditation, as pursued in Ch'an (Japanese: Zen) Buddhism, and that of devotional piety and prayer, as recommended in Pure Land Buddhism. Indeed, these two sects survived and continued to prosper even after the great persecution of A.D. 845, which virtually wiped out the dominant influence of the Buddhist religion together with other foreign religions such as Zoroastrianism and Manichaeanism.

THE TRANSLATION OF BUDDHIST SCRIPTURES

The translation of Buddhist literature from Pali and Sanskrit into the Chinese language hastened the process of acculturation of Buddhism in China. This may sound simple, but it was not, on account of the enormous vastness of the corpus of books called Buddhist scriptures, and the fact that the translation effort itself took over a thousand years.

Already, sometime during the two centuries between the death of the historical Buddha and the birth of the first great Buddhist emperor, Ashoka (third century B.C.), some sort of Buddhist canon in the form of *oral* tradition had appeared. Indeed, one difference between the Indian and the Chinese civilizations is that the change from the oral tradition to the written one was slower to be effected in the case of India. It therefore took longer for Buddhist scriptures to be put into writing than it took the Confucian classics.

When Buddhism first came into China, the people there knew nothing of its previous history. The Chinese were ignorant of the fact that Buddhism had already splintered into sects in India and Central Asia, and that the scriptures that had been written down were to a large extent sectarian writings attributing various teachings to the Buddha himself. Instead, the Chinese imagined that the scriptures were the Buddha's *ipsissima verba,* recorded by disciples around the time of his death and stored in caves and libraries before they were discovered and taken to China. The facts, actually, were quite different, especially where Mahayana is concerned. There was no fixed corpus, no original Tripiṭaka (Sanskrit: three baskets referring to Buddhist scriptures) that was gradually being translated. The ensuing difficulties experienced by Chinese converts led to the creation of a *Chinese* Buddhism, a response in part to the problems of hermeneutics and textual interpretation.

As the Chinese Buddhists were happy to lay hands on everything and anything translated, they welcomed the scriptures which were brought in with foreign monks, sometimes as gifts to the court, other times just in their memory. (The Indian tradition had always encouraged oral recitation, and the learning by heart of sacred texts.)

We are interested in those Buddhist scriptures that were introduced into China and translated into Chinese. We shall start with the translation process, dwelling upon the choice made of texts for translation, the quality of the work, and who did the work of translating. (Many of the translations are all that remain of the texts that have become lost in their original languages, whether Pali or Sanskrit. Indeed, with its 3,053 entries—entries which include many commentaries as well as so-called original scriptures—the Japanese Taishō edition of the Chinese Tripiṭaka has become essential for the study of the Buddhist religion.*

How were Buddhist texts chosen for translation? In the beginning, the Chinese exercised little choice about what to translate

---

* Note that this is an edition by scholars and for scholars. Thus, the collection includes those non-Buddhist texts that had, in the past, been mistaken as Buddhist, such as those of Manichaean or Nestorian origins.

and what not. This was left to the foreign monks. As the translations were read, however, there was little doubt as to which books were preferred. So choice can be discerned in repeated translations of more popular texts, a repetition that would mark the character of Chinese Buddhism.* The number of times depends also on how early the scripture was first introduced, and the versions each time were usually different.

What did the Chinese find so attractive about these scriptures? This is a vast question, and it holds the key to understanding *Chinese* Buddhism. We must limit ourselves to a few words here, to the few things shared by the scriptures: the Mahayana doctrine of the bodhisattva (a savior figure who refrains from entering Nirvana in order to help more people) including the lay bodhisattva as in the *Vimalakīrti sutra,* and the teaching of the universal accessibility of Buddhahood. Chinese Buddhists developed these doctrines further to include, in the pale of salvation, indeed all sentient beings, even the stubborn unbelievers, and expressing this metaphorically to embrace also the entire universe.

By the end of the T'ang dynasty (906), the formation of the Chinese Buddhist canon was practically completed, even if a few scattered translations were made during the later periods. The earliest scriptures were copied by hand, but the importance of wide dissemination of the Buddha's teachings inspired from very early on the use of printing. Besides, as new books were written— always *attributed* to the Buddha himself—they were taken to China for translation, sometimes, literally, "before the ink was dry." So to the Chinese, it must have seemed a miracle that so many texts should claim to give the Buddha's own words. We might even speak here of some kind of "sutra industry" in India, seeking to satisfy the demand in China for Buddhist scriptures for translation!

With regard to Mahayana Buddhism in China, let us remember that the word "canon" does not have the same normative sense it has with the Hebrew or Christian scriptures, or even with the

---

* We are thinking of the *Great Perfection of Perfect Wisdom* (four times), the *Vimalakīrti sutra* (nine times), the *Suraṇgama sutra* (nine times), and the *Lotus sutra* (three times). The *Small Perfection of Perfect Wisdom,* introduced earlier, had been translated nine times.

Theravada (Pali) scriptures. There was, for example, never a serious effort to define scriptural *authority*. The Chinese Mahayana canon still keeps something of the tripartite structure of the Pali canon with the *vinaya* (monastic discipline), *sutta* (sermons) and *abhidamma* (further discourses) sections, but this became artificial on account of the great influx of new discourses or sutras composed much later, claiming to be the words of the historical Buddha, and translated as such into Chinese. Besides, the Chinese themselves added new works to the corpus, including one work given the status of a sutra (without being ascribed to the historical Buddha)—the *Platform Sutra of the Sixth Patriarch,* a Ch'an treatise—as well as many other philosophical treatises and numerous scriptural commentaries.

Why would the state patronize Buddhism to the extent of helping with the translations, and seeing to the spreading of its good words? There were, of course, pious sovereigns who did this for merit and devotion, or to please the believing multitudes. Besides, patronizing was one way of controlling the religion. The Buddhist canon was useful to the state, serving as a "constitution" for the *sangha* (community), and the state exercised its prerogatives by making the final decision about which translations were fit for inclusion in the canon. Such decisions were made, of course, on the advice of the experts. But it was the state's imprimatur that made a collection of books the Buddhist canon. And the state used the canon as a sanction; it could and did punish members of the *sangha* for moral or ritual transgressions against the prescriptions and proscriptions of the scriptures.

We have little information regarding the authors of the Confucian classics, and even less regarding the authors of the Taoist scriptures, or of the Pali and Sanskrit Buddhist scriptures—outside of the fact that the Buddha himself did not write them. We possess by comparison ample information about the *process* of translation that built up the Chinese Buddhist canon, and about those men who translated the Buddhist scriptures into Chinese. We know the names of over two hundred translators, not to mention their assistants—since, in most cases, the translators cannot be said to have personally done the work word for word, but instead worked with collaborators or teams of collaborators.

Serious work in translation only began in the second century A.D., with the arrival of certain learned Buddhist monks from Central Asia. With help from native collaborators, these monks translated scriptural works—some from the Abhidharma, most from the Āgamas or Nikāyas—which were authoritative for Theravada, as well as scriptural writings from the Mahayana corpus.* So Theravada teachings such as the Four Noble Truths, dependent origination, and retribution, as well as Mahayana teachings on "emptiness," Buddha-lands, the Six Perfections, and the like, became more accessible even though translations tended to be only of a part of a whole text. (Zenryū Tsukamoto, *A History of Early Chinese Buddhism: From Its Introduction to the Death of Hui-yüan,* trans. Leon Hurvitz [Tokyo, 1979], vol. 1, pp. 78–112.) Other monk-scholars followed in their footsteps: men such as Dharmarakṣa (232–309), born in Dunhuang, who translated over a hundred Mahayana texts. He dictated, often from memory, for his Chinese copyists. His important contribution was the *Lotus sutra,* called in Sanskrit the *Saddharmapundarika* (A.D. 286), a text of paramount importance for the development of Mahayana.

A succession of Chinese monks traveling west on pilgrimage, as well as the arrival of foreign monks in China, spurred the work of translation on. The first of these Chinese monks actually to reach India was Fa-hsien, who went in search of an original monastic code in the company of a group of monks (399). Till then, it appears that the *vinaya* was passed down only by oral transmission. (James Legge, *A Record of Buddhistic Kingdoms: Being an Account by the Chinese Monk Fa-h[s]ien of His Travels in India and Ceylon [A.D. 319–414] in Search of the Buddhist Books of Discipline* [Oxford and Clarendon, 1886; reprint, New York: Paragon, 1965]. This book includes his biography in Chinese.)

By the time of Fa-hsien's return to China, and unknown to him, the entire *vinaya* had already been translated by someone else. That it should be translated so late indicates that before the fifth century, the Chinese only had some of the doctrinal sutras and were without a collection of scriptures faithfully reflecting the structure of the Buddhist Tripiṭaka.

* This included a no longer extant translation of the *Suraṇgama sutra.*

TWO TRANSLATORS: KUMĀRAJĪVA AND HSÜAN-TSANG

The translation of Buddhist scriptures into Chinese was a monumental task, to be accomplished only with the support of the state and its enormous resources. Even then, the work called for a certain kind of genius, and one such was the famous Kumārajīva (344–c. 413). Born in Kucha (Central Asia), the son of a Brahmin father and a devout Buddhist princess, he was trained in Afghanistan in both Theravada and Mahayana texts. His fame as a scriptural scholar reached the northern Chinese court (the country was then politically divided), and the ruler literally plotted wars to "kidnap" him. Kumārajīva was brought to Ch'ang-an (402), honored with the title of national preceptor, and surrounded by a thousand monks and lay people (including some of the best scholars in the country) in daily sessions. His task was to retranslate those most influential of Mahayana scriptures and produce definitive editions with authoritative interpretation. Until his death around 413, Kumārajīva and his collaborators poured forth a steady stream of translations, including not merely scriptures, but also commentaries that helped to explain the primary texts. Their output included the *Amitābha sutra,* basic text of the Pure Land school in China (402), the *Perfection of Wisdom in 25,000 Lines* (404), the massive *Treatise on the Great Perfection of Perfect Wisdom* (405), and the two important Mahayana scriptures, the *Lotus* and the *Vimalakīrti* (406).

Until that time, translators had sought mainly to make use of words and concepts coming from Taoist texts to make the Buddhist scriptures more comprehensible as well as more acceptable. This was the method called *ko-yi* (matching of meanings). But it did not always permit the accurate communication of the content of the original texts, and sometimes even distorted them. Readers noticed the difference with Kumārajīva's translations.

Actually, with his undeniably important contributions, Kumārajīva appears not to have been able to read or write Chinese. His greatness lay in his immense learning and understanding, and the leadership he exercised in the translation of the scriptures. But his reputation as a genius was such that the Chinese ruler in the North thought it a waste for him not to have progeny, and offered him concubines. Kumārajīva acquiesced to the royal wishes, for which he has been severely criticized by the Buddhist monks. We know, however, of no genial children from him.

The T'ang dynasty (618–906) also witnessed a flowering of translation activity. The most famous person in this respect was Hsüan-tsang, pilgrim and translator himself, who had brought back to China hundreds of sutras. He remained after that for twenty years in the capital, Ch'ang-an. A man of peerless energy and determination, Hsüan-tsang took care to translate entire works, rather than being content with partial translations.* With him, the corpus of Mahayana scriptures was made available, as well as its most important treatises and commentaries. In the twenty years before he died, he completed the translation of seventy-five works.

Hsüan-tsang left China for India without official permission, but he returned to a royal welcome and had to decline the offers of high office. His adventures as a traveler and a pilgrim (he was nearly killed on his way from China to India by some cannibals, who only spared him at the last minute for fear of reprisals from a higher power) inspired eventually the famous novel *Travel to the West.* In this piece of fiction he was given as companions a monkey, representing quick wit and loyalty, and a pig, representing sensuality. Indeed, the monkey became the hero in the novel, whereas the monk seemed quite helpless in difficulty, having resort only to prayer and meditation.

To return to the subject of translations: the Buddhist texts were coming from India at an uninterrupted rate, leaving no leisure for reflection. But once people realized the complexity of the doctrines, other problems presented themselves. What should one do when contradictory teachings are all ascribed to the Buddha himself?† How to sort out, how to coordinate, how to systematize these new strands of Buddhist doctrine was the burning question.

---

* He brought out, for example, a six-hundred-*chüan Prajñāpāramitā* (Perfection of Wisdom) and other lengthy treatises of one hundred or two hundred *chüan.* (A *chüan* is a Chinese chapter.)
† The translation of two huge scriptures, the *Mahāparinirvāṇa* and the *Avataṃsaka,* especially presented problems of understanding.

THE GROWTH OF BUDDHIST SECTS

Against this background, we may understand the flourishing of Buddhist sectarianism, with different schools selecting one or another scripture to represent the true or chief teaching of the historical Buddha. These were Mahayana schools that knew no parallels in India; they developed the Buddhist philosophical genius in a Chinese context while also preaching the practical methods of meditation and devotion. In so doing, they were helped by the Mahayana emphasis on *upāya* (skill-in-means), which relativizes the importance of dogma as such in favor of practical results. The best-known schools, such as T'ien-t'ai, Hua-yen, Ch'an, and Pure Land, exemplify the Chinese response to Indian religiosity, and their influence would spread outside of China to Korea and Japan. Thus the Hua-yen (Japanese: Kegon) school built its doctrines on the *Avataṃsaka sutra,* which they believed to contain the teaching of the historical Buddha right after his enlightenment. It presents a noumenal world of *li* and a phenomenal world of *shih* which interpenetrate each other, with all phenomena manifesting the one unchanging noumenon, thus establishing a totally integrated philosophical system, in which everything leads to the Buddha in the center. It thus strengthens the Mahayana emphasis that the absolute or Nirvana can be found in the here and now of the cycles of rebirth called *saṃsāra.* On the other hand, the T'ien-t'ai (Japanese: Tendai) school sought to harmonize the many differences found in the diverse scriptures by formulating a classification of the sutras and their teachings according to successive periods in the Buddha's life, and according to his pedagogical genius; T'ien-t'ai claimed that *its* most venerated *Lotus sutra* represented the culmination of his final and mature teaching. In reconciling the contradictory teachings of the Buddhist religion, it established a great eclectic school recognizing all forms of Buddhism. It also testified to the Chinese propensity for the harmonization of opposites as well as to the emphasis on historicity. Both schools paved the way for Ch'an Buddhism, which borrowed from their philosophy, to focus more practically on the practice of meditation itself.

CH'AN AND PURE LAND BUDDHISM

The word Ch'an is the Chinese transliteration of the Sanskrit *dhyāna,* meaning "meditation." It is also known by the Japanese pronunciation of "Zen" and refers basically to the religious discipline aimed at calming the mind and permitting the person to penetrate into his or her own inner consciousness. Continual practice can allegedly conduct one to an ecstatic experience or a blissful state of equanimity and wisdom. As exercises of meditation, *dhyāna* had been developed in India over the ages, but as a Buddhist school, Ch'an is a Chinese development. Its later spread to Korea and Japan, and its recent popularity in both Europe and America, have made Ch'an or Zen the best-known form of Buddhist religion.

In common with other Mahayana systems, Ch'an teaches that ultimate reality—*śūnya* (emptiness), sometimes called Buddha-nature—is inexpressible in words or concepts, and is apprehended only by direct intuition, outside of conscious thought. Such direct intuition requires discipline and training, but is also characterized by freedom and spontaneity. This has led Ch'an to become somewhat of an iconoclastic movement, relativizing such other practices as studying or reciting the Buddhist sutras, worshiping the Buddha images, and performing rituals, which are regarded as of no avail to the goal of spiritual enlightenment (Chinese *wu;* Japanese *satori).*

From its distaste for book learning Ch'an became known as a special tradition "outside the scriptures," that is, not dependent on words or letters, but pointing directly at the human mind or heart to enable its followers to see into their own natures. Such a tradition is only transmitted "from mind to mind," that is, from master to disciple, without the intervention of rational argumentation. It advocates the "absence of thoughts" to free the mind from external influences. Here it is useful to recall a "competition in verse" between the young monk Hui-neng (638–713) and the older and more learned Shen-hsiu. The latter emphasizes the need for careful preparation for the enlightenment experience in the following words:

The body is the *bodhi* tree,
The mind is a bright mirror.
At all times diligently clean it,
Keep it free from dust.

To which Hui-neng's response, asserting the nonduality of mind and body, and the immediate character of enlightenment, is:

Bodhi is originally no tree,
Nor has the bright mirror any frame.
Buddha-nature is always clear and pure,
Where is there any dust?*

Against a background of sectarian multiplication, Ch'an itself divided into many subsects or branches, depending on the varying emphasis on methods and techniques, involving also different beliefs regarding whether the goal of spiritual enlightenment is a sudden experience, or one that is achieved after a gradual process of cultivation. The "sudden" school is especially associated with Hui-neng, allegedly illiterate, whose southern branch of Ch'an focused on the abrupt character of the enlightenment and an iconoclastic attitude toward Buddhas and bodhisattvas, Buddhist literature and rituals. Till then, Ch'an Buddhism had given an important place to specific Buddhist sutras, especially the *Laṅkāvatāra* (in the "gradualist" school) and the *Diamond* (in the "sudden" school). But Southern Ch'an produced its own *Platform Scripture*—with a sermon ascribed to Hui-neng himself—which ranks as the only Chinese Buddhist work with the status of a sutra, and which has become most important for the movement. In relating the simple life of the young monk Hui-neng performing menial tasks in the monastery, such as carrying water and firewood, it stresses the importance of the ordinary life, and even the possibility of finding enlightenment outside of meditation. This was a logical development for the Mahayana movement within Buddhism, which acknowledges the presence of the absolute in the relative, of Nirvana in *samsāra*, and of the sacred in the pro-

---

* From the *Platform Scripture*.

fane. It had the result of affirming the value of this life and this world, and particularly of secular life itself. Besides, in accordance with its emphasis on freedom and spontaneity, Southern Ch'an calls on its followers to "kill everything that stands in your way" of achieving enlightenment. So too, "if you should meet the Buddha, kill the Buddha. If you should meet the Patriarchs, kill the Patriarchs. . . ." Indeed, many great Ch'an masters were vigorous and original personalities who sought to bring their disciples to new levels of insight and understanding with the use of shocking and even, sometimes, violent methods. (Consult Chang Chung-yüan, ed., *Original Teachings of Ch'an Buddhism* [New York, 1969].)

The problem is, should Ch'an be considered Buddhist, as it does not give a prominent place to scriptures, images, and even the Buddha himself? The Ch'an masters would of course reply in the affirmative. According to them, the religion is defined, not by its scriptures, but by the realization of the experience of enlightenment, and this can be best done by looking inside one's own nature. If Ch'an shows the philosophical influence of both T'ien-t'ai and Hua-yen Buddhism, it also discloses a good deal of Taoist sympathy: the emphasis on spontaneity and the natural, on living ordinary lives, and on the wordless transmission of wisdom. Ch'an represents an effort to return to the sources of Buddhist inspiration—and hence to certain features of Theravada Buddhism, especially that of saving oneself by one's own efforts, what the Japanese call *jiriki* (self-power). It involves as well a Taoist effort of discovering one's own original nature that would also influence Neo-Confucianism. Such Taoist affinity, as well as Ch'an's practical bent, has led to its being called a Chinese religion.

Pure Land Buddhism is named after *Sukhāvatī,* a Sanskrit word representing an ideal Buddhist paradise this side of Nirvana. This paradise is believed to be presided over by the Buddha Amitābha (in Chinese, Omitofo; in Japanese, Amida), who is assisted by the bodhisattva Avalokiteśvara (in Chinese, Kuan-yin; in Japanese, Kannon). It is based especially on the *Pure Land sutra,* which has two versions: a lengthier one emphasizing the equal importance of faith and devotion to the Buddha as well as good works, and a shorter one (the *Amitābha sutra)* which says specifically that only faith in the infinite compassion of the Buddha, shown in prayerful and meditative repetition of Amitābha's name, is necessary.* This refers to the practice called *nien-fo* (Japanese *nembutsu*), by which the faithful invoke, with faith, the name of Amitābha. Eventually, the belief emerged that one such single act of faith, when performed with one's whole heart, could become sufficient for salvation. Nevertheless, believers tended to multiply these acts hundreds and thousands of times—frequently with the help of beads, and somewhat technically, if only to reinforce their disposition of faith and surrender. This religion of faith exemplifies what the Japanese call *tariki*, or "other-power," as distinct from the reliance on "self-power" *(jiriki)*.

While Pure Land beliefs can be traced back to Indian sutras, this school began in China probably in the fifth century A.D.; it would spread everywhere in East Asia and, through East Asian migration, to Southeast Asia and the West as well. As a Chinese religion, Pure Land Buddhism has especially appealed to the masses seeking not only ultimate salvation but also a power that responds to their ordinary needs. In this respect, the figure Kuan-yin attracts the most devotion. Originally a male figure, it eventually became transformed into a female in religious iconography, probably through Tibetan influences (tenth century). Clad in white, this "goddess of mercy" became rather early a symbol of the "giver of children" to which women pray for issue. This development offers a curious contrast to the otherworldly thrust of Indian Buddhism, and shows how *Chinese* the religion has become in a totally different cultural environment.

With its emphasis on faith in Amitābha, who becomes very much a God-figure and a dispenser of grace and salvation, Pure Land differs immensely from Ch'an and its more pantheistic tendencies. However, in spite of obvious differences between Ch'an and Pure Land, the Chinese tendency toward syncretism led to a gradual harmonization of Ch'an with Pure Land, of meditation and the study of scriptures; by this harmonization devout Buddhists combined the Ch'an practice of meditation with the Pure

* A third important scripture regards the meditation of Amitābha, also known as Amitāyus.

Land practice of *nien-fo* (Japanese *nembutsu*): reciting the beads while calling on the name of the Amitābha with faith. By such means, the western paradise became interiorized, just as the ultimate or the Buddha-nature itself had become interiorized in Ch'an, T'ien-t'ai, and Hua-yen Buddhism.

FOLK BUDDHISM AND THE MAITREYA CULT

Such syncretism took place especially on the folk level, leading to a harmonization within Buddhism, as well as between Buddhism and Taoism, and between all the three religions of China, until we have a folk religion embracing various strands from all three traditions. Here a well-known Chinese development is the metamorphosis of the Maitreya cult.

Maitreya, the Buddha of the Future, is a well-known figure in the Buddhist sutras and may also represent messianic influences from beyond India, perhaps from Persia. Because of such connotations, it has been the focus of certain political rebellions even in China itself, including that which eventually led to the founding of the Ming dynasty (1368). But the image of Maitreya also underwent a transformation somewhat akin to that of Avalokiteśvara or Kuan-yin. I refer here to the earlier large and heroic figure before the seventh century, which reappeared in the fifteenth century and afterward in the shape and appearance of a wrinkled, laughing monk with an exposed potbelly, carrying a hemp bag but in a reclining posture, with small children climbing on top of him and surrounding him. This image is extremely popular, not only in a devotional cult in the whole of East Asia, but also as an artistic decoration in the world at large.

In this guise, we see once more the embodiment of Chinese values within a Buddhist image. This Maitreya figure, called Mi-lo, affirms the importance of worldly happiness and prosperity and performs the same function as the goddess-figure Kuan-yin, since Mi-lo is alleged to have the power of giving children to those who pray to it. And this desire for posterity, so much a part of the Chinese ancestral religion, stands in diametrical opposition to the Buddhist call for renunciation of all desire. In this light, the metamorphoses of both Kuan-yin from Avalokiteśvara and Mi-lo from

Maitreya are good indications of the Chinese appropriation of the Buddhist religion. If Buddhism survived in China, it did so by serving Chinese goals, including Confucian family values, thus confirming a basically Chinese affirmation of the importance of this life and this world.

And so an Indian religion has taken on Chinese faces, giving reinterpretations of certain essential, earlier teachings. With the emphasis on the bodhisattva ideal, the idea of Nirvana became virtually obsolete, to become replaced in practice by desire for rebirth in the Pure Land. With the teachings of meditation and enlightenment, as given in Ch'an, the scriptures were relativized, while biographies of Ch'an masters and their recorded conversations multiplied, offering riddles *(kung-an;* Japanese *koan)* that help force the mind to go beyond the rational and discursive to the nonrational and intuitive.

THE BUDDHIST LEGACY IN EAST ASIA

According to the census of 845, there were a quarter of a million monks and nuns, forty-six hundred temples, and over forty thousand lesser shrines in China. The wealth and power of the *sangha* invited envy and provoked persecution. The questions may be asked: What has happened to Buddhism since the ninth century? What has happened in the last millennium? Is it still a great religion in China today? How is it faring in the new, Marxist society? In short, what is the Buddhist legacy in China, and what importance does it still have?

It should first be mentioned that Buddhism usually fared better under governments of non-Han Chinese or mixed ethnic backgrounds, such as during the so-called Six Dynasties (317–581), the T'ang dynasty (618–907), and also the Yüan or Mongol dynasty (1279–1367), when Tantric Buddhism became the privileged sect. This is understandable, since, in spite of its steady pace of acculturation, the Buddhist religion remained a testimony to alien cultural influence. Besides, for those conquerors of China from the steppes, Buddhism (like Islam after it) helped to fill a spiritual vacuum. In the case of Tantric Buddhism, it also offered a sense of special power. During the other times, such as the Sung (960–1279) and the Ming (1368–1644) periods, when the Han Chinese were once more in control, Confucianism was again dominant. But the two traditions learned and borrowed from each other. The central Mahayana insight, that Nirvana is to be found in *saṃsāra*, that is, *in* this life and this world, had made the religion more acceptable to the Chinese and the Japanese. In the words of the eleventh-century monk Ch'i-sung, author of the essay "On the Original Way" *(Yüan-tao):*

> The Buddhist follows a monastic rule and cultivates his mind and heart. . . . achieving a high degree of virtue. He also extends his way [Tao] to others, wanting to do good to all with no distinction of things, achieving also a sublime Tao. . . . Although he does not marry, he serves his parents with his virtue. Although he destroys his appearance, he serves his kin with his Tao.*

Of course, we have come a long way since the Sung dynasty, when Buddhism was showing its mature Chinese form—but also when decline had already set in. Further developments did not prevent the continued decline of Buddhism, as well as the persisting amalgamation of the three religions. The Buddhist legacy in China represents a religion which has taken on many Chinese moral values while retaining its concern for deliverance from suffering, and its various monastic lineages and communities as centers for the transmission of the teaching or *dharma.* But the legacy includes as well the Buddhist contribution to Chinese culture, which has never been the same again. I speak here especially of Buddhist contributions to the development of Neo-Confucian metaphysics and spirituality; to the fine arts and to sculpture, such as we see today in the rock-cut "cave temples" of Yunkang, Lungmen, and of course Dunhuang; to the architectural styles of temples and pagodas—the latter being an evolved form of the original Indian stupas, where relics were kept. Within today's boundaries of the People's Republic, there are also the many temples and monasteries of Tibet, as well as the famous Potala Palace of Lhasa,

---

* See his collected writings, given in the Taishō edition of the Buddhist canon, no. 2115, ch. 1, p. 651.

former residence of the Dalai Lama. And there are various genres of Chinese literature, including poetry and folk literature, which could not have developed in the way they did without Buddhist impetus and influence. Interestingly, in the 1920s, when Chinese intellectuals were calling for intellectual pluralism and a greater openness to Western ideas, the monk T'ai-hsü started a reform movement within Buddhism, while prominent lay devotees, dedicated to the furthering of the knowledge of Buddhism, extended their activities to social work and popular education.

The Buddhist legacy is also present in both Korea and Japan—as East Asian Buddhism, that is, mediated through China and using Chinese translations of the Buddhist scriptures. In Japan, we still find a wealth of diverse Buddhist sects, whereas in Korea there is much less sectarian difference in doctrine or ritual, and more evidence of syncretism with local shamanic religion. Also, except for some Japanese influence, the Korean monks have largely remained celibate, whereas the Japanese now have mostly a married clergy—their practical application of the Mahayana insight that Nirvana is to be found in *saṃsāra*, that the ultimate is to be found in the relative, and that salvation is to be found here and now.

Three important sects of Japanese Buddhism are not known in China. They include the esoteric Shingon (True Word) sect of Tantric Buddhism, which went from India to China and was introduced from early ninth-century China by the Japanese monk Kūkai, although it has since disappeared from China; the Jodō Shinshū or True Pure Land sect, started by Shinran in the thirteenth century, with its exclusive faith in and devotion to the Buddha Amida, its principal focus upon the exercise of *nembutsu,* and its greater readiness to adapt itself to modern exigencies; and the Nichiren (literally, Sun and Lotus) sect, named after its founder and started somewhat later in the thirteenth century, and known for its exclusive exaltation of the *Lotus sutra* and its association with Japanese nationalism.

It should be mentioned that Buddhism is uniquely Japanese in Japan, as it became Chinese in China. This is an important dimension of *all* Japanese religions, in spite of discernible Chinese influences. Theoretically, one finds more continuity between China and Japan, in the case of both Confucianism and Buddhism. Practically, however, the blending of the traditions, such as of Shinto and Buddhism, has given Japanese Buddhist sects a new visage, different from their Chinese antecedents. Besides, it is interesting to see the greater Tantric influence on various Japanese Buddhist schools, including Tendai.

In today's Japan, Buddhist sects tend to be associated with the rituals surrounding death and mourning, and the temples have shrines which honor the ashes of the departed. Indeed, Japanese Buddhism is so closely associated with the memory of the dead and the ancestral cult that the family shrines dedicated to the ancestors, and still occupying a place of honor in homes, are popularly called the Butsudan, literally, "the Buddhist altars." For the same reason, Buddhism is frequently called the religion of the dead, whereas Shinto is labeled the religion of the living on account of its association with the joys of life. It has been the custom in modern Japan to have Shinto weddings (or, more recently, Catholic weddings, followed by a honeymoon journey to Hawaii or Switzerland), but to turn to Buddhism in times of bereavement and for funeral services.

Has Buddhism any contemporary relevance in Japan, aside from mainly ministering to the memory of the departed? The question has sometimes been asked. Buddhism's influence is certainly present—even speculatively, as discerned in the modern Japanese philosophy developed by Nishida Kitaro and his followers, which blended Buddhism with European (Continental) philosophy. And Buddhism is regarded as representing a conservative force, more associated with nationalism, and little interested in the problems brought about by social change.

And so, what of the importance of Buddhism today? The West may still be aware of the role of Buddhism in Japan and Korea, with its traditional sects and temples—even if its influence is subtle and ill defined. In Japan more than in Korea, there is the richness of sectarian transmissions, although in Korea, the monastic discipline has been better preserved. The West knows also of the enduring Buddhist influence in Southeast Asia: especially in Burma and Thailand, but also, to some extent, in the Chinese circles of Taiwan, Hong Kong, and Singapore, where folk religion shows a very eclectic face. But what of mainland China with its Communist society?

Here, it must be said that Buddhism, in its Tantric form, remains the dominant religion of the Tibetans and the Mongols, and is once more showing itself after the end of the Cultural Revolution (1966–77). Among the Han Chinese, there are still devotees of Pure Land and of Ch'an, and of so-called folk Buddhism. Temples are once more open, and novices are being trained. But it is definitely a minority religion, on the periphery of the society.

As a religion which has survived the Cultural Revolution, Chinese Buddhism faces peculiar problems. I am referring not merely to the fear of renewed persecution, but to certain changes that the religion has sustained. It appears, for example, that many secularized monks are returning to the temples—but as married men. Although novices are presumably trained to remain celibate, one cannot help but wonder what the future form of the Chinese *sangha* will be like. Questions can also be raised about the content of Buddhist belief in East Asia. For example, it appears that many Chinese, Japanese, and Korean Buddhists are less than clear about their belief in the cycle of rebirth. Their accounts of *saṃsāra* include the presupposition of a wandering *soul,* which is not in accord with strict Buddhist teaching, and they tend to perceive life in linear terms. Besides, they frequently equate Nirvana with the Pure Land, and the Buddhas with the bodhisattvas.

And yet, can we say that Buddhist influence is over? Has Chinese Buddhism not as well moved to the West, especially to North America? In those areas where an immigrant community is well established, be that in California, New York, or Toronto, we find Buddhist communities, not only from South or Southeast Asia, but also from Japan and China; they are active, and they even assume a role of leadership in organizing communal religious life and in spreading the knowledge of Buddhism beyond the ethnic community. Just as Christianity has evangelized East Asia, so too Buddhism is evangelizing North American and Western Europe. Its gains may be numerically small, but the converts are frequently among the intellectually sophisticated.

The historical transformation of Buddhism in China leaves behind many questions for students of the history of religions. On the one hand, as we have seen, Buddhism adapted itself to Chinese culture to the extent of becoming a Chinese religion, while maintaining its distinct identity in the company of Confucianism and religious Taoism. On the other hand, it was never completely accepted by the country's political and intellectual elite, it suffered severe persecutions, and it was threatened with near extinction. Has the Buddhist openness to acculturation served the religion well? What would have happened if the religion had been less adaptable?

My own answer is, Buddhism could not have survived in China the way it did, had it not adapted itself culturally to the environment. Acculturation also accounts for its transformation, and its ability to contribute positively to Chinese civilization. True, Buddhism had been on a steady road of decline ever since the ninth century, and, with all its efforts of renewal and revival, it has generally been regarded, in the twentieth century, as peripheral to the concerns of Chinese society and even as irrelevant to modern life. However, without acculturation, such decline could have set in much earlier, perhaps more than a thousand years ago. Besides, in spite of Buddhism's decline, its strength may be discerned in its continual ability to resurrect itself after persecutions. We need not overestimate the importance of Buddhism in today's China; but ought we to overlook its resilience?

Besides, may we see in the Buddhist acculturation to Chinese civilization a kind of model for other foreign religions, including Christianity? Would the Christian religion have fared better had it adapted itself more consciously to Chinese cultural values?

CHRISTIANITY: A FOREIGN RELIGION IN EAST ASIA

In the course of some thirteen centuries, Western Christianity sought to penetrate China at least four times, only to be driven off each time. I shall not dwell on it, as Hans Küng will present this history in his response. But historically, the efforts of Christian acculturation did not endure long enough for us to discern properly their consequences. From the lessons of the Buddhist example, we might adduce a better acceptance of Christianity, as well as a deeper influence on Chinese culture, had things been different. I doubt that mass conversions, whether among the elite or among the peasants, would have occurred. Sixteenth- and seventeenth-century China was not sixth- or seventh-century Gaul, or even sixth-, seventh-, or eighth-century Central Asia. As an ancient civilization, China was difficult to penetrate. Moghul India would be another instance. After sweeping across North Africa and eastward into Persia with the help of war and conquest, Islam was unable to win over the majority population of Hindu India. And, after taking over the place of the Moghuls, the British Raj did not offer a better occasion for the Christian evangelization of India.

Many mistakes were made—as for example by the missionaries who quarreled among themselves over methods of evangelization, and by their leaders in Rome. These mistakes retarded and rendered difficult their task of evangelization. But the unique claims of the Christian religion, as well as the sense of cultural superiority maintained by the Chinese, were such that a confrontation between Christianity and the dominant religions of China could not have been avoided. In my mind, the worst mistakes were those made latest, when the missionaries relied on the gunboat diplomacy of the Western powers for their protection. More than even the earlier mistakes, this political compromise labeled them as opportunists and even as imperialists.

Until the Communist takeover, the Christian religion had remained a missionary religion, which Buddhism had long ceased to be. Was there, and is there, however, any chance of Christianity's ever becoming a Chinese religion?

Here, we observe that Buddhism penetrated sufficiently into Chinese culture to influence its ways of thinking, and to become, in turn, influenced by it, whereas Christianity did not. As a latecomer, Christianity remained a foreign religion, finding adherents among those who were Western-educated, or at least Western-oriented, but not hostile to religion. Indeed, there were many among the Western-oriented who regarded religion and science as irreconcilable, and rejected both traditional Chinese culture and Western religion.

Besides in China, Christianity was also introduced into Korea and Japan. Korea has frequently been perceived as a country of conservative inclinations; yet the number of Christians has stead-ily risen, till it is now about 25 percent of the total population. Even the growth in Taiwan and Hong Kong, and elsewhere among Chinese communities in Southeast Asia, cannot match this phenomenal upsurge. In Japan, on the other hand, except for the so-called Christian century (1550–1650), with mass conversions followed by severe persecutions, Christian missionaries have met with occasional curiosity and general indifference.

Why such difference regarding acceptance of Christianity in Korea and Japan? Some association may be made with the differ-ences between Korean shamanism which favors a kind of mono-theism, and Japanese Shinto, with its eight million gods. Possibly, the stronger Confucian influence in Korea has also been favorable to the development of Christianity, whereas the stronger Bud-dhist influence in Japan is more of a deterrent. And then, differ-ences in national character can also be alleged between the Kore-ans and the Japanese.

In any case, the differences between Korea and Japan leave us also guessing regarding the future of Christianity in China, should this religion be permitted to function without official prohibitions or limitations. A better indication may be found in the relative openness of the Chinese population in Taiwan and Hong Kong as well as Singapore: their response has been more positive than the Japanese, and less enthusiastic than the Koreans.

Besides, the question may also be asked, what *difference* has Christianity, as a universal religion, made to Japan and Korea? In the case of the Second World War, the Japanese Christian churches, with some exceptions, rallied to the support of the gov-ernment, perhaps all the more in their desire to prove their own patriotism, whereas the strongest opposition group, in spite of their numerical and political weakness, was the Socialists.

The minority status of Christians in the various East Asian coun-tries brings with it a feeling of insecurity. It is not known whether the postwar Japanese Christians have overcome this feeling. The insecurity appears less the case in Korea, where Christians are also prominent in the dissident movement. But it remains very true of the Christians in China today, who are sorely aware of the accusa-tion leveled against them that they are collaborators with "cul-

tural imperialists." But the recent upsurge in the number of conversions, indicates however, that the consciousness of cultural
imperialism appears to be subsiding.

"CHINESE RELIGION": ONE OR MANY?

We have spoken of *three* (or perhaps, four) Chinese religions:
Confucianism, the "moral" and "ritual" religion; Taoism, the "theistic" or even "polytheistic" and "alchemical" religion; and Buddhism, the "devotional" and "mystical" religion, besides the religion of antiquity. And we have briefly discussed the situation of
Christianity as another foreign religion in China.

However, are there really several—say three—principal religions in China? Here we need to keep in mind the entire heritage
of Chinese culture, from which the religions cannot be separated.
This inseparability between religion and culture has led many to
the conclusion that the Chinese have no religiosity of their own.
But it also explains how much common ground can be found
between the religions of China. To the extent that Confucianism
and Taoism came out of the same spiritual roots, sharing in certain
beliefs, rituals, and values, one may speak here of *one* Chinese
religion, but with multiple forms of expression. But this cannot
include Buddhism, even when Buddhism has influenced so much
the religion of the folk. Therefore it may be better to consider
Buddhism a religion of foreign origin.

It is perhaps to be expected that the ruling dynasties of native
origin tended to favor Confucianism (and Taoism), whereas those
of alien or mixed backgrounds offered more protection to Buddhism. Taoism and Buddhism offered a sense of escape and consolation during the times of disunity, whereas Confucianism contributed more directly to social and political cohesion during the times
of national unity. The three religions actually complemented one
another, since they attended to different areas of human concern.
During and after the Ming dynasty and until today, they have
tended to converge in a syncretistic movement; and Confucius,
Lao-tzu, and the Buddha have sometimes been joined in veneration and worship by the adherents and this movement.

Certainly, there had been rivalry, even acrimony, between

these three traditions, and yet it appears that they were eventually able to coexist and complement one another. We see here a spirit of harmony and reconciliation which is perhaps most characteristic of traditional Chinese culture—a harmony of parts within a whole, in which each religion serves a socially useful function. In Confucianism, such harmony has been directed to human social relationships; in Taoist philosophy, it has been turned to man's relationship with the rest of nature. Taoist religion presents a difficulty, since the desire for physical immortality prompted proto-scientific experiments which were consciously undertaken *against* the spirit of harmony and in the name of *wresting* from nature itself the secrets of life and longevity. (And this means a "proto-scientific" spirit of exploitation of nature.) On the other hand, Buddhism offered an entirely new outlook on life and the world, only to become itself conditioned by the pervading Chinese culture. It filled a certain spiritual vacuum by addressing itself to questions largely ignored by both Confucianism and Taoism. Even outside of any particular syncretistic cult, many Chinese have found it possible to follow all three teachings at the same time. For example, a man could be a Confucian in his active life, responding to multiple social responsibilities; a *philosophical* Taoist in his leisure hours, reading poetry and enjoying nature and wine, practicing some health regimen associated with *religious* Taoism; and both he and his wife—or, at least, she—would frequent the Buddhist temple to offer prayers for special intentions. The coexistence of all three religious traditions, and the possibility for the same persons to be involved in all of them, testifies to a certain pluralism within the Chinese—and the East Asian—civilizations, a pluralism that was not known by Europe and the Middle East.

MARXISM AND RELIGION

The happy harmony of traditional Chinese society existed, of course, more as an ideal than as fact. Among other factors, the three major teachings were never the *only* religions in China. The country has also known Islam and Christianity, although the adherents of these Western religions have always been a minority in the population, and Muslims have usually come from specific ethnic groups, refraining from making converts from the majority. In any case, China faced the onslaught of Western intrusions, both political and cultural, especially from the late nineteenth century onward. This was the age of imperialism, when Asian and African nations were confronted by Western European—and also North American—ambitions of domination, supported by modern science and superior military technology. The onslaught of Western imperialism has been a most severe test for Chinese culture and society, and the occasion for a long period of self-doubt and self-criticism, which has not yet ended. As traditional society found itself in the process of disintegration, Western philosophical and religious ideas were introduced together with Western ideas of science and government. The Chinese dilemma has been how to modernize without losing a cultural identity and a rich heritage. In the ensuing struggle, as we know, a particular Western ideology, that of Marxism, emerged victorious. It would combat traditional religious values, considered as outmoded; feudal forces, which were keeping the country backward; and the more recently introduced Christian religion, considered an ally of Western political and cultural imperialism.

What exactly happened to religion after the Communist victory? Where Christianity is concerned, we know of the exodus of missionaries, some having left before 1949. Actually, the Constitution of 1954 and each constitution promulgated since guaranteed religious freedom. This was in line with classical Marxist teachings, which assert that religion would wither away in a classless society, even if its demise might take many years. During the 1950's, a certain measure of freedom—narrowly defined as freedom of religious belief—is therefore allowed for political reasons. The most recent constitution, that of 1982, would offer an improvement, including a stronger guarantee of freedom for religious practice.

Christianity in China appears divided, even after its resurrection since the end of the Cultural Revolution. We are left openly wondering: Will it now be able to *become Chinese,* that is, indigenized, under the control of the Communist government, but without the interference of Western missionaries? And, with all its claims of patriotism, is Chinese Christianity losing its universality?

Will it become too much of a *political* religion, too ready to compromise with official Marxism?

Marxism earlier showed a certain Western doctrinal intransigence and even militant aggressiveness that had not been found to the same extent in China's traditional religions. But the Cultural Revolution proved to be too extremist for most people, including most Communists. The death of Mao (1976) was followed by the fall of the Gang of Four and the implementation of a radically new policy; this policy included a growing openness to the West (including tolerance for Western religions), and an increasing readiness to permit a critical inheritance of traditional heritage. Under these circumstances, what future can we project for religion, or religions, in China?

What future can be forecast for religion in China? Will religious life survive under official tolerance, will it prosper and develop, or will there yet be harassment and persecution? It appears at present that religion is both surviving and prospering, while a measure of harassment and persecution is also persisting in specific quarters. Obviously, the experiences of the recent past have created a real spiritual vacuum, and the revival of religious life, however minor, is one way by which this is being filled. With government support, Taoist and Buddhist temples, Islamic mosques, and Christian churches have been repaired and reopened, and the various groups are once more permitted and encouraged to educate recruits. Conversions to Christianity are being reported, and these are said to occur sometimes in secret, with the young people converting one another. Not surprisingly, religious ignorance is widespread, and folk "superstitions" are returning.

With the greater efforts at modernization, even Westernization, will the country also find Western religion, especially Christianity, more attractive, or will it prefer the religions of its own traditional past? This question had been raised in the recent past but was superseded by the dominance of Marxism. Today, with the realization that Marxism does not offer all the answers, it is once more being asked.

In this context, what role can we see for Marxism? It appears to situate itself somewhere between the revival of the religions and the influence of Western liberalism. So long as the government remains Marxist, the ideology will also be relevant, if only in a theoretical sense. Here the history of Buddhism in China may even contain a lesson for Marxism as an ideology of Western origin, now in power, that yet needs to make itself indigenous.

Tang Yijie, a professor from China, a specialist in Buddhism and Taoism, once told me that the history of Buddhist acculturation in China offers as well a clue to the future of Marxism in China. According to this prognosis, Marxism will first have to take account of traditional Chinese values and assimilate these into itself, and then, gradually, will become itself absorbed by this great Chinese culture sometime in the future. *My* question here is, when Marxism has become entirely Chinese, will it remain Marxist?

What are theology's responses to this situation, especially as it touches Christianity in China? I believe that these will also have to be both universal (from the perspective of the world outside China) and particular (from that of Chinese Christianity). And I wait to hear from Hans Küng.

CONCLUSION: THE THIRD "RIVER SYSTEM"?

Let us return to a "global" consideration of Chinese religion by recalling to mind traditional China's self-consciousness as the center of the civilized universe, indeed, of "all under heaven" *(t'ien-hsia),* and its concomitant disdain of anything peripheral to this civilization. Chinese values were considered to be *universally* valid, and Chinese culture had spread to the regions adjacent to the country, especially in the case of Japan, mainly as a result of the civilizing efforts of these regions themselves. The late nineteenth century witnessed a rude awakening, as the Chinese discovered that theirs was only one country among others, and indeed, that their survival was being threatened by others. Consequently, the twentieth century has been a struggle for survival, the manifestation of Chinese nationalism—very much like nationalism elsewhere in Asia—vis-à-vis the imperialistic nationalism of the Western powers and of Japan. As a consequence of this struggle for national survival, the entire cultural legacy was scrutinized.

In this historical context, the religious situation of China takes on new perspective. I speak of the tension between the universal and the particular. For example, Confucianism, a tradition with universal claims, was rejected as irrelevant to national survival. Instead, Marxism was favored—a system with universal claims but of foreign origin. And Marxism was given a particular task, that of saving China. In the process of carrying out this task, Marxism might increasingly assume a Chinese face, or rather several Chinese faces, identifying itself with the particular goals of this country, and of the stated policies of its successive leaderships.

As we look at China through the dimensions of time and space, we may conclude that religion was strongest in the earliest centuries and is currently strong only in the peripheral regions (Tibet, Central Asia). Does that mean that religion is no longer *central* to Chinese culture, and has not been for a long time? And is this not the result, at least in part, of the tendency toward harmony and syncretism, which makes "secular humanism" out of formerly religious traditions?

But can we not also say that Chinese humanism itself, with its doctrine of self-transcendence in different forms (Confucianism, Taoism, Buddhism), points to *another* expression of human religiosity, which cannot simply be dismissed with the word "secular"?

Here, could we not point to the "third river system" (to use Hans Küng's words) of a humanism open to religion, which emerged more than two thousand years ago and is still alive? In this sense, it is in the same company as the Semitic (or Abrahamic) traditions (Judaism, Christianity, Islam) and the Indian (or South Asian) traditions (Hinduism and southern Buddhism). It remains a great living tradition, although not without its own problems in the modern world.

If this is accepted, then this "third river system" also challenges all of us to redefine the word "religion" itself—to see this phenomenon not only as something not necessarily linked to a belief in God (as Buddhism has shown to be possible), but also and especially as a striving for self-transcendence that remains open to Heaven, to the Great Ultimate, to the True Self, and to the Pure Land. Seen in this way, this third "river system" with its inherent humanism, urges its followers to self-transcendence, not only with regard to one's fellow human beings, but also with regard to another reality: to the highest reality (in Confucianism), to the deepest reality (in Taoism), and to the final reality (in Buddhism).

2. *Hans Küng:* A Christian Response

MISSED CHANCES—NEW POSSIBILITIES?

In the introduction to this book, I already emphasized that, in this final response, I would not discuss the theological challenge of Buddhism. What Christian theology may have to say to Zen or Amida Buddhism will not be repeated here and can be found in an earlier publication ("Buddhism and Christianity," pt. C in *Christianity and the World Religions,* Küng et al.). This response concentrates on something that is even more important for the future of Christian theology, namely the history of the encounter between Christianity and China, and the possibilities for a contextual Christian theology in Chinese garb. The former is fascinating in both its opportunities and its failures; the latter attracts hardly any attention in Europe.

It is curious to think that Christianity might have become right at home in China, much like the first great foreign religion, Buddhism! An organic combination of Christian religion and Chinese culture would have come into being. It is barely conceivable: the Chinese landscape would have been as unimaginable without Christian churches as it is without Buddhist pagodas. Like Buddhist art, Christian painting and sculpture would have influenced Chinese art; Christian rites and practices would have become thoroughly Chinese. There would have been an original characterization of Chinese culture through the Christian faith, Christian ethics, and Christian piety, much as was the case with Buddhism.

Or was it the case that Christianity was from the beginning not as open as Buddhism, not as tolerant, not as adaptable? It is senseless to get caught up in a lot of hypotheses about this. All this did *not* happen. Let us stick to the actual history.

If we are to believe such a highly knowledgeable Sinologist as the Frenchman Jacques Gernet, then the differences between the European and Chinese views of humanity and the world are so fundamental that the Christian missions of modern European times (the Jesuits since 1583) had to fail. The decisive factor, therefore, was not political suppression, but essential differences between Chinese and Christian morals and religion themselves! Gernet's original French publication carries the straightforward title *Chine et Christianisme: action et réaction* (Paris, 1982). The German translation, by contrast, carries the fancy and false title of "Christ Came All the Way to China: A First Encounter and Its Failure" *(Christus kam bis nach China: Eine erste Begegnung und ihr Scheitern* [Zürich, 1984]; similarly, also, the book by Young, cited in Response II above, *The First Encounter).* The encounter of the sixteenth and seventeenth centuries was in fact not the *first,* as Gernet tells us in his book. However, in a single footnote he dismisses the earlier encounters between Christianity and China as "historical curiosities."

But wait a minute! The encounters before the sixteenth century are also worthy of historical and theological attention. They are also *models for possibilities and methods* of encounter between such different religions in the context of the single "religious history of humankind" (W. C. Smith). Using seven historical models of encounter, I want to describe the specific characteristics of each historical encounter and thereby systematically analyze methods of interreligious relations for today. For the contemporary situation, using historical models is the best critical way of finding out how Christianity should approach China theologically and what is possible or impossible in this context. As much as possible, the goal is a contextual, indigenized, locally rooted Christian theology for Chinese Christians and churches that can be justified in today's terms.

MODEL 1: OUTWARD ASSIMILATION

Too few Europeans are aware of the fact that it was not the Roman Catholic or even the Byzantine church that was the first to bring the gospel to China. It was rather that Christian church which, for a long time (even though in the minority wherever it existed), was the most widespread Christian confession and certainly by far the most enthusiastic mission church: the *Nestorian* church. The name is misleading. This church is none other than Syrian-Persian Christianity. During the great Christological controversy at the end of the fifth century, it opposed Alexandrian Monophysite tendencies and took the side of Nestorius of Syrian Antioch, who had been deposed as patriarch of Constantinople. It eventually separated from the imperial church in 488. Since, it has lived separated from the Eastern church. Nevertheless, it was the only Christianity that had the opportunity to be spread across Asia very early on, mostly by merchants. Accordingly, it boldly pushed forward into India, Indochina, Java, Tibet, Central Asia, and even, in 578, China.

In 635—a year in which the Irish-Scottish monk Aidan brought Celtic Christianity to England and in which some German tribes were still far from being Christianized—the Nestorian monk A-lo-pen arrived in Ch'ang-an (today Xian), the western capital of the Buddhist and cosmopolitan T'ang dynasty. Here, the Nestorians were honorably received by Emperor T'ai-tsung, a man as eager to learn as he was tolerant. Here, their writings were translated; of these, a treatise on the Messiah and three monotheistic discourses were found in the already mentioned caves of Dunhuang (Yang Lian's poem!). Here, a monastery was built for them, followed by further monasteries here and elsewhere, including one in the eastern capital. An edict of toleration for Christianity was also issued.

Following persecution instigated by Buddhists at the turn of the eighth century, a new Golden Age dawned toward the middle of that same century. Indeed, it was a time of amazing *ecumenical cooperation*. The learned Bishop Adam, working with the Buddhist monk Prajna, had thirty-five Biblical and Nestorian writings as well as several Buddhist sutras translated into Chinese. The famous stele of Xian from the year 781 (written in Syriac and Chinese and excavated in 1623) reveals the most important particulars about the spread of Nestorian Christianity. Of course, since many among the people regarded Christianity as a Buddhist sect, it was included in the Buddhist persecution. Its revival under the Yüan dynasty toward the end of the thirteenth and beginning of the fourteenth centuries is attested by the notes of Marco Polo, the Chinese annals, and many graves and crosses.

This Nestorian church had its *own Christology, liturgy, and symbolism*. Instead of the crucifix, which was also largely despised by the rest of the first-millennium church, its central symbol was the "cross of victory." Indeed, one even finds crosses that emerge from the (Buddhist) lotus flower. It is therefore not surprising that Western Christians reproached these Nestorians for a *too excessive accommodation* to Buddhist and Taoist conceptions. "The impartial reader of A-lo-pen's texts will no doubt be surprised by the Buddhist atmosphere that he encounters; but the essence of the Christian proclamation, for instance in the description of Jesus' passion or the prominence given Christian monotheism, persistently and inescapably breaks through the Buddhist concepts and trains of thought" (G. Rosenkranz, *Die älteste Christenheit in China in den Quellen-Zeugnissen der Nestorianertexte der T'ang-Dynastie* [Berlin, 1939], p. 6).

It is one of the ironies of history. The Franciscan John of Monte Corvino, a former soldier, doctor, and judge, arrived as papal legate in Khanbaliq (Peking) in 1294 after an extremely difficult overland journey through Armenia, Persia, and India. There, as the first Roman Catholic bishop, he translated the Psalms and the New Testament into Mongolian and built three churches. But first, in good Roman fashion, he tried to "convert" the Christian Nestorians! In order to create an indigenous clergy, he gave Latin and liturgical instruction to boys that he had bought. This tactic already reveals a different, namely Roman, missionizing method that in this case remained a mere episode. The fall of the Mongol dynasty in 1368 also meant the *decline of Mongol non-Chinese Christianity*. The Nestorian church was wiped out in the fourteenth century in the wake of the Islamization of the Mongols and Turks, and then especially by the horrible persecution of Tamerlane in 1380. Only a few tens of thousands of Nestorians remained in South India and Mesopotamia—until today.

MODEL 2: SYNCRETIC MIXTURE

Likewise in the seventh century (perhaps already in the sixth century), *Manichaeans* came to China from East Turkestan by way of the Silk Road. Is Manichaeism a Christian sect? More than this, it was a *world religion* with its own dualistic and Gnostic style. Founded by Mani (third century) in the Judeo-Christian milieu of Mesopotamia, it spread to Spain in the West all the way to China in the East. *Mani?* He died in chains but understood himself as *God's final prophet,* following all the prophets since Adam, Zoroaster, Buddha, and even Jesus. He, Mani—the Apostle of Light, the supreme Enlightened One, and the Paraclete promised by Jesus— replaced with his religion the churches of Zoroaster in Persia, of Jesus in the West, and of the Buddha in the East. He was in fact celebrated as the new Buddha in the East.

Indeed, this "religion of light" had its heyday in the West of the fourth century (Augustine was himself a former Manichaean!), and in the eighth century it became the *state religion* of the Central Asian empire of the old Turkish Uighurs. It also took root in Chinese Turkestan and in Gansu. It was a *mixture of Christianity, Buddhism, and Persian traditions!* The "Catechism of the Religion of the Buddha of Light," put together by a Manichaean bishop on the order of the Chinese emperor, shows how much original Manichaeism was saturated with Buddhist (and Confucian!) elements. The Manichaeans already followed the same vegetarian regimen as the pious Buddhists. They wore the same color—white, the color of Buddhist laypersons, of the lotus, and of the future Maitreya Buddha. Manichaeans worshiped the sun and the moon; they performed secret rituals during the night or before sunrise to celebrate the victory of light over darkness, something also common in Buddhism to celebrate the enlightenment of the Buddha. Later, the Manichaeans survived some very serious political catastrophes. Eventually, however, the Mongolian assault of Genghis Khan in the thirteenth century weakened it critically.

In what was a complicated history, the Manichaean faith

blended with a very remarkable movement: the late medieval lay
Buddhist millenarianism of the White Lotus sect. This sect combined the expectation of the Maitreya Buddha at the end of time
with the regular invocation of the Amitābha Buddha, that Buddha
of the Immeasurable Light through whom one hoped to be reborn
in the Pure Land. Proscribed, persecuted, and transformed into a
secret society, the White Lotus sect played an important role in
rebellions and recurrent uprisings of the thirteenth to fifteenth
centuries. In 1368, it helped to overthrow the Mongolian Yüan
dynasty and to raise the emperor T'ai-tsu, founder of the national-
Chinese Ming dynasty, to the throne as "king of light" (Ming =
light). T'ai-tsu was an ex-Buddhist monk who, however, later
turned against the rebellion. He extended the Great Wall and
raised Neo-Confucianism to the status of state philosophy. It was
this more Sinocentric China that the European Jesuit missionaries
encountered when they arrived in China at the end of the Ming
dynasty (1368–1644) to found the modern China mission.

MODEL 3: COMPLEMENTARY LEVELS

The *first Portuguese ship* appeared in Chinese waters in 1514.
The event ushered in a new era for China. The Portuguese gained
a foothold in Canton and, a little later, in other port cities as well.
In 1567, they acquired formal permission to settle near Canton in
Macao, which was to become the oldest European colony in China.

Already in 1543 some Portuguese also found themselves on the
coast of Japan, where they spread the knowledge of firearms. Only
six years later, the *first Catholic missionaries* followed. *Francis
Xavier* won numerous followers by converting a few Japanese
chiefs (feudal lords) who expected their territories to benefit from
the trade relations between Macao and Europe. Later he decided
to try his luck in China, but died alone at the age of forty-six on a
small island within sight of the Chinese coast. This was in 1532, the
same year that the Italian Matteo Ricci was born. At fifty, the latter
went to Macao as a Jesuit missionary, there to become the really
great missionary to China. Ricci, along with Michele Ruggieri,
began to missionize in South China in 1583, a decisive date whose
four hundredth anniversary in 1983 was commemorated in the

People's Republic. Taiwan even organized a large international Ricci symposium in 1983 (an almost one thousand page Chinese and English volume with all the contributions to the symposium has been printed: *International Symposium on Chinese-Western Cultural Interchange in Commemoration of the 400th Anniversary of the Arrival of Matteo Ricci, S.J. in China*).

Indeed, *Matteo Ricci* was the outstanding figure of the Christian mission to China. Yet he did not even come onto the scene as a "Christian missionary." Having mastered written and spoken Chinese, he was rather presented as a philosopher and moralist, a mathematician and astronomer. Armed with learned books and new instruments (a much admired realistic map of the world, a telescope, prisms, clocks, but also religious paintings), he and his entourage linked themselves to the *ideal of the Confucian scholar*. They began to wear the dress of these scholars after having first associated themselves with popular Buddhism and having wandered about in the costume of Buddhist monks. In this mighty empire with its age-old incomparably high culture (printed books since the tenth or eleventh century)—about which they reported to an astonished Europe—these Jesuits were thus the first much admired representatives of a still premodern (pre-Copernican) European science that was nevertheless to develop extraordinarily rapidly in the succeeding century.

To put it differently, although Ricci and his people were entirely motivated for their missionary work, *mission* for them was *in no way identical with massive confrontation.* On the contrary, they attempted to accommodate themselves diplomatically to the Chinese scholarly milieu. They made themselves as familiar with the complicated forms of Chinese manners as with the old traditions, particularly the Chinese classics. They hoped thereby to be better able to proclaim the message of the one true God, the "Lord-on-high" or the "Lord of Heaven" in Chinese garb. They hoped in this way (and they were later reproached for this) to win for Christianity, not so much the masses, as primarily the elite—the political and social ruling class of educated officials (mandarins), and, where possible, the emperor himself. One could call such a procedure *indirect mission from above.*

What this means is that Ricci and Ruggieri, from 1601 in the imperial city of Peking, increasingly understood that Buddhism (its egoistic quest for wisdom was criticized) was not then the dominant *Weltanschauung* in China. It was *Confucianism,* renewed in the face of politico-moral decadence. Because of its undogmatic openness, its high individual and social ethic, its veneration of parents and ancestors, and its reverence for a highest essence (without a pantheon or divine myths), Confucianism seemed to be a much *better ally for Christianity* than popular Buddhism with its "idolatry" and its basically quite un-Chinese doctrine of the transmigration of souls. We have heard about this already.

Altogether the scholar from the West, Ricci at first did not build a church, but rather taught in a private academy, as was normal in China. At first, he did *not* want to initiate people into the (overly rational) *"mysteries" of the Christian faith* (Trinity, Incarnation). Was this illegitimate? Rational "fundamentals" such as God the creator of heaven and earth, immortality of the soul, reward of good, and punishment of evil are, after all, also basic to the Christian faith. Was this then Jesuit dishonesty, as some Chinese opponents along with Jacques Gernet suppose?

No, Ricci only practiced what has been normal in some Roman colleges until today: the *distinction* between *natural theology and revealed theology.* Educated in Thomistic theology, Ricci and his people did not want to offer a *Summa Theologiae* but rather, in a certain sense, a *Summa Contra Gentiles.* They wanted to start with *praeambula fidei,* the antechambers of faith, and this with critical recourse to original Confucianism. In his famous writing *The True Idea of the Lord of Heaven (T'ien-chu shih-i),* Ricci showed that the original Confucian texts, before they had been influenced by Buddhism and anti-Buddhism, already contained very rudimentary forms of analogous concepts to the Christian ideas of God *(Shang-ti* = Lord-on-high, or *T'ien* =Heaven) and life after death (cf. *The True Idea of the Lord of Heaven,* trans. Douglas Lancashire and Peter Hu Kuo-chen, S.J. [St. Louis, 1985]). There were indeed substantial differences between the Confucianism of the beginning and the Buddhist-influenced, philosophical Neo-Confucianism of the eleventh and twelfth centuries, which reduced Heaven to an abstract principle (paired with earth). Ricci himself preferred the more Biblical, personal God-concept of ancient China to the transpersonal principle *(li)* or the Great Ultimate *(T'ai-chi).* Nevertheless, the approach of the Jesuit missionaries was less popular than scholarly, less existential than objective, less theological than philosophical. Ricci was in fact able to win a few important and scientifically oriented literati as converts. Of course, in order to convince the Chinese more readily, the missionaries not infrequently reinterpreted the Chinese classical texts to suit their own purposes, while at the same time arguing from the standpoint of scholastic-Thomistic philosophy. *Thomistic building-block thinking brought with it all its problems:* in Ricci's "catechism," the name of Jesus is only mentioned once, in the margin! When some Chinese later discovered that Christians held a man named Jesus, who lived in the time of the Han dynasty, to be the Lord-on-high that the Chinese worshiped, they found this strange, even unbelievable. And it is more than a little irritating that Ricci, who was so tolerant on the "natural" level, was as intolerant when it came to baptism as any Tridentine Catholic: he demanded a complete break with the Confucian, Taoist, and Buddhist past, hence the burning of Buddha figures and tablets.

It is therefore not surprising that, in time, *opposition* arose to this so daringly executed *pedagogical and diplomatic adaptation.* Unfortunately, the opposition came from all sides. There was, first of all, the opposition of Buddhists who defended Buddhism against attack. Later there was also opposition from Confucians who questioned the Christian interpretation of the classical writings. Finally, there was the opposition from home. For oftentimes transparent reasons having to do with colonial, church, and religious order politics, Ricci's method was accused of being a sellout of Christianity.

MODEL 4: MISSIONARY CONFRONTATION

Around the year 1600, twenty years after Ricci's beginnings in China, there were ostensibly about three hundred thousand converts in Japan already. In China itself, of course, where Ricci and his friends had already toiled for two decades, the number of new converts barely exceeded one thousand. These, however, included many high officials, such as Li Chih-tsao and Hsü Kuang-ch'i, the later prime minister. As a German study has shown, the latter in particular was interested in Christianity not least as a means of enlightenment (as opposed to magic and superstition among the people) and for filling of the religious vacuum created by Confucianism. He, and undoubtedly many others with him, saw the Christian religion as something "to complement Confucianism and replace Buddhism" (cf. Monika Übelhör, *Hsü Kuang-ch'i (1562–1633) und seine Einstellung zum Christentum* [Hamburg, 1969], esp. p. 98).

In Macao, however, the church became increasingly impatient. Already during Ricci's lifetime, other missionaries such as Niccolo Longobardo began to preach in a simpler way to crowds. The Chinese must have increasingly seen this as *vile double-dealing:* for the educated, the Christians offered philosophy, morals, and science in harmony with Confucianism; for the simple people, however, they offered the most remarkable dogmas and miracle stories, which stood in contradiction to Confucian rationality. The Chinese authorities began to notice how, under the direction of foreigners, illegal Christian associations formed under the name of the "Doctrine of the Lord of Heaven" and sometimes launched into secret activities. The result was the *first expulsion of missionaries* in 1617, seven years after Ricci's death. The missionaries, meanwhile, either remained in secret or came back in greater numbers. A serious conflict was foreshadowed.

In response to the objections raised by new Japanese converts, Ricci's successor, Niccolo Longobardo, spoke up *against the prevailing use of Chinese names for God.* To avoid misunderstandings of content, and through fear of adulteration, the missionaries permitted *Latin theological concepts* to be translated into Chinese as well. In Japan, Francis Xavier already had experience introducing the Latin word for God, Deus, with a made-to-order Japanese-sounding "Deusu." Buddhist bonzes associated "Deusu" with the similar-sounding *daiuso,* which in Japanese means, of all things, "great lie." As a result, for the sake of the orthodox doctrine, not only were the three persons of the Trinity given Japanized forms (Deusu Patere, Deusu Hiiryo, and Deusu Supiritsu Santo), but also key theological concepts such as *persona* (person), *susutanshija* (substance), *garasa* (grace), and even *diidesu* (faith). All in all there were about fifty of these. In consequence, and in total contrast to Ricci's missionary method, the message of the Christian God had to appear to the Asians as a completely *foreign, Latin European import.* Christianity as a grafted-on religion! It did not seem to occur to anyone that using the original Greek and Hebrew words of the Bible would have been more consistent. Since the advent of the medieval paradigm, the equation "Christian = Catholic = Latin = Roman" had come to be taken for granted in the West. Now, with the Counter-Reformation, it became an actual necessity.

At first, however, Longobardo could not prevail among the Jesuits in China. Ricci's strategy continued to be followed. The big conflict, the actual *rites controversy,* only broke out later when, in 1634, Spanish Dominicans and Franciscans began to missionize in China (cf. Ludwig von Pastor, *History of the Popes* [St. Louis, 1941], vol. 33). These were at first offended by the fact that Chinese Christians were allowed to venerate their ancestors and Confucius, but then also by the use of the traditional Chinese names for God. Aside from arrogant and ignorant papal envoys, the rivalry between orders (Dominicans and Franciscans versus Jesuits) and different nationalities (Spain and France versus Portugal) undoubtedly played an often greater role in the subsequent showdown than the theological arguments themselves. In any case, the Jesuits were denounced in Rome by their rivals; and, once again, endless proceedings began in the *Sanctum Officium Sanctissimae Inquisitionis,* today rebaptized as the Sacred Congregation for the Doctrine of the Faith. Especially in France, where the Jansenists felt every argument against the Jesuits was justified, the conflict became a political issue. A flood of polemical writings and rejoinders washed over Europe.

In the meantime, the *mission in China* had made some *progress:* in 1670, a good one hundred years after Ricci's beginnings, one could count 273,780 Catholics, and the prospects for the future seemed good. In 1692, the greatest emperor of the new Manchu dynasty, *K'ang-hsi,* a man much admired in Europe as well, opened all of China to the preaching of the gospel with a renewed *edict of toleration.* Some Jesuits at the emperor's court even hoped for the conversion of the emperor, whom the philosopher, ecumenist, and diplomat Leibniz held to be the greatest prince of the contemporary world. As the Jesuit difficulties with respect to the Chinese rites and terms increased in Rome, Emperor K'ang-hsi sent the pope the requested official answer of the Chinese rites tribunal. It arrived in Rome in 1701 and made clear that, in China, Confucius was venerated not as a god but as a teacher; that the veneration of ancestors was a commemoration and not a worship service; and that the divine names T'ien and Shang-ti did not refer to the physical heavens, but to the Lord of heaven and earth and all things.

All of this was to no avail, as is well known. In 1704, Pope Clement XII, under threat of excommunication, forbade the Chinese Christians their ritual practice, the veneration of the ancestors and Confucius, and the use of both traditional names for God, Shang-ti (Supreme Lord) and T'ien (Heaven). Only the more recent Christian expression, T'ien-chu (Lord of heaven) was permitted. However, since the veneration of ancestors was in fact fundamental to Chinese social order, and the Confucian ethic was basic to its scale of values, this ruling actually meant that whoever wanted to become or remain a Christian had to cease being a Chinese.

There is no question that the pope made a wrong decision of historic proportions. The consequences for Christianity in China were catastrophic. Even Baron Ludwig von Pastor, a historian more inclined to be well disposed toward the papacy, could not comment on this decision without critical undertones: "The prohibition of the rites was a decision of incalculable consequences. Things were forbidden to the Chinese Christians which, in their estimation, were demanded by decency and good manners, and on the basis of an interpretation that was at variance with that given by Emperor Kanghi [sic] and the Chinese scholars" (Pastor, History of the Popes, vol. 33, p. 428). In 1710, over the objections of the Chinese apostolic vicars and the Jesuits, all this was confirmed and aggravated by a new decree from the Roman Inquisition. And the threat of excommunication issued against all authors of publications about rites and rites controversies has until today not been formally withdrawn.

It was under Emperor K'ang-hsi that the *Chinese reaction* to this provocation gradually set in. In 1717, the ruling of the nine highest courts in China was handed down: expulsion of the missionaries, proscription of Christianity, destruction of the churches, forced abjuration of Christian faith. The number of Catholics shrank quickly and restricted itself for the most part to farmers and fishermen, who lived separated and despised. The defense against oppositional currents and Christianity ended in a *dogmatization of Confucianism* along Roman lines, with similar fateful consequences for future development.

But it was only five years later, after the death of K'ang-hsi, that the real persecutions started. Rome remained unimpressed. In 1742, the energetic Benedict XIV confirmed the earlier decisions of the Inquisition with the bull *Ex quo singulari,* and "definitively" prohibited the Chinese rites. Two years later, the special Indian (Malabar) rites were also proscribed, and with them the missionary method of the Jesuit Roberto de Nobili, who had, like Ricci in China, led the way in India. These rites had likewise earlier been permitted. Was this then the end of the Christian mission in China? The lifework of Ricci and the Jesuits was certainly destroyed—by Rome. The missionaries, however, were to return, of course this time in an entirely different context.

MODEL 5: CULTURAL IMPERIALISM

In the nineteenth century, at the height of European nationalism, colonialism, and imperialism, there was a renewed wave of missions to China. This time, it included *Protestant missionaries* as well, usually of pietistic origin and fundamentalist faith. In the first half of the century, they met with the strong resistance of the Catholic countries and the British East India Company. The Protestant "weapon" was the Bible and the conviction was that, once translated, it would work all by itself. The first missionary to China sent by the London mission, *Robert Morrison,* had to reach China via America. He was able to do very little missionizing between 1807 and 1834 in Canton. Nevertheless, he was able to lay the groundwork for others with his Chinese grammar and Chinese translation of the Bible.

The missionary breakthrough came later. Even today, the Chinese remember the year 1842 only too well as a year of national disgrace, pure and simple. After the infamous British *Opium War* waged for the benefit of British opium exports from India to China (with massive profits for the English and horrendous consequences for the Chinese) and the so-called peace treaty of Nanking, in this year of 1842 China not only had to withdraw from Hong Kong, but also had to open five seaports to the Christian missions. An unspeakable humiliation exactly 150 years after Emperor K'ang-hsi's edict of toleration! The "unequal treaties" now juxtaposed two conditions: foreign merchants could sell opium all over China; and missionaries could spread the gospel all over China! And the Catholic church? For its part, the Roman curia likewise threw in its lot with the European powers. And the mission, whether Catholic or Protestant, was now an integral *part of the imperialistic calculations of the great European powers.*

Christianizing therefore now meant colonizing: the merchant, the soldier, and the missionary worked hand in hand! The *merchant* conquered new markets, so sorely needed by a depressed European industry. In the battle of economic competition, he was the outrider of the European quest for world dominance. The *soldier,* diverted to external conflicts from the internal social tensions of the European colonial powers, secured the economic and political interests, if necessary with naked military force. The *missionary*—like most whites, convinced of his racial superiority; all too often uncomprehending, tactless, and arrogant when dealing with indigenous traditions—was not selective about the means he used (treaty rights, litigation, bribery). He assured the dominance of Western civilization and culture in the church, the school, and the hospital.

Nor do the Chinese deny certain *benefits* of this European "colonization." From a scientific, technical, economic, and military point of view, the agrarian and bureaucratic society of China had fallen behind in the preceding centuries. The missions in particular brought benefits in the areas of education, worker and farmer welfare, and public health. Many missionaries and sisters selflessly took the part of the people in schools, hospitals, and churches. In the thirties of our century, around 35 percent of the Chinese elite still received a Christian education, while 90 percent of the nurses and 70 percent of the hospitals were Christian (D. B. Barrett, ed., *World Christian Encyclopedia* [Nairobi and Oxford, 1982]). But all this cannot hide the basic fact that China entered the twentieth century as a country that was economically exploited, highly restricted in its national independence, and threatened in its cultural identity—even though, owing to competition among the great powers (Russia and Japan had now entered onto the stage) and its own economic-cultural potential, China was never a real colony.

MODEL 6: ANTIMISSIONARY REACTION

This history of political, racial, cultural, and also religious colonialism and imperialism, combined with internal political stagnation and a conservative officialdom that resisted all modernization, provides the background. In such a context, is it any wonder that, within the space of a century, five very different *revolutionary movements* broke out in the country? And that, to a greater or lesser extent, they displayed a hostility to foreigners and were antimissionary?

First, there was the *Taiping movement* from 1850 to 1866. Combining misunderstood Christian ideas with old Chinese and Taoist elements, this movement proclaimed a "heavenly kingdom of ultimate peace" which it tried to bring about by force, in particular against missionaries and Christians. Here we already have a peasant revolt that demanded the abolition of private property and equal rights for women. In the process, large parts of China were completely devastated, Nanking was conquered and Peking threatened, and up to 20 million human lives were sacrificed. Ultimately, troops from eight "Christian" European states crushed the revolt in the service of the Chinese government and compelled enormous reparation payments before they withdrew.

Second, after all the coerced "unequal treaties" and the partition of China into European spheres of interest (the Tientsin massacre of 1870 was a warning), the great *Boxer Rebellion* broke out in 1900 under the banner of the "Fists of Uprightness and Concord." The Rebellion was full of hatred for the foreign legion from the imperialist West. Not only were the German envoy, Klemens von Ketteler, and many diplomats killed, but so were perhaps 250 foreign missionaries and around 30,000 Chinese converts, both branded as foreign or half-foreign "devils." And again, after the military intervention of an international expeditionary corps (Germany, France, England, Japan, the United States), a dictated peace (1901) was declared, complete with a Chinese expiatory legation to Berlin. While Japan, after 1867 (Meiji Restoration), opened itself to Western thinking, technology, and industry and laid the foundations for a modern industrial state, China still closed its doors to modernization, notwithstanding a few rudimentary beginnings.

Third, only a decade later, the great *national revolution of the Young Chinese* broke out in 1911–12. These were fascinated by Western secular science and democracy. The movement was led by Dr. Sun Yat-sen, a baptized Christian like his successor, General Chiang Kai-shek. The demands were democracy, nationalism, and public welfare. The world-historical consequences were the fall of the Manchu dynasty, the end of the 4,000-year-old empire, and the establishment of a republic. And yet, in 1924, Christian instruction was forbidden in the schools so that non-Christians would not be forced to take classes in Christian religion. After all, in the 1930s and 1940s, the Catholic church alone controlled around two thousand schools, three universities, and around two hundred hospitals. On the other hand, part of the picture was also that, during the Japanese war of aggression against China (1931–45), the Roman curia stood "neutral" on the side of militaristic Japan (early recognition of the Japanese puppet state Manchukuo). This was, after all, the same curia that, in 1933, made Hitler diplomatically presentable with a concordat, and that collaborated with fascist regimes in Spain, Portugal, and Vichy France.

The European missionaries had still barely comprehended what it meant for their missions that, with the First World War, China caught up with an *epochal change to a modern paradigm:* to modern science, technology, industry, and democracy. Antireligious, secularistic, and anti-Christian thinking were widespread. Yet the Protestant and Catholic missionaries could not even agree on the most basic issues, the names of God. The Protestants opted for Shang-ti (Lord-on-high), while the Catholics held to T'ien-chu

(Lord of heaven), the name introduced by Ricci. The result is that, in our century, Protestantism and Catholicism still use different Bibles and appear to many Chinese (including many Christians) to be two religions with two different Gods. The Catholics are the "believers in T'ien-chu" while the Protestants are the "believers in Shang-ti" (called "Christians" = "believers in Chi-tu"). There is therefore no common Chinese name for all Christians. No one wanted to listen to insightful Christian missionaries such as the Anglican Roland Allen (1869–1947). Already during the First World War, he appealed to the New Testament in demanding indigenous churches that would support themselves in complete independence, would administer themselves, and would propagate themselves. Thus, already here, long before the Communists, we have the Three Selfs!

Only in 1939, around 350 years after Ricci's death, did Pius XII finally revise those "definitive" papal decisions in the sense of Ricci and de Nobili: he published decrees of toleration regarding the veneration of ancestors and the names of God. The implementation of these was, however, the object of official ecclesiastical delay in China itself for many years. Other concerns had come to the fore there in the meantime. The question was no longer whether one worshiped Confucius or the ancestors. The central problem was the resistance against the Japanese conquerors and also the unchecked rise of the Chinese *Communist Party* (1924–34; 1947–49). Indeed, once again a revolution, the *fourth* revolutionary movement in our count, was under way. This one had both a national (against the Japanese) and a social (mobilization of the peasants) dimension. Because of the whole previous history, it too was radically opposed to Christianity as an "imperialistic foreign religion," and especially to Rome.

As nuncio in Germany, cardinal secretary of state, and pope, Pius XII carried the main responsibility for the "neutral" stand of the Vatican in the face of Nazism (concordat with Hitler, silence on the Jewish question), Southern European fascism, and Japanese imperialism. In 1946, after the Second World War, this same Pius XII finally established an independent Chinese ecclesiastical hierarchy (in good Roman fashion, with 20 archbishops, 79 bishops, 38 apostolic prefectures, and 1 "mission"): it was "definitively" too late. Three years later, instead of Christianity, Marxism-Leninism became the official religion—rather, the quasi-religion, the official ideology—of a billion Chinese and their neighbors. On September 21, 1949, Mao Tse-tung proclaimed the *People's Republic of China* along Soviet lines. This was an epochal event whose permanent significance should be recognized by Christians today as well. For the first time in the modern era, China was freed from the influence of foreign powers, had gained its complete independence (ultimately even from the "fraternal" Soviet Union), and had once again discovered its national pride! This of course included the sacrifice of millions, the extensive destruction of the family group ("people's communes"), and the battle against Confucianism and the Christian church.

For the anti-Communist Christian churches in China, this was a *catastrophe.* In 1950-51, all foreign missionaries were expelled, often under ignominious circumstances (over 5,000 Catholic priests and religious). The Catholic press was banned, and all schools were confiscated, as were the hospitals, charitable institutions, and all church property. The Roman internuncio was expelled. All Chinese priests and laypeople were called upon to speak out against imperialism, feudalism, and bourgeois thinking, and to join the so-called *Three Self Movement:* self-support, self-administration, self-propagation of the churches. Most *Protestant* Christians (1.3 million Protestants, especially in the cities and among the educated, when the Communists came to power) saw no difficulty in 1951 in declaring themselves for these three autonomies. They had already largely disengaged themselves from foreign influence in the previous decades. The state therefore gave them official recognition. And what did *Rome* do?

Pius XII, who in 1950 condemned all the newer directions in Catholic theology and then proclaimed a new Marian dogma, also ceremoniously condemned the Three Selfs in 1952-54. He forbade Chinese Catholics (3.25 million, mostly in the countryside and among simple people) any cooperation with the Communist regime. Also forbidden was of course membership in unions or Communist associations, as was reading of Communist newspapers, magazines, and books. In 1951, in the midst of the Chinese battle against Americans in Korea, Rome named an American the archbishop of Yangchow! As if enough epochal errors had not already been committed, the Vatican now turned completely toward Taiwan. In 1952, the regime there received diplomatic recognition, the Vatican chargé d'affaires who was expelled from Peking was accredited in Taipei, and Taipei was erected as an archbishopric.

The break between Peking and the Vatican was complete. Once again, it seemed to be impossible in China to be both Christian (at least Catholic) and Chinese. And after all missionaries were either expelled or imprisoned (in 1958, around 30 bishops who remained loyal to Rome were in prison), no bishops were appointed anymore. Since 1957, the Chinese Catholics have been officially grouped in the Catholic Patriotic Association. When, following the old church tradition, these finally elected their own bishops and notified the Vatican, these bishops (at the time, around 50) were hit with excommunication, even though they had been validly consecrated. The upshot of this, as is so often the case, completely insensitive Roman policy was a split within the Chinese Catholic church itself into an official "patriotic" church and an unofficial, underground church (with priests, but virtually no more bishops).

The suffering of the church in China was to increase still more. In 1966, Mao initiated the *Great Proletarian Cultural Revolution* of the youthful Red Guards, the *fifth* revolutionary movement. Under the banner of the fight against the Four Olds (old customs, old manners, old ideas, old culture), this movement also turned against everything religious. Like Buddhist monasteries, Taoist temples, and Muslim mosques, the Christian churches were closed, destroyed, or turned to profane uses. The "patriotic" church, bishops, priests, and many faithful were also affected: they were persecuted for their faith or condemned to forced labor or imprisonment. For example, the spiritual leader of the official Catholic church in China, Bishop Jin Luxian of Shanghai, was imprisoned from 1955 to 1973. Like other institutions of Chinese society, the Christian churches outwardly collapsed completely along with the other religions. Only in Hong Kong, Taiwan, South Korea, and Southeast Asia was Christianity able to progress in the decades after the Second World War.

And yet, on Mao's death ten years after the beginning of the Cultural Revolution (1976), the state and the party struck out in a new direction, adopting a *pragmatic policy toward religion.* Then it became evident that Chinese Christianity had not disappeared completely, but had remained alive through smaller groups and "house meetings." These have to a large extent been maintained. Nevertheless, at the same time, currently around seven hundred Catholic churches (including the cathedrals of Peking and Shanghai) are once again open to the public (cf. Jean Charbonnier, *Guide to the Catholic Church in China* [Singapore, 1986]). It is the same with hundreds of Protestant churches. Also, both churches have seminaries at their disposal and are increasingly able to publish translations of the Bible (and, before long, the Documents of the Second Vatican Council). And so, after an exceptionally difficult, horrendous test of their faith—the only thing beneficial about the state oppression was that it forced unity—the churches are apparently moving toward a "postdenominational," ecumenical era.

But let there be no illusions. Article 36 of the revised 1982 *constitution* reads, "The citizens of the People's Republic of China enjoy freedom of religious belief. No organ of the State, [no] public organizations or individual shall compel citizens to believe in religion or disbelieve in religion. The state protects legitimate religious activities." Yet it also says (and here lies the problem for the Vatican), "No religious affairs may be dominated by any foreign country." This new policy will therefore not lead to renewed permission for European and American missions and to foreign domination. Even in the future, every Chinese government may well adhere to the demands of the Three Selfs of 1950: self-support, self-administration, and self-propagation of the Chinese church.

What should one do now? According to my understanding of the local situation, and following many discussions, only the pressing appeal to the Vatican now remains. Rome should consent to the liberalization in China and take a step toward reconciliation in order to end the split between the official and the underground church. The validly consecrated bishops should be recognized as legitimate, and the selection of new bishops by indigenous ecclesiastical groups should be permitted.

Is the Chinese revolution an event without analogy in history? In this case, *parallels from the time of the French Revolution* come to mind. It is well known that the revolutionary regime that came to power in 1789 nationalized all church property, dissolved various monasteries and orders, and absorbed ecclesiastical administration into the functions of the state. The choice of pastors was transferred to the citizens, and that of bishops to the governmental administrations of the *départements*. When the clergy resisted and almost every second one refused to take the required oath to the new constitution, around forty thousand priests (refusing to take the oath) were driven out of France in 1792. This resulted in two churches: a "constitutional" one and an underground church with its own episcopate. This, as everybody knows, did not prevent Rome from negotiating a concordat with Napoleon in 1801, one that revealed a pragmatic accommodation to the historical circumstances. Rome recognized the republic as the legitimate government of France; the Catholic church received governmental recognition not as the state religion, but as the *de facto* "religion of the vast majority of French citizens." The clergy was to take the state oath of allegiance; the bishops were to select the pastors (subject to government approval). The bishops would be nominated by the state but canonically installed by the pope. This is what happened in France. And in China? Some pragmatic resolution of the problems may well not be out of the question there either. And the more quickly it comes, the more help it will be to Chinese Christianity.

At the same time, though, the plea is also directed to the *Catholics in China:*

• Let the priests and the faithful of both the official and the unofficial, underground churches forgive each other.

• Let the injustice and suffering inflicted on Chinese Catholics from without (by the Vatican and the imperialist powers) and within (by the government, the Red Guards, or each other) be forgotten.

• Let them become reconciled with each other, with Rome, and with the Chinese Communist Revolution and thereby offer the world a witness of Christian love that clears the way for sensible political action. For China is also waiting for the realization of a new model of Christianity.

MODEL 7: CONTEXTUAL INCULTURATION

Between outward harmonization (model 1: Nestorianism) and syncretic mixture (model 2: Manichaeanism) on the one side, and missionary confrontation (model 4: seventeenth and eighteenth centuries), cultural imperialism (model 5: nineteenth and twenti-eth centuries), and antimissionary reaction (model 6: twentieth century) on the other, a further type of encounter between Christianity and China is conceivable. Such an encounter would envisage not only a complementary synthesis (model 3: Ricci), but also a genuine *indigenization,* the *taking root* of Christianity in Chinese soil. This is contextual inculturation (model 7).

The text is one and the same everywhere; the Gospel, but in the context of Chinese culture. More than an outward accommodation or acculturation, this gospel would achieve a deep rooting, an *inculturation,* of Christianity in Chinese society. This model wants no more missionary import of Christianity from the outside, no more simple translation of Western theology into Chinese concepts. Rather, we should seek a reflection and realization of Christian faith from within the sociocultural context of contemporary China and in the framework of an independent (self-supporting, self-administering, self-propagating) church.

What do we mean by culture here? The culture of the past? Not primarily. It is, after all, quite questionable to what extent, for instance, the Chinese classics or even Neo-Confucian thought as such still influences contemporary thinking. Certainly no one wants to return to prerevolutionary China, despite all the revolutionary excesses. No, what we mean is the *culture of the present.* This is a culture that, even outside the People's Republic, has been to a large extent secularized; and yet it is still under the subterranean, strongly individualizing influence of the old religions and earlier paradigms of Chinese history. As such, Marxist ideologies and faith in positivistic science are spiritual challenges to be taken as seriously (cf. Küng, *Does God Exist?*) as the traditional religious-intellectual currents of Confucianism, Taoism, and Buddhism.

This *process of secularization,* characterized by the industrialization, urbanization, and modernization of life and the broad development of communication techniques, is of course a fact. This is not only the case for large urban industrial agglomerations from Shanghai to Chengtu. Even in previously isolated village culture all the way to Central Asia and Tibet, it has progressed amazingly far. A return to premodern circumstances is out of the question. The presence of radio, television, videocassettes, and transportation media is already enough to assure this. Many religious usages have disappeared as a result, even outside of the People's Republic; but quite a bit of superstition, crippling fear, and slavish obedience also—along with a lot of other things associated with "religion" that were there for the diversion, intimidation, or consolation of the people.

Yet, after forty years of Communist rule, the Confucian legacy persists in the form of the Chinese sense of the family, cosmic unity, and personal conscience of the individual. In the wake of the Cultural Revolution, the enthusiasm even of the youth (and around half of China's population, about five hundred million, are young people under sixteen) for the old Communist ideals has cooled considerably. Suppressed religiosity is returning in various forms. Unlike Mao, his predecessor, Deng Xiaoping is seeking a certain synthesis of Marxism and Confucianism.

The field research of the young German scholar Thomas H. Hahn offers an impressive corroboration of the *reawakening of religiosity* in China today. Over the course of two years (September 1984–September 1986), Hahn collected data from thirty-eight Buddhist and Taoist monasteries all over China, an unprecedented and unique empirical investigation. His results are in fact amazing. First, at least on the local level (if not on the provincial or even national level), there are manifestations of old religious beliefs and practices. Second, many of these manifestations are not in accord with the laws of the state; but the state authorities can no longer keep up with the pace of development. Third, the state authorities quietly tolerate such developments according to the motto "First build the temple, then make a report." Fourth, the revival of old traditions is connected with economic questions ("When the land blooms, then so do its gods"). To be sure, the numbers cannot be compared with those of the year 1940. What is also important, however, is that the advanced secularization of the modern cities apparently has only had a limited effect on the mass of people with respect to their attitude toward religion. In sum, "thirty-seven years of communist rule have not quite quenched the common people's thirst for security, peace, wealth and health. If those basic questions remain unanswered, the turn to supernatural authority is only natural and stringent" ("New Developments Concerning Buddhist and Daoist Monasteries in the People's Republic of China" [unpublished manuscript]).

Therefore, rather than lament the manifest breakdown of the tradition in the spirit of an undifferentiated cultural pessimism, one should rely on the *adaptive, assimilative, and integrative power of the great religions* that has proven itself over the millennia. Accordingly, the Chinese classic authors and the Neo-Confucian thinkers should not simply be repeated, but rather interpreted "forward" from the critical hermeneutical viewpoint of today. The deeply humanistic spirit of the Chinese tradition should be taken up, and at the same time, its transcendent dimension should be made clear again for today, as we heard at the end of Julia Ching's exposition. After what has been said thus far, it would seem beyond question that valuable impulses and support exist for the encounter of traditional Chinese religions with Christianity. The latter underwent and to some extent survived secularization a great deal earlier. And it is precisely in the face of modern secularity and threatening atheistic banality that ecumenical dialogue among the religions has its particular significance.

A contextual Chinese Christian theology does not need to refer primarily to the classical authors. Rather, what is required is an *analysis of the complexity of the present* for the sake of *survival in the future.* And today, this analysis definitely includes a *critique of the development of modernity.* In China, after all, the modern paradigm was delayed, but then it was introduced and enforced with breathtaking speed, radicalness, and universality, so that ultimately it ran into crisis quickly with a Cultural Revolution that wound up negating culture. In the light of this history, it must be asked whether, in China especially, the ambivalence of modern development—the already variously emphasized ambivalence of modern development—the already variously emphasized ambivalence of modern science, technology, industry, and democracy ("people's democracy")—has not become so visible that henceforth one will have to follow a twofold policy:

• On the one hand, one must continue the current propagation of "modernization" in the underdeveloped areas (agriculture, industry, science—and the military?).

• On the other hand, one must realize and take into account that "alternative" tendencies *toward a postmodern society* can be observed on a global basis already.

Put differently, because of its greatly delayed modernization, China has the opportunity to learn from the negative experience of the highly modern states and to mitigate in its own development the immanent destructive forces of modern science, technology, industry, and democracy. Critical voices such as that of the physics professor Fang Lizhi, called by many the Sakharov of China, deserve to be heard in the interest of China. This is especially true when, undoubtedly speaking for a great many intellectuals, he calls for more democracy, for reform, and for academic freedom. All too infrequently have the intellectuals in Chinese society filled the function of the "conscience of civilization," as the student newspaper of Peking University pointed out in its sensational article about Fang Lizhi in July 1985. This newspaper emphasized the high moral character of this important scholar and recalled a long tradition of intellectuals who have resisted authority out of moral conviction and have been ready to accept personal disadvantage for the sake of the truth. What is amazing is above all that the question of religion received a new valuation in this article: "Our attitude to the entire religious question bears rethinking. We naively assume that Western religions reveal ignorance, but fail to realize that modern Western religion is a vigorous tradition infused with contemporary meanings. Western religion is also a means of experiencing such emotions as love, friendship and compassion. On the other hand, was not the Cultural Revolution, which we claimed to be a greater boon to mankind than the Western Renaissance, an effort to deify certain people in the name of revolution? And did not the Cultural Revolution drag China into ignorance and darkness?" (Quoted in *China Spring Digest* 1 [March/April 1987], p. 8. Cf., in this regard, the life story of a woman from the Cultural Revolution, Nien Cheng, "Life and Death in Shanghai," *Time,* June 15, 1987.)

In the China of modern times, religion has understandably been seen as outdated, antiprogress, and immoral because of its opposition to science, technology, industry, and democracy. Often it has been ignored, suppressed, and persecuted. But, in fact, *religion has a new chance:* the chance to renew society, provided that it renews itself internally and orients itself toward the future. For the Christian churches and their theology in China this means concretely

• the maintenance and further development of the *moral and spiritual integrity of Christians,* (so marveled at by non-Christians during the chaotic Cultural Revolution), working together with many Chinese intellectuals who feel themselves committed to moral values;

• a Christian *basic movement* entirely from below, consisting of small communities that are concretely concerned with the living human person, without the rigid authoritarianism of before;

• an *alliance* of especially the Protestant denominations into a church with common leadership and common training facilities; hopefully, also a certain ecumenical opening of the Catholic church. And what does this mean for theology?

A CHINESE THEOLOGY FOR THE POSTMODERN AGE

Indeed, what does it mean for *theology and the church to take root* with a view to the postmodern situation in China? Four basic hermeneutical premises seem to me to be indispensable for a postmodern theology, whether it functions more in an ecclesiastical or a university milieu, in a sociopolitical or a cultural-religious setting.

1. There must be a clear reorientation to the *original, Biblical faith* and not to some confessional, Western-ecclesiastical doctrine

such as has caused so much division in Chinese Christianity over the centuries. The Christian message that came out of Judaism does not need a traditionally Hellenistic, Roman, Germanic, or Anglo-Saxon garment. It can and should be clad—postmodern means postcolonial and postimperialistic!—in Chinese garb.

2. Therefore, there must also be a broad-minded *reformulation* of the original faith from people's contemporary experience, from the contemporary sociopolitical situation. Just as, in the West, it is no longer necessary in order to be a Christian to be against Galileo and Darwin, against the French and Russian revolutions, so too in China today, it is no longer necessary to be oriented against Mao and the Chinese Revolution in order to live as a Christian. Even in China, being authentically contemporary and being authentically Christian are no longer mutually exclusive.

3. There must be an orientation toward *practical example.* If the church's proclamation is to be both scriptural and contemporary, it must be oriented more toward concrete realization in Chinese society than toward dogmatic correctness and strict orthodoxy. The time of persecution was a hard lesson in this regard. The practical Christian witness of the individual and the Christian community had and has particular significance even today in this secularized Chinese society. In China, Christian communities that concentrate on the welfare of people and not just on themselves can be a ferment of societal development.

4. There must be a *renewal of culture through religion.* A contextual Chinese Christianity, with all its aesthetic, moral, and political implications, can make a constructive contribution to ethics and education, to the discovery and preservation of the humane values in the lives of the nation and the individual. Today obviously, this only makes sense in the spirit of a dialogue between partners, and in working together with people and groups from other religions and ideologies—without an exclusive claim to salvation. Yet a contextual Christianity could come to function as an example for all of Asia. For what happens when growing economic progress is accompanied by religious indifference and apathy, by positivism in science and utilitarianism in everyday life? In short,

what happens wherever a purely materialistic attitude begins to assert itself, whether this be in China or Japan, in Korea or Taiwan, in Hong Kong or Singapore? There is an increase in the sense of meaninglessness, in lack of commitment, in moral permissiveness, and in the loss of a spiritual home. Christian theology and church could help the East avoid the notorious errors of the West.

The few Chinese theologians just beginning to appear are today faced with a task of historic proportions. But they do not stand alone—not even the Taiwanese theologians, who have until now given more thought to inculturation than those on the mainland (pioneers include Bishops Ch'eng Shi-kuang and Stanislaus Lokuang, as well as the theologians Paul Welte, Luis Gutheinz, Fang Chih-jung, Chang Ch'un-shen, and Wang Hsien-chih). In all of Sinicized territory—especially in Japan (the great pioneers there are Heinrich Dumoulin and Maurus Heinrichs) but also in the rest of East Asia (Philip Shen and Peter Lee are representative for many others)—individual Christian theologians (still far too few of them women) and many study groups and faculties are working on an *independent* Asian Christian theology. The 1987 report of the Committee on Theological Concerns (CTC) of the Christian Conference of Asia (CCA) remarked in a retrospect (by General Secretary Wang Hsien-chih) on the eight years of its existence, that various *Asian theologies* have developed out of their national contexts which are quite different from those of Europe and America, but also from Latin American theology. Among them:

- the *minjung* (=people's) theology of Korea;

- the homeland theology in Taiwan;

- the theology of struggle in the Philippines;

- the theology of captivity in Sri Lanka;

- the theology of development in Indonesia. . . .

A contextual *Chinese* theology will be distinct from all these theologies. Yet it would do well to keep in mind the larger problems of an Asian theology in the broad sense.

PROBLEMS OF ASIAN THEOLOGY

According to the just-mentioned report, the five *problems* in the forefront in these Asian theologies are as follows:

1. *People and Country.* Why? Because these theologians are often dealing with people who are economically exploited, politically oppressed, culturally despised, and socially marginalized. They are also dealing with countries that are divided (Korea, Sri Lanka), internally insecure (Hong Kong, Taiwan), or subject to strong ethno-religious tensions (India, Malaysia, Indonesia). A contextual Christian theology must attempt to lead the way in a multi-racial and multireligious situation.

2. *Religion and Ideology.* Why? Because in many Asian countries, Christian theology is faced with a situation in which political ideologies (such as communism) have become quasi-religions—or in which, on the other hand, the indigenous religion (above all in the form of folk religion) all too often has the effect of enslaving the people rather than freeing them psychologically and politically (for example, the Philippines or Korea). These religions encourage powerlessness, resignation, the yearning for consolation, and even a false need for security. A contextual Christian theology will have to distance itself from both secularist ideologies and religions that enslave; and it will have to take the part of religion in the interest of social, individual, and spiritual liberation.

3. *Technology and Ecology.* Why? Because increasingly, Asian theology is finding itself in opposition to developments that declare technology and industrialization to be "national goals" but actually only benefit the ruling elites of the respective countries. For the natural environment and the people, on the other hand, the developments often have catastrophic consequences. A contextual theology has to prepare the ground for the awakening of a greater sensitivity in the people themselves to the ecological damage caused by the economy. This would apply to highly developed countries such as Japan, to threshold countries, and in the end to underdeveloped countries as well.

4. *Militarization and Power.* Why? Because increasingly, Asian theology is finding itself having to oppose state ideologies that identify the state and the people, and that result usually in militarism, sometimes in state terrorism. Even in Asia, a bloated military-industrial complex is gobbling up enormous quantities of money, intellect, and technology. It is also increasing dependence on the superpowers. It must be resisted out of religious conviction; so must that concentration of economic and political power that leads to absolute control over mass media and the educational system, and thus *de facto* to corruption and the suppression of human rights. This resistance would also apply in the case of a remilitarization (introduced under cover of the old *tenno* ideology) of Japan (raising of the defense budget above and beyond the hitherto constitutionally stipulated norm).

5. *Women, Youth, and Workers.* Why? Because a contextual Asian Christian theology is seeing itself increasingly confronted with the problem

• that the life of Asian women suffers under a patriarchal authoritarianism;

• that young people feel oppressed in a repressively hierarchical educational system (brain drain as a result of brainwashing);

• that, finally, the workers in particular will increasingly begin to feel the exploitative structures of the economic system.

Therefore, a Christian theology in an Asian context will have to work for a change of consciousness so that women, young people, and workers will be able to avail themselves of their full human rights—and so that the quality and opportunities of life will be guaranteed for all.

The question is therefore whether, after the horrific experiences of modern and recent times in all these problem areas, religion in *China* will not prove to be more of a constructive force for social change than a backward-looking institution. Undoubtedly the situation is different in China than, for instance, in the Philippines or Korea. Yet, however that may be, it must be kept in mind that Christian theology can only properly tackle the problems just discussed if it also reflects on *what is proper to it,* if it seeks to gain a new contextual understanding of its own *text:* the *Christian message* (cf., in this regard, Küng, *Theologie im Auf-bruch).* In the process, what is outdated should rightly be dropped, and the new should just as evidently be integrated. Now, particularly in the Chinese context, what should be the main focal points of such a critically constructive theological self-reflection?

FOCAL POINTS OF CHINESE THEOLOGY: UNDERSTANDING OF GOD, CHRIST, AND SPIRIT

The Chinese Christian Fu P'ei-jung, one of a generation of young philosophers in Taiwan, lists ten theses for Christian-Chinese dialogue. My "Christian responses" in this book have in large part tried to discuss these. I hope that these will render a service as well, especially to my Christian brothers and sisters in East Asia. The discussion must indeed determine the relation between specifically Chinese and specifically Christian concerns (cited from A. B. Chang Ch'un-shen, *Dann sind Himmel und Mensch in Einheit. Bausteine chinesischer Theologie* [Freiburg, 1984], pp. 70–73);

• between the goodness of human nature (China) and the doctrine of original sin, between human capabilities (freedom) and the gracious action of God;

• between the unity of Heaven with the human being (China), between God and the human person, between immanence and transcendence;

• between being cocreator on the one hand (Chinese preference for process) and human awareness of being a creature on the other;

• between universal harmony (China) and the mystical union with God;

• between the figure of Confucius on the one hand, and the figure of Christ on the other; between the *jen* of the Confucians and the love of the Christians;

• between morals and religion, the unity of knowing and doing (China); between faith and action, between theory and practice.

This is all a kind of "agenda" for a further dialogue between Christianity and China. In what follows, I want to try and point to certain more classical focal points of a theological self-reflection in the very different Chinese (but also in the wider East Asian) context. What could all this mean for a Chinese understanding of God, Christ, and the spirit?

1. A Chinese *understanding of God?* "Heaven" is of course the key word here. Obviously, a Christian can say "heaven" instead of "God"; for what else is heaven than a symbol for God himself? Judaism from early on also did not dare to pronounce the name of Yahweh out of reverence. It used other, indirect titles so that, for instance, the Gospel of Matthew, which originated in a Jewish-Christian milieu, could say "Kingdom of heaven" instead of "Kingdom of God." Would this not be a way for the "correspondence of the human person and Heaven," the ideal of China, to be an expression for the Christian notion of the correspondence of the human person and God?

And yet the Chinese talk of Heaven as much as the Christian talk of the Father in heaven will have to be scrutinized to determine whether today, in the era of space exploration, this word is still what it once was; whether it does not evoke too many erroneous associations; whether it has not lost some of its power for symbolizing ultimate reality. One will have to consider whether it would not sometimes be better to work with philosophical concepts such as the Great Ultimate *(T'ai-chi)* or the Great One *(T'ai-i)*, which allow a transcendent dimension, God, to be felt in the macrocosm and in the microcosm, *in* ourselves.

Moreover, it must be borne in mind that, although Chinese thinking has from its origins been very closely tied to the recurring natural rhythms, its contact with Marxism (and Marxism's secularized eschatological view of history) has brought it to much closer contact than one might assume with the original Judeo-Christian way of thinking. But Judeo-Christian historical thinking has a forward orientation: it uses the prophetic anticipation of God's future to change the present. Accordingly, a Chinese-Christian understanding of God and the world would have to take into account not only the natural harmony of the whole, the correspondence of heaven and earth that is a given from the beginning. In addition, while continuing and at the same time religiously overcoming the Marxist notion of the future, such an understanding would have to include a future that is actively to be created in a changing world with an impulse toward development.

As far as the *symbolism* for a Chinese understanding of God is concerned, the suggestion of the Japanese theologian Masao Takenaka will have to be taken into consideration. He has written a small but very thought-provoking book with the title *God Is Rice.* Does this suggest a solution? In the first place, the title, taken from the poem of a Korean, would seem to be subject to misunderstanding. Obviously, Takenaka does not simply want to make rice, as a food, into God (rice Christians—this word immediately awakens the worst associations). On the other hand, however—and this is the essential point—rice in Asia is in fact a more natural food than bread and therefore the more comprehensible religious symbol. For the Chinese, bread is nothing but a European import. Significantly, the Japanese even use the Spanish-Portuguese word *pan* to designate it. To put it concretely, for all of Sinicized Asia, the supplication from the Lord's Prayer would be more meaningfully translated as "Give us this day our daily *rice.*"

- Rice symbolizes life, the gift of Heaven, the gift of God.

- Rice symbolizes harmony with nature, with the entire cosmos.

- Rice symbolizes the togetherness of people, eating together and sharing together.

Could this not therefore be expressed in the celebration of the Eucharist? Where the rice cake is *broken,* it becomes the sign of the self-sacrifice of Christ. Indeed, it brings to mind the "living rice-bread which came down from heaven" (Jn. 6:51). Rice would thus be in the symbolic center of the Christian Chinese community as necessity of life and as sign of the sacrifices of the one for the many and of the many for each other.

2. A Chinese *understanding of Christ?* Such an understanding ought to dispense with abstract conceptualizations using Greek and Latin terms. These were often the danger of the Western metaphysical tradition. Rather, in accord with the European historical-narrative tradition in Christology, such understanding should be oriented more strongly to the living historical figure of Jesus Christ (on this tradition, cf. Hans Küng, *On Being a Christian* [Garden City, N.Y., 1976]). Has Chinese thinking not been primarily historically oriented for around three thousand years? What we are after is therefore not a conservative, speculative, and metaphysical interpretation of Jesus. Rather, we want a historical and practical, a contemporary interpretation. The Korean theologian Ahn Byung-Mu has set forth an impressive version in his exegesis of the Gospel of Mark. Here, Jesus Christ is the man of the *minjung,* of the alienated "people" without power or possessions. He is one of these people; he speaks their language. All his life, he identified himself with them right up to his violent end. And in his announcement of the coming Kingdom of heaven, he ushered in the end of the old world and the creation of a new world. This is a Jesus, therefore, who "together with the suffering minjung" fights "at the front of this advent." It is from him that God's will is revealed "in the event of the love of Jesus for the minjung and in the identification of Jesus with the minjung" (Ahn Byung-Mu, *Minjung: Theologie des Volkes Gottes in Südkorea,* ed. Jürgen Moltmann [Neukirchen, 1984], p. 132).

Generally speaking, the proclamation of the Kingdom of God and the passion should be centrally placed in a contextual Asian Christology. Jesus is the crucified

• whose spirit can already now transform society and the heart of the individual;

• who, as the living one, has something decisive to say to all the crucified people of Asia who are so often in a life-and-death struggle;

• who is the incarnated demand for more humanity against the divinization of traditions, institutions, organizations, and persons;

• who stands for the one God; who identifies with the weak, the powerless, the downtrodden, and the persecuted; who demands justice for children, widows, strangers, and the poor; who promises deliverance from all evil and also victory over death.

Victory over death because death is not the last thing, but rather God, the last and the first. This is already expressed in very different ways in the New Testament. Luke gives us a visible representation. Jesus is awakened to new life and raised to God. Using a legendary form of the story that is unique to Luke, the crucified one is designated as the one who "ascended into heaven." Does this version not to some degree justify the discussion among Chinese theologians as to whether the risen Jesus Christ could not be characterized with the designation *"man of heaven"?* Such considerations were occasioned by the interpretation of the "man of heaven" given by the non-Christian philosopher Fang Tung-mei: "The 'man of heaven' perfects his life. He fulfils his own nature as well as those of human beings and things. He supports the generation of life by 'heaven-earth' and partakes in 'heaven-earth.' In the Confucian view, the human person reaches his goal in being a creator with God. In the Taoist view, according to Chuang-tzu, it is that person who has 'heaven' as his or her deepest origin, the inner strength *(te)* as her source, and the *tao* as his or her form of expression. Taoism also calls him the 'man of the summit,' the 'holy,' the 'authentic man.' He can accompany the divinity, savor 'heaven-earth,' nourish all things, be connected with all things under heaven. He instructs the simple folk, knows about the beginning and the end, is identical in every direction, with large and small, coarse and fine. He is present everywhere, i.e., the influence of life fills every place in the world" (quoted in Chang Ch'un-shen, *Himmel und Mensch*, p. 87).

The Sinologist Robert P. Kramers relates another fascinating attempt at Christology, this time not from the Taoist, but from the Confucian tradition. This is the attempt of the Taiwanese theologian Hu Tsan-yün. He seeks to understand the figure of Jesus in the light of the Confucian conviction that Heaven and the human are essentially the same. In Jesus, the "possibility of the human becoming one with God" found its most complete expression. He, Jesus, is the answer to what the Chinese have been seeking for thousands of years, the "unknown person." He is the "solution to the problem of the identity of the human essence and the way of Heaven" (in *Evangelische Missionszeitschrift* 23 [1966], pp. 87–101, esp. p. 92).

Naturally, every title such as "man of heaven" or the "unknown person" raises numerous Christological questions that cannot be taken up in this description of theological focal points. Yet it should not be overlooked that the Jesus who was rescued from death can in fact be understood in different ways. According to Paul, Jesus, as the one raised to God, possesses God's power, strength, *spirit* to such an extent that he not only has the spirit at his disposal, but, through the resurrection, can even himself be understood as spirit (1 Cor. 15:46; 2 Cor. 3:17). This means that the Lord who has been awakened to God's life now has the existence and mode of action of the spirit. Yet, what does this mean? Here we see a new theological focal point of the coming Chinese theology.

3. A Chinese *understanding of spirit?* The Chinese theologian Chang Ch'un-shen has translated "Holy Spirit" with *ch'i.* He has thus chosen one of those ancient Chinese words that can hardly be rendered adequately in the Western world. It means air, breath, breath of life (one is reminded of Taoist medicine), an inner energy, psychological power connected with blood and breathing. It is a vital, dynamic, original power that permeates the entire universe, indeed, all things (macrocosmic and microcosmic), and leads to an ultimate unity. *Ch'i* must therefore be understood like the "spirit" of the Biblical witness. The spirit, of course, never appears as an independent being but always needs a substrate as support and basis of action. As an utterly dynamic, living, and vital force, it works throughout all the dimensions of the All, from matter up to the level of the human spirit. For the believer, it should be the subject not so much of conceptual analysis as of living experience. "On both sides, *ch'i* or spirit belongs not only to the cosmic and natural life-world, but is also closely connected with the moral dimension of human life. And over and above this, it serves as the mysterious bridge between God and the human person" (Chang Ch'un-shen, *Himmel und Mensch*, p. 122).

Such a "spiritual" view of reality makes it possible to take *transcendence and immanence,* God being in the world and the world being in God, seriously without falling into a pantheism on the basis of a justifiable rejection of dualism. No, God is not a particular object within reality. Although not apersonal, he is still more than personal. One could call him transpersonal. A hidden God who is inherent in the world is—to use the daring comparison of Thomas Aquinas *(Summa Theologiae* I, 8, 2–3)—like the soul, the principle of life that is inherent in the body. Through his presence *(praesentia),* power *(potentia),* and essence *(essentia),* God is in all things. He is to be compared with the Chinese vision of unity in which the "heaven-humanity-harmony" is both the hidden foundation and the manifest goal. In this way, the Chinese "category of unity" (correlation, continuum, harmony) comes more sharply into play for the understanding of God, as opposed to an all too anthropomorphic accentuation of the concept of person.

To be sure, for believers, the spirit of God as the spirit of Jesus Christ is active especially in the community of faith: in the *church.* To this extent, ecclesiology flows from pneumatology. In China particularly, one will have to maintain a sober attitude with regard to all spiritual superelevations of the church. After all the experiences of the Chinese nation in the last decades, church will be understood less than ever as institution, but rather entirely as *communio,* as the community of the faithful. It will be understood as a church that is not, as it was so often during all the centuries, a hindrance to the Glad Tidings, but a reliable witness to the Glad Tidings in theory and in practice. This is church as a community of faith

• that is open for new forms (house churches) and new configurations (Chinese art, poetry, liturgy, organizational forms);

• that works loyally together in service to society with people of other faiths and convictions;

• that is, to use an Asian formulation, both "people-oriented" and "Christ-centered."

For the Catholic church, the question of inculturation also touches especially on matters of church discipline. For instance, the problem of celibacy poses itself with peculiar sharpness in a society such as the Chinese, in which the family is a fundamental element in life's experiences, and in which everything depends on the continued flow of life, on descendants.

Infinitely more could be said from a Christian perspective on the themes addressed here: from folk religion, to Confucianism, to Taoism, to inculturation and the individual themes of contextual Chinese Christian theology. What a wealth of ideas for Western Christian theology to take up in its own task! And what a theological awakening there will be when the young generation of Chinese theologians begins to develop its creative, intellectual, and spiritual potential on a broad front! China, or specifically, Chinese traditions, are certainly a challenge not only for Christianity, but also for the secular West as a whole. The last section of this response will deal with this.

WHAT THE WEST CAN LEARN FROM EASTERN THOUGHT

We have already cited the 1958 manifesto of Chinese scholars calling for a reevaluation of Sinology and a rebuilding of Chinese culture. *Five values* are listed there that the West could learn from the East:

• as a complement to the Western drive for progress, the spirit and ability nevertheless to be able, self-contentedly, to sense what is in every single moment of the present, and to give up what one could have;

• a profound and all-encompassing understanding or wisdom that is not oriented toward abstract general concepts and principles, but toward an intuitive, elastic, dialectical, and authentically spiritual grasp of reality;

• a feeling for mercy and compassion that is superior to false Western enthusiasm and its possessive "love";

• a historical sense of responsibility for the further development of one's own highly technicized culture which, without spiritual life, will decline like those of the ancient Greeks and Romans;

• the basic attitude that regards the whole world as a family in which there is no room for original sin and hell.

All this will have to be discussed. Of course, one thing has not been mentioned, and this problem is already an indicator of the radically changed situation. It is the problem of the preservation of creation, of ecology, of humanity's relation to and understanding of the world as such.

I have mentioned a number of times that, since the seventeenth century, modernity has entered upon an unparalleled triumphal march over the world under the banner of four powers: science, technology, industry, and democracy. To be sure, this has happened at different times on different continents. This lack of simultaneity in development from a premodern to a modern world had particularly drastic consequences in China. We know that currently we are witnessing an epochal transformation from a premodern agrarian society to a highly industrialized modernity that, for a country such as China, involves every opportunity and risk. And after all that we have said about the task of a contextual Christian theology in Chinese garb, about the mutual theological challenges of Christianity, Confucianism, and Taoism, we want to conclude this response by concentrating on the following questions: What challenge emanates from China itself, particularly regarding the mastering of the Western ecological crisis? What challenge can Chinese spirituality in particular pose, not only for Christianity, but also for Western society as a whole in the face of environmental crisis and "growth sclerosis"?

Taiwan is in this regard perhaps more instructive than mainland China. Here, industrialization and urbanization, the entire process of modernization, have proceeded at a rate that has already frightened critical observers. All the errors from which the West has had to suffer in the process of its modernization threaten to be repeated. For many in China, all of Western modernity stands for "the mechanistic world, the world of plastic concepts, computers, calculation, social complexity, this ultimate wanting-to-control-everything." These are the words of the Jesuit Luis Gutheinz, a German-speaking theologian who has decades of experience on Taiwan. Speaking in Chinese terminology, this is all *yang,* and in fact so much *yang* "that a subliminal tendency to scepticism is revealing itself in the modern Western world." But even in the West, this scepticism is at bottom a yearning for *yin,* a yearning that Taoism as a rule answered better. It is not least for this reason that Taoism has proven to be so attractive to many Europeans (Luis Gutheinz, *China im Wandel. Das chinesische Denken im Umbruch seit dem 19. Jahrhundert* [Munich, 1985], pp. 118f.).

One could therefore also describe the transitional situation in which the Western world has found itself since World War I (paradigm change from modern to postmodern) as follows: as the transition from a masculine-aggressive, rational-analytic *yang* age to a more feminine-preservative, receptive-synthetic *yin* age. Naturally, this is not just a matter of slogans on placards. Yet it is no accident that more and more people in the West today, including natural scientists in the tradition of Max Planck, Albert Einstein, and Werner Heisenberg, are emphasizing the complementarity of analysis and synthesis, rational knowledge and intuitive wisdom, research and ethics, indeed the complementarity of science and religion.

Eastern thought (particularly of Chinese origin) has become increasingly influential in the circles of the exact sciences as well. Fritjof Capra's much discussed book, *The Tao of Physics* (Boulder, Colo., 1982), was able to demonstrate a certain convergence between Western physics and Eastern wisdom in impressive fashion. Put negatively, this means that substantive-static thinking such as in Greek medieval and modern Cartesian philosophy has been superseded because it is no longer adequate for a new understanding of reality. If, instead, we express this positively, then it means that contemporary natural science, like Eastern thought, is conscious of the *fundamental unity* as well as the *inner dynamic of nature* in the macrocosm as well as the microcosm; it is conscious of the universal interdependence and interaction of all things, events, and phenomena that manifests itself even in the spheres of elementary-particle physics and molecular biology. For even in Western physics, reality can no longer be seen as a collection of in-principle identical physical objects. Reality is an infinite, inseparable, *complex, dynamic network of relations* that, even in the subatomic domain, comprises a complementary unity of all possible differences, contrasts, and oppositions. It allows itself to be known, not through objective observation, but only through objectively subjective participation. It is to be described with concepts that are not copies of reality, but rather creations of our mind.

In multiple respects, *The Turning Point* (Fritjof Capra; 1982) has thus been reached, a turning point of truly epochal proportions, even if, as a calm, dispassionate European and Christian, one does not exactly believe in a New Age of Aquarius. In any case, it is understandable why today many people are calling for a change of paradigm from *yang* action, oriented to the self, to a new *yin* action, in accord with nature. We know that, for Western thought, which has resulted in both capitalism and communism, conflict, polarization, irreconcilable and antagonistic positions are characteristic: contradiction and antithesis. Taoistically influenced thought, on the other hand, is very much more consensus-oriented, very much more interested in cooperation and natural harmony. *Yin* and *yang* are not irreconcilable opposing forces, are not to be understood as dualistic principles. Rather, they are polar forces that flow into one another, that constantly balance each other in dynamic equilibrium. They refer to each other and complement each other within the framework of a harmonious whole. And Christian theology?

Even in *Christian theology* today, people on all sides are realizing that exaggerated anthropocentricity and the conquest and exploitation of nature by man are wrong. As opposed to these, the protection and preservation of creation, along with the cocreativity of humanity with the rest of creation, is being reestablished as the mandate of the creator. Conscious of a fundamental unity of humankind and the cosmos, a new harmony is being sought. The spiritual challenge of China is especially noticeable here. Jürgen Moltmann, more than other theologians, has concerned himself with an up-to-date doctrine of creation *(Gott in der Schöpfung. Ökologische Schöpfungslehre* [Munich, 1985]). Under the title "China Between Tao and Mao," he has justifiably called for a new concept of progress in the context of a new concept of equilibrium. Instead of the continued integration of nature into the human history of progress, the reverse is now advocated: the integration of the human history of progress into the rhythms and cycles of earth's ecosystem, which alone can guarantee the survival of humanity. Basing himself not only, as did Capra, on Eastern wisdom, but especially also on the Judeo-Christian (and, I would add, also the Islamic) conception, Moltmann advocates the following: "It seems to make sense to expand the community of human beings to a community of human beings and nature." For, "according to the Judeo-Christian conception, the God of creation and the covenant placed the community of creation, consisting of human beings, animals, plants, and the earth, into one community of rights. —From ancient Chinese culture, the Taoist harmony with nature through integration of humanity into nature and action through non-intervention into nature is very much in tune with the modern search for a culture that is capable of surviving. 'Not acting against nature furthers the thriving of things' *(Tao-te ching,* 43)." ("China Between Tao and Mao," *Evangelische Kommentare* 20 [1987], p. 154.)

Of course, this development is also a return question directed to Chinese thought, Marxist thought not excepted. The modern subjectivization of the human person has undoubtedly led to a reification, decomposition, disintegration, pillaging, and destruction of the world. Nevertheless, this subjectivization should not be reversed. Instead, it should be more strongly integrated with the overall continuity of the world. In the entire Sinicized world, it is obvious that an increasing importance is being given to the individual and his or her needs—as opposed to family, the job, and the state. This fact alone cannot be readily condemned as Western individualism. It is a matter of the *human person* and his or her dignity: not the person in isolation, but rather the person in his or her being-in-itself and in his or her being-with. At this point, I should reverse the process and allow Eastern thought to be challenged by Western, especially Christian thought. As everywhere, learning, cross-fertilization, and enrichment go hand in hand.

Hans Küng: Epilogue

DUAL RELIGIOUS CITIZENSHIP: A CHALLENGE TO THE WEST

We should not be under any illusions about the difficulties presented by the question we have saved for this epilogue. Julia Ching
has touched upon it in her presentations. It is one of the most
challenging questions for interreligious dialogue, but of course
only for a dialogue of existential significance that tries to take
seriously the truth of every religion. Can one, may one, belong to
two or more religions at the same time? Is there such a thing as
dual religious citizenship? What is legitimate or illegitimate here?
What are the criteria? What does one have to learn to make distinctions? To conclude this book, I want to consider briefly how
this problem can be critically examined further. It is a final point;
and yet it is not final. It is an epilogue that will at the same time be
a prologue—for ever deeper understanding of the religions.

THE PROBLEM

For Europeans and for Christians, all this does not seem to be a
question. Dual religious citizenship? For whom is this supposed to
be a problem? But whoever can relativize his or her Eurocentric
or Christian worldview will quickly notice that what seems utterly
impossible to the adherents of prophetic religions such as Christianity, Judaism, and Islam is not at all foreign to those of East

Asian religions. Our Western experience has been that one is either a Jew *or* a Christian *or* a Muslim, but not two of these at once, let alone all three. In East Asia, however, it is quite possible to be both Confucianist and Taoist, both Buddhist and Shintoist. Take *Japan* for example. Nowhere in the Sinicized countries is the question of religious adherence solved as pragmatically as there. Thus, curiously enough, Japan in 1983 was statistically reckoned to have around 120 million inhabitants but, at the same time, 220 million believers. It is well known that in Japan, Shintoists, Buddhists, Christians, and followers of newer religions coexist. This statistical incongruity, of course, is amazing only for someone who does not know that 72 percent of Japanese consider the goal and content of all religions to be more or less identical—and that many do not even know to which religion they concretely belong! (Statistical information in Josef Kreiner, "Religion in Japan," in *Japan,* ed. Manfred Pohl [Stuttgart, 1986], pp. 378–92).

In Europe, things are completely different. As a result of Europe's historical and intellectual development, especially since the advent of the critique of religion in the seventeenth century, people in Europe either remained religious and Christian or they moved from being nonreligious to being atheistic. The problem of dual *religious* citizenship could not therefore even arise. It is only with the appearance of new churches and religious communities in our century that the question could emerge for Europeans as well. If all these religions do not simply replace the earlier ones, but are rather conceived as suitable supplements for the purpose of mutual interpenetration, is there then a legitimate form of dual religious citizenship? One that results less from naïveté, ignorance, or even indifference than from genuine tolerance, irenicism, and ecumenicity? Let us therefore not be deceived. With the presence of religious communities of, for instance, Neo-Hindu or Buddhist origin, the question of dual citizenship is becoming increasingly unavoidable for the West as well. A growing number of people in Europe, but above all in North America, claim to be and advocate being both Christian *and* Buddhist, Christian *and* Taoist, Christian *and* the member of some new religion.

But how is such dual citizenship to be judged? Is it to be declared heresy? Should one strive for clear delineation, as more recent Christian apologetic literature does? (So said a church commission about the new religious wave. "Die neue religiöse Welle," *Una Sancta* 41 [1986], pp. 320–38, esp. p. 331.) Whatever the answer, the first, still unsatisfactory reactions from the churches appear to make more precise theological argumentation more necessary than ever. As a Christian, can one, may one really be a dual religious citizen? Both Christian and Confucian, Christian and Taoist, Buddhist, Shintoist? Moreover, this question is more multilayered than fundamentalists on the right and liberals on the left assume. What is needed is differentiation. We shall therefore try to approach the heart of this problem in three steps, starting with the cultural and then proceeding to the ethical and the genuinely religious dimensions.

Cultural Dual Citizenship?

In the first instance, it makes an appreciable difference whether the problem of dual citizenship is raised by an Asian who comes from a country with Confucian, Taoist, or Buddhist traditions, or by a European from a relatively unitary Christian tradition. For it seems to me to be completely inconceivable that someone whose origin is Chinese would not have absorbed an appreciable portion of Confucian culture in terms of surroundings, lifestyle, expectations, language, upbringing, and national characteristics. An example? "I am a Confucianist. I was thirteen when I was put in the foreign language school in Shanghai by my father and I have never completed the full course of traditional Chinese studies. What does it matter! I had already been imbued with the intellectual and spiritual tradition of Confucianism, the worship of the All-High, the practice of filial piety, zeal in performing acts of virtue in order better to understand man and to make practical progress towards the acquisition of virtue, everything that goes to make up the soul of the Chinese race. . . . The Confucianist spirit prepared me to see the evident superiority of Christianity." These are the words, representative for countless others, of the first foreign minister of the Republic of China and three times the prime minister, Lou Tseng-tsiang, a convert to Christianity (quoted in *Concilium* 126 [1979], p. 88). What this means is that it has long been the practice (historical examples were cited) for a Chinese who wished religiously to be entirely Christian to remain at the same time entirely Confucian in culture, without thereby betraying or suppressing his Christian faith in the least.

It is similar in *Japan*. There Shinto is not a confessional religion (only 2.8 percent of Japanese designate themselves as adherents of Shinto), but an ancient folk belief. Although it has been abolished as a state cult since 1945, it continues to be something like a national custom. Many Japanese Christians therefore see no difficulty in participating in the Shinto ritual as part of the social life of their country. Of course, this does raise the problem of religion and culture as such.

Whatever is to be said in criticism of isolated problematic practices—for instance, in Japan (visits to shrines and appeals to specific divinities for acceptance by a specific university or company) —there can fundamentally be no argument that, if Christianity is to be at home in Asia at all, it must become rooted, incarnated, indigenized, inculturated in the culture and society that is so greatly marked by Buddhism, Confucianism, Taoism, and Shintoism. It is well known that, in Asia, this has only occurred in rare instances: in Korea and the Philippines.

The situation in *Europe* was no different. Christianity had a chance at spiritual survival only when it proved capable of changing paradigms: from the Jewish-Christian to the Greek-Hellenistic, to the Latin-Roman, and finally to the Germanic-Reformation paradigm. As we heard, "inculturation" is the magic word around which everything revolves theologically and ecclesiastically. Then as now, it has been a controversial problem especially in a church such as the Catholic church. For Rome still treats its "provinces" like a Roman Empire instead of like a Catholic commonwealth. Accordingly, it still attempts to colonize and Romanize the Asian and African peoples in doctrine ("universal catechism"), language, dress, gesture, and custom (celibacy). We cannot stop here, however; for culture and *ethos* can no more be separated than religion and culture.

ETHICAL DUAL CITIZENSHIP?

Let us now take a second step. The culture of a people is to a great extent determined by its religious ethos. The culture is ethically secured—just as, conversely, the ethos is stamped by the culture. In other words, it is impossible that someone of Chinese origin would not also have adopted much from the Confucian (Taoist, Buddhist) tradition in terms of basic ethical attitude, behavior, and norms (with respect to fellow human beings, nature, and God). This is all the easier since Confucianism (like Buddhism) is understood more as an ethos than as a dogmatic faith. This ethos can, so to speak, be tied to a very different idea of God and transcendence. One can therefore ask why it should not be possible for a Chinese to be a full Christian in his or her faith, *in rebus fidei*, in terms of dogma, but also be a Confucian or a Buddhist *ethically, in rebus morum*, provided that this does not contradict the fundamental Christian ethos of the gospel. An example?

As far as Confucianism is concerned, the Chinese Christian *Stanislaus Lokuang*, archbishop of Taipei and rector of Fu-Jen University, has left no doubt about the compatibility of Christian faith and Confucian ethic. In dealing with the question "How can one be at the same time authentically Chinese and Christian?" he writes: "An authentic Chinese must have a deep esteem for matters of the spirit. He must respect Heaven and his Ancestors. He must observe the Confucian moral code. He must cultivate the five virtues of charity, justice, temperance, fidelity, and prudence. He must have filial piety to build family. An authentic Christian must love God above all things, and his neighbor as himself. He must observe the Ten Commandments. He must put eternal life as the final aim of his life. When we compare the conditions of these two types of life, we find that they are not contradictory to one another. They reciprocally complete one another" *(Concilium* 126 [1979], p. 89). For this sort of basic attitude, dual citizenship in the cultural and ethical sense would not seem to be a problem. Of course, the religious questions that were addressed require separate and critical reflection.

Basically, what has to be kept in mind here is that, if Christianity really wants to become at home in Asia, it has to mesh with the ethos given by the indigenous religion. This ethos might, for instance, concern the attitude of the individual to himself, to society, and to all of nonhuman nature. One of the pressing concerns of our time is to bring to light the fact that all *the great religions of humanity share fundamental ethical principles.* This must be done for the sake of religious and political peace in the world. The commonality of ethos in particular could become a unifying, peacemaking bond in the community of peoples. It could contribute to a freer, more just, and more peaceful coexistence in our increasingly uninhabitable world.

The great religions have a unique responsibility for humanity; but they also have a unique opportunity—and a unique authority which, if used, is greater than that of all the politicians combined. An impressive expression of this is to be found in the declaration of the World Conference of Religions for Peace held in 1970 in Kyoto, Japan. Here the ethical agreement among the different religions is convincingly presented: "Having come together to deal with the paramount theme of peace, we discovered that the things that unite us are more important than the things that divide us. We found that we had in common:

• a conviction of the fundamental unity of the human family, of the equality and dignity of all people;

• a feeling for the inviolability of the individual and his or her conscience;

• a feeling for the value of the human community;

• a recognition that might is not equal to right, that human power cannot be self-sufficient and is not absolute;

• the belief that love, compassion, selflessness, and the power of the spirit and of inner truth are ultimately more powerful than hatred, enmity, and self-interest;

• the feeling of an obligation to take the side of the poor and oppressed against the rich and the oppressors;

• the profound hope that good will ultimately triumph."

Yet, a last and most difficult question can now no longer be put off. If culture and ethos can be made compatible with Christian faith, must not a third and last step also be ventured? Should it not be possible for a Christian to be a strict *religious* Confucian, Taoist, or Buddhist as well? Beyond the mere cultural or ethical, is dual *religious* citizenship in the strict sense not therefore possible?

DUAL CITIZENSHIP IN FAITH?

Such a question can be approached from very different fundamental positions.

1. A Christian of Asian origin can *take not only his or her own Christian religion quite seriously,* but also the indigenous Asian religion to the extent that it does not contradict the Christian faith. This combination could allow a deeper understanding of ultimate reality, the absolute, God—but also of the world, humanity, and nature. Indeed, it could eventually lead to a deeper appreciation of practices such as meditation. Our interreligious dialogue demonstrated again and again that better mutual information reveals significant parallels and convergences in spite of all divergences and differences. It showed that enrichment through cross-fertilization is possible. It is not necessarily a contradiction in itself if a Christian wants also to be a Confucian, Taoist, or Buddhist—if, in following Christ, he or she also wants to take the concerns, conceptions, and practices of other religions seriously (to the extent that they do not contradict his or her Christian faith). Such a Christian is, in the best and broadest sense of the word, an *ecumenical Christian.*

2. It is also entirely possible for a Christian—and this concerns Asians as well as Europeans and North Americans—to be a Buddhist, Confucian, Taoist, or whatever because he *takes neither of the religions completely seriously.* He or she does not really practice the discipleship of Christ or follow the Eightfold Path of the Buddha. Rather, he or she selects from the two religions according to his or her taste, taking what he or she likes and unconcernedly leaving what seems burdensome behind—a commandment of Jesus here, an injunction of the Buddha there. He or she mixes

himself or herself a kind of religious cocktail, often ostensibly "mystical," prepared above all for the consumption of Europeans and North Americans who are often all too understandably fed up with their own religion and are looking for something new. Such private religion, mostly nurtured in small groups of the enlightened elite, may satisfy the religious needs of some people; but with such a private, optional religion, one can no longer talk about a genuinely ecumenical attitude. In this case, genuinely ecumenical Christianity appears rather to have disintegrated into a pseudoecumenical syncretism.

But let us not be led astray. Such folkloric consumer religions hardly play a serious role anymore in the ethics and faith of the younger generation. Consequently, only around a third of all Japanese describe themselves as religious (even though two thirds, indeed, 76 percent, affirm the necessity of a religion). If, however, the religious foundation is missing or remains nonobligatory, there will be unforeseen consequences for education and the basic ethical values that hold a society together. Increasingly, politicians from Tokyo to Singapore are seeing this as a serious challenge. Social criticism is, of course, very unpopular in the countries concerned. Such criticism has been openly and frankly leveled against contemporary Japanese society by the well-known Japanese intellectual Shuichi Kato

• on account of the short Japanese memory with respect to the ugly past, and the total absorption in the present;

• on account of the widespread consumerism that devalues all values;

• on account of the unaltered group mentality and the neglect of individuality;

• on account of the absence of a strong intellectual elite and on account of the danger of the gradual erosion of political rights.

These are all ethical and also veiled religious problems with which, of course, other countries besides Japan, similarly highly technologized and urbanized, have to do battle. There is therefore no cause for Christian self-righteousness. After all, parallel phenomena (or pure folklore religiosity) exist in the West as well. And if an upwardly mobile Japan currently has more career- and success-oriented people, our saturated Europe and North America, after all the modern achievements, have more dropouts. We refer to practically insoluble problems for parents, educators, teachers. Total value indifference, hopeless loss of orientation, and the abyss of a practical nihilism threaten on both sides. They can hardly be overcome by a purely rational ethic such as has been attempted throughout all of European modernity. No, it is not beneficial for the people of the Far East or of the West if none of the religions occasionally sampled is really taken seriously. Religions, even Confucianism and Buddhism, are more than mere ethos.

3. Therefore, one can be a religious Christian and a religious Buddhist, and so forth, by attempting *to take both religions entirely seriously.* Obviously, one will quickly come to the realization that, in spite of all the convergences and parallels, being a Christian and being a Buddhist are not simply identical: the way of discipleship in Christ and the path of the Buddha cannot simply be traveled at the same time. Certainly reconciliation can be pursued and understanding deepened in the future; and everything that has been written in this book is intended to contribute to this understanding. However, now as before, the experts particularly cannot ignore that, when all is said and done, Christianity and, for instance, Buddhism are not just two different paradigms, but two different religions. The conversion from the one to the other therefore represents not a mere change of paradigm, but rather a change of religion.

Therefore, even with every cultural and ethical possibility for integration, the truth of every religion extends to a depth that ultimately challenges every person to a yes or no, to an either-or. This is not just the case for the primarily exclusivist prophetic religions of Semitic origin. It is also valid for the more inclusivist mystical religions of Indian origin, and basically also for the more wisdom-oriented religions of Chinese tradition. An Indian religion that does not see its own truth exclusivistically as the only one (something that also no longer holds today for an ecumenically open Judaism, Christianity, or Islam) nevertheless likes to regard its own truth inclusivistically as the highest or most profound one, with the truth of the others as at best a propaedeutic or an aspect of the whole truth. A convinced Confucian or Taoist will also accordingly not simply let Christianity stand as a truth of equal importance beside his or her own native religion. Therefore, as much as cultural and ethical dual citizenship is possible and ought to be made possible ever anew, a religious dual citizenship in the deepest, strictest sense of faith should be excluded—by all the great religions.

This, however, again raises the question of Christian existence in the context of another culture and a non-Christian ethos with peculiar clarity. *Christian inculturation, not dual religious citizenship,* must be the watchword! And it is especially on this point that self-criticism of Christian theology is in order. The reason is that the question of dual religious citizenship is a critical question directed at Christianity itself. Already in 1979, the French theologian Claude Geffré made this clear in a contribution to the international journal *Concilium,* one of the first to recognize "China as a Challenge for the Church." The question of whether one can be a Taoist or a Buddhist and simultaneously a Christian points in fact to the more radical question of what it is that is most important in Christianity. Geffré justifiably points out that, for Christianity, the "event of Jesus Christ" takes precedence over every tradition and remains the original point of reference for all Christian action. Every historical configuration of this event must be distinguished from the event itself. "One could go so far as to say that Christ did not found a new religion if by religion is meant a system of symbols, a set of rites, a catalogue of moral prescriptions or a programme of social practices. Christian existence cannot be defined in advance. It exists wherever the Spirit of Christ raises up a new form of being for man individually and collectively" ("China as a Challenge for the Church," *Concilium* 126 [1979], p. 79).

In point of fact, what is at issue is not the "mission" of the "church" with colonial-imperialistic intentions. What is at issue is the *inculturation of the spirit of Jesus Christ* for the whole of humanity. Christians are challenged to allow this spirit of Jesus Christ to become visible all around this globe in ever new cultural expressions, forms and configurations. Resolute Christian identity in the discipleship of Christ and the greatest possible openness to the cultural, ethical, and religious values of non-Christians belong together! In both large and small things, Christianity, a minority, should stand in the service of humanity, the majority.

Basic Literature

GENERAL

1. Bauer, Wolfgang. *China and the Search for Happiness.* Translated by Michael Shaw. New York, 1971.

2. Wing-tsit Chan. *Religious Trends in Modern China.* New York, 1954.

3. De Bary, William Theodore. *East Asian Civilizations: A Dialogue in Five Stages.* Cambridge, Mass., 1988.

4. Eder, Matthias. *Die Religionen der Chinesen.* Vol. 3 in *Christus und die Religionen der Erde,* edited by F. König. Vienna, 1951.

5. Eichhorn, Werner. *Die Religionen Chinas,* Vol. 21 in *Die Religionen der Menschheit,* edited by C. M. Schröder. Stuttgart, 1973.

6. Eliade, Mircea. *A History of Religious Ideas.* Chicago, 1978. Vol. 1.

7. ———. *Shamanism: Archaic Techniques of Ecstasy.* New York, 1964.

8. Forke, Alfred. *Geschichte der alten chinesischen Philosophie.* Hamburg, 1927.

9. Franke, Herbert, and Rolf Trauzettel. *Das chinesische Kaiserreich.* Frankfurt, 1968.

10. Franke, Wolfgang, and Brunhild Staiger. *China Handbuch.* 2nd ed. Opladen, 1978.

11. Fung Yu-lan. *A History of Chinese Philosophy.* Translated by Derk Bodde. Princeton, N.J., 1952. 2 vols.

12. ———. *A Short History of Chinese Philosophy.* Edited and translated by Derk Bodde. New York, 1962.

13. Granet, Marcel. *The Religion of the Chinese People.* Edited and translated by Maurice Freedman. London, 1975.

14. Jaspers, Karl. *The Great Philosophers: The Foundations.* Translated by Ralph Manheim. New York, 1962. Vol. 1.

15. Kitagawa, Joseph M., *Religion in Japanese History.* New York, 1966.

16. ———. *Religions of the East.* Philadelphia, 1963.

17. Köster, Hermann. *Symbolik des chinesischen Universismus.* Stuttgart, 1958.

18. Lewis, I. M. *Ecstatic Religion: An Anthropological Study of Spiritual Possession and Shamanism.* Harmondsworth, 1971.

19. Needham, Joseph. *Science and Civilisation in China.* Cambridge, 1954–86. 6 vols.

20. Smith, D. Howard. *Chinese Religions.* New York, 1968.

21. Thompson, Laurence. *Chinese Religions: An Introduction.* Encino, Cal., 1975.

22. Wach, Joachim. *Sociology of Religion.* Chicago, 1944.

23. Waldenfels, Hans, and Thomas Imoos, (eds.) *Fernöstliche Weisheit und christlicher Glaube: Festgabe für Heinrich Dumoulin.* Mainz, 1985.

24. Waley, Arthur. *Three Ways of Thought in Ancient China.* London, 1939.

25. Weber, Max. *The Religion of China: Confucianism and Taoism.* Translated by Hans H. Gerth. Glencoe, Ill., 1964.

26. Yang, C. K. *Religion in Chinese Society.* Berkeley, Cal., 1961.

FOR CHAPTER I

1. Blacker, Carmen. *The Catalpa Bow.* London, 1975.

2. Chang, K. C. *Art, Myth and Ritual.* Cambridge, Mass., 1983.

3. ———. *Shang Civilization.* New Haven, Conn., 1980.

4. Tsung-tung Chang. *Der Kult der Shang-Dynastie im Spiegel der Orakelinschriften.* Wiesbaden, 1970.

5. Eichhorn, Werner. *Das alte chinesische Religion und das Staats-Kultwesen.* Leiden, 1976.

6. Elliott, Alan J. A. *Chinese Spirit-Medium Cult in Singapore.* London, 1955.

7. Keightley, David. *Sources of Shang History.* Berkeley, Cal., 1978.

8. Kitagawa, Joseph M. and Alan L. Miller, eds. *Folk Religion in Japan: Continuity and Change.* Chicago, 1968.

9. Vandermeersch, Léon. *Wangdao ou la voie royale.* Paris, 1980. Vol. 2.

FOR CHAPTER II

1. Wing-tsit Chan. *Chu Hsi and Neo-Confucianism.* New York, 1985.

2. Chang, Carsun. *The Development of Neo-Confucian Thought.* New York, 1962. 2 vols.

3. Ching, Julia. *Confucianism and Christianity: A Comparative Study.* Tokyo, 1977.

4. ———. *To Acquire Wisdom: The Way of Wang Yang-ming (1472–1529).* New York, 1976.

5. Creel, Herlee G. *Confucius: The Man and the Myth.* New York, 1949.

6. Eber, Irene, ed. *Confucianism: The Dynamics of Tradition.* New York, 1986.

7. Graf, Olaf. *Tao und Jen. Sein und Sollen im sungchinesischen Monismus.* Wiesbaden, 1970.

8. Rowley, H. H. *Prophecy and Religion in Ancient China and Israel.* London, 1956.

9. Schwartz, Benjamin I. *The World of Thought in Ancient China.* Cambridge, Mass., 1985.

10. Vandermeersch, Léon. *Le Nouveau monde sinisé.* Paris, 1986.

FOR CHAPTER III

1. Creel, Herlee G. *What Is Taoism?* Chicago, 1970.

2. Huard, Pierre, et al. *Chinese Medicine.* Translated by Bernard Fielding. New York, 1968.

3. Kaltenmark, Max. *Lao Tzu and Taoism.* Translated by Roger Greaves. Stanford, Cal., 1969.

4. Lagerwey, John. *Taoist Ritual in Chinese Society and History.* New York, 1987.

5. Maspéro, Henri. *Taoism and Chinese Religion.* Translated by Frank A. Kierman, Jr. Amherst, Mass., 1981.

6. Naundorf, Gert, et al., eds. *Religion und Philosophie in Ostasien. Festschrift für Hans Steininger.* Würzburg, 1985.

7. Robinet, Isabelle. *Méditation Taoïste.* Paris, 1979.

8. Saso, Michael, and David Chappell, eds. *Buddhist and Taoist Studies.* Honolulu, 1977. Vol. 1.

9. Schipper, Kristofer. *Le Corps Taoïste.* Paris, 1982.

10. Sivin, Nathan. *Chinese Alchemy: Preliminary Studies.* Cambridge, Mass., 1968.

11. Strickmann, Michel. *Le Taoïsme de Mao-shan.* Paris, 1980.

12. Welch, Holmes, and Anna Seidel, eds. *Facets of Taoism: Essays in Chinese Religion.* New Haven, Conn., 1979.

13. Welch, Holmes, et al. "Symposium on Taoism." *History of Religions* 9, no. 2/3 (1969–70).

FOR CHAPTER IV

1. Cary-Elwes, C. *China and the Cross.* London, 1957.

2. Charbonnier, Jean. *Guide to the Catholic Church in China.* Singapore, 1986.

3. Ch'en, Kenneth S. *Buddhism in China: A Historical Survey.* Princeton, N.J., 1964.

4. Dumoulin, Heinrich. *Geschichte des Zen-Buddhismus.* Bern, 1985. Vol. 1.

5. Gerber, Uwe. "Kontextuelles Christentum im neuen China." *EZW-Texte,* Information No. 94, Stuttgart, 1985.

6. Gernet, Jacques. *China and the Christian Impact.* Translated by Janet Lloyd. Cambridge, 1985.

7. Kreiner, Josef. "Religion in Japan." In *Japan,* edited by Manfred Pohl. Stuttgart, 1986.

8. Küng, Hans, et al. *Christianity and the World Religions.* Translated by Peter Heinegg. Garden City, N.Y., 1986.

9. Orr, Robert G. *Religion in China.* New York, 1980.

10. Rosenkranz, G. *Die älteste Christenheit in China in den Quellen-Zeugnissen der Nestorianertexte der T'ang-Dynastie.* 1939.

11. ———. *Der Nomos Chinas und das Evangelium.* 1936.

12. Tsukamoto, Zenryū. *A History of Early Chinese Buddhism: From Its Introduction to the Death of Hui-yüan.* Translated by Leon Hurvitz. Tokyo, 1979. Vol. 1.

13. Zürcher, Erik. *The Buddhist Conquest of China.* Leiden, 1955. 2 vols.

TRANSLATIONS FROM CLASSICAL TEXTS

1. De Bary, William Theodore, et al., eds. *Sources of Chinese Tradition.* New York, 1960. 2 vols.

2. Hawkes, David. *Ch'u Tz'u: The Songs of the South.* Oxford, 1959.

3. Köster, Hermann. *Hsün-tzu.* Kaldenkirchen, 1967.

4. Lau, D. C. *Lao-tzu: Tao-te ching.* London, 1963.

5. ———. *Mencius.* London, 1970.

6. Legge, James. *The Chinese Classics.* Oxford, 1861–72. 5 vols.

7. ———. *A Record of Buddhistic Kingdoms.* Oxford, 1886. Reprint. New York, 1965.

8. Tsunoda, Ryusaku, et al., eds. *Sources of Japanese Tradition.* New York, 1958. 2 vols.

9. Waley, Arthur. *The Analects of Confucius.* London, 1938.

10. ———. *The Book of Songs.* London, 1954.

11. ———. *The Nine Songs.* London, 1955.

12. Watson, Burton. *The Complete Works of Chuang-tzu.* New York, 1968.

13. ———. *Hsün-tzu: Basic Writings.* New York, 1963.

14. ———. *Mo-tzu: Basic Writings.* New York, 1963.

15. Wilhelm, Richard, and Cary F. Baynes. *The I Ching or Book of Changes.* 3rd ed. Princeton, N.J., 1967.

NEW REFERENCE WORK IN THE STUDY OF RELIGION
   Eliade, Mircea, ed. *The Encyclopedia of Religion.* New York, 1987. 16 vols.

The quotations from the Old and New Testaments are taken from the Revised Standard Version (RSV).

Acknowledgments (1)

My thanks go first to Hans Küng for his friendly invitation to me to give the joint lectures with him at the University of Tübingen in the summer semester of 1987, and for the initiative to expand the lectures (by quite a bit) as a joint book. Besides, I must thank Willard G. Oxtoby for all his assistance and encouragement, without which my part of the book might not have been ready for the press. As it now appears, my work represents especially the collaboration between myself and both Hans Küng and Willard Oxtoby, as well as the editors at Doubleday in New York, while the parts by Hans Küng reflect also the skills of his translator, Dr. Peter Beyer, who is also my colleague in the Department of Religious Studies, University of Toronto.

In writing a book such as this, I cannot but remember my own personal odyssey: growing up in China, and becoming, eventually, a "China scholar," able at last to return from time to time to that country—even if I now belong to the "Chinese diaspora" overseas, with some of the advantages of this bicultural situation. My consciousness of roots and family is especially strong at present, with the publication of my brother Frank Ching's book *Ancestors: Nine Hundred Years in the Life of a Chinese Family* (New York: William Morrow, 1988).

My thoughts also go to Mrs. Elisabeth Luce Moore, my dear and great friend, who is herself so attached to the subject treated in this book, and who has been an inspiration to me in many ways.

There are, of course, countless other friends, colleagues, and students from whom I have learned so much. And, on the eve of the submission of the manuscript to the English-language publisher, I look forward to learning even more from the readers of this book.

JULIA CHING
May 31, 1988

Acknowledgments (2)

This book would not have been written without the help of many people, too many to mention individually here. It was first of all Julia Ching who, already in the sixties, challenged me to deal with Chinese thought as a Christian theologian. Two subsequent trips to the People's Republic of China then had a critical role in revealing to me the significance of China as a spiritual superpower. I had my first concrete look at China shortly after Mao's death. In 1979, as part of a delegation from the Kennedy Institute for Bioethics in Washington, I had the opportunity to deliver a lecture on the function of religion in society to the Chinese Social Science Academy in Peking. The other trip, in 1987 (together with Julia Ching and Willard Oxtoby), gave me a living impression of the current political and social upheavals in mainland China, and made me concretely aware of the situation of the church there. Also not to be forgotten are my trips to Japan, Korea, and Taiwan, and the important conversations I had there, especially with many university and church colleagues. My heartfelt thanks to all those who helped me penetrate more deeply into the spirit and history of China, whether men or women of the church, theologians, scholars of religion, or representatives of the diplomatic service.

The completion of the manuscript would not have been possible without the reliable assistance of my co-workers in Tübingen, to whom I cannot express enough gratitude. There is, first of all, Mrs. Eleonore Henn, who, assisted when necessary by Mrs. Hannelore

Türke, showed infinite patience and great perseverance in making the many drafts of the manuscript technically possible. This is often a tedious task that cannot be appreciated too much. I also wish to thank Mrs. Marianne Saur, above all for her help and encouragement in making the language of the manuscript more comprehensible. Further, I want to thank my academic colleagues at the Institute for Ecumenical Research for their energetic support both in the technical preparation of the lectures and in the final revision of the manuscript. And last but not least, I want to thank Dr. Karl-Josef Kuschel, academic advisor to our Institute, who for many years, as a good colleague, has helped me with the form and content of my "responses."

HANS KÜNG
Tübingen
July 1987

Indexes

INDEX OF NAMES

(Alternative forms of a name are given in parentheses.) This index was prepared by Madina von Bülow and Joachim Zehner.

INDEX OF SUBJECTS

HANS KÜNG, born in 1928 in Sursee, Switzerland, is professor of ecumenical theology and director of the Institute of Ecumenical Research at the University of Tübingen. He is a world-renowned theologian and author of many books, including *Theology for the Third Millennium, Christianity and the World Religions, Eternal Life?, Does God Exist?,* and *On Being a Christian.*

JULIA CHING, born in 1934 in Shanghai, China, is professor of religious studies at the University of Toronto. She has taught in Australia, at Columbia and Yale Universities, and is the author of many books, including *To Acquire Wisdom* and *Confucianism and Christianity,* the latter a winner of Outstanding Academic Book of the Year (1977) from *Choice* magazine.